Good News About
Sex & Marriage

Good News About Sex & Marriage

Answers to Your Honest Questions
about Catholic Teaching
UPDATED, REVISED & EXPANDED EDITION

CHRISTOPHER WEST

Foreword by
Archbishop Charles J. Chaput, O.F.M. CAP.

servant
AN IMPRINT OF
FRANCISCAN MEDIA
Cincinnati, Ohio

Nihil obstat: Rev. Joshua R. Brommer, S.T.L.
                   Censor Librorum
Imprimatur: Most Rev. Ronald W. Gainer, D.D., J.C.L..
                   Bishop of Harrisburg
                   October 4, 2018

The *nihil obstat* and *imprimatur* are official declarations that a book is free from doctrinal or moral error. No implication is contained therein that those who grant the *nihil obstat* or *imprimatur* agree with the contents, opinions, or statements expressed.

LIBRARY OF CONGRESS CATALOGING-IN-PUBLICATION DATA
West, Christopher, 1969—
Good news about sex and marriage : answers to your honest questions about Catholic teaching/ Christopher West.
Includes biographical references.
ISBN 978-1-63253-274-9 (alk. paper)
1. Sex—Religious aspects—Catholic Church. 2. Marriage—Religious aspects
Catholic Church. 3. Catholic Church—Doctrines. I. Title.
BX1795.S48 W47 2004
241´.66—dc21   00-043182

ISBN 978-1-63253-274-9

Published by Servant, an imprint of Franciscan Media
28 W. Liberty St.
Cincinnati, OH 45202
www.FranciscanMedia.org

Printed in the United States of America
Printed on acid-free paper
18 19 20 21 22 5 4 3 2

To my beloved bride, Wendy.
Without her love I would not be who I am,
nor could I have written this book.

Contents

Author's Note on the Updated, Revised & Expanded Edition

While the *good news* about sex, gender, and marriage remains the same as ever, cultural attitudes have shifted dramatically since this book was first released in 2000. Since that time, the logic of the sexual revolution hasn't only marched forward—it has sprinted.

Smartphones have made hard-core pornography our main reference point for understanding sex. "Hookup" culture has nearly obliterated the notion that sexual activity need have anything to do with love and commitment. Same-sex marriage has become the law of the land, and a "gender theory" that makes one's sex completely malleable has been enshrined in law, making those who question it or raise concerns liable under hate speech legislation.

This new cultural landscape necessitated an updated and expanded version of this book. New insights, nuances, and questions have been added throughout, especially in chapter eight on same-sex marriage, and a brand-new chapter addressing questions of gender identity has been added.

My goal in this new edition is the same as that in the first: to answer people's honest and sometimes gritty questions in light of the teachings of Christ. But what, really, do Christ's teachings have to say in response to today's challenges? Here, I can make St. John Paul II's words my own:

> I think that among the answers that Christ would give *to the people of our times* and to their questions, often so impatient, *fundamental would still be the one* he gave to the Pharisees [when he spoke to them of God's original plan for creating us male and female]. In answering these questions, Christ *would appeal first of all to the "beginning."* He would perhaps do so all the more decidedly and essentially, inasmuch as man's inner and simultaneously cultural situation seems to move away from that beginning and assume forms and dimensions that diverge from the biblical image of the "beginning" to points that are evidently ever more distant.[1]

Yes, the problems and situations of men and women today are distant indeed from the image of harmony portrayed in the "beginning" when man and woman embraced their humanity "naked without shame." But, as John Paul II added, "Christ would not be 'surprised' by any of these situations." And in responding to them, "he would continue to refer above all to the 'beginning.'"[2] And so will we. For therein, in Christ's appeal to God's original plan for creating us male and female, lies also the hope of our restoration.

Everyone experiences an "echo" in his or her heart of that original plan. Everyone still longs for it. And the good news about sex and marriage is that Christ came into the world "to restore creation to the purity of its origins."[3]

It's been very encouraging to receive so many testimonies from around the world of how this book has changed people's lives. I pray this fresh edition will help a new generation to rediscover that God's plan truly is *good news*!

—Christopher West

Foreword to the Original Edition

Here's a safe bet: I'd wager that most of you who open this book have heard about a "vocation crisis" in the Church. Over the past thirty years, it's been a popular topic of conversation. Thousands of articles have been written about it. You've probably seen your share.

Here's another safe bet: I'd wager that nearly all those stories and conversations dealt with priests or religious—how few we have, and why we'll have even fewer in the future. And of course, we do need more priests and religious, and in many areas of the United States, the decline in their numbers is extremely serious.

But here's a third safe bet: I'd wager that very few of those articles and conversations dealt with the most fundamental vocations crisis of all: marriage and family life. God calls every one of us by name to participate in his work of creation, each in his or her own way. We *all* have vocations. Marriage is a vocation. Parenthood is a vocation. It's no accident that most priests and religious emerge from believing, practicing, loving Catholic families. In fact, in many ways, the love between a husband and wife is the foundation stone upon which every other Christian vocation is built. Strong marriages and families make a vital, joy-filled Church. The opposite is also true: Families who are lukewarm in their love for God and indifferent in their worship weaken every other dimension of Catholic life. That's why the Church so urgently needs men and women who can provide the example and guidance our families need.

You'll find that Christopher West is exactly that kind of man: articulate, joyful, faithful to the Church, and absolutely passionate about Jesus Christ and the Gospel. As a husband and father, he writes from experience. He knows the pressures and joys of married life. He knows the objections to Catholic teaching firsthand, because he struggled through them himself. He has the marvelous gift of making important truths easily accessible—demonstrating the "whys" behind the "whats" of Catholic teaching in fresh and persuasive ways.

Surely the most tender and exhilarating bond in married love is sexual intimacy. It's also the most easily misunderstood and misdirected. That's why the witness of a person like Christopher West is so valuable. In *Good News About Sex and Marriage*, he takes John Paul II's "theology of the body" and makes it understandable, compelling and relevant for married couples today. His reflections on the Church and contraception are simply outstanding. In effect, this little volume is a kind of "catechism of Catholic teaching on sex and marriage"—and therefore perfect for marriage prep courses, RCIA, adult education and marriage enrichment.

But it's not a theoretical work, nor a textbook. Rather, it's a source of *practical nourishment,* because it continually shows that dealing honestly with issues of sex and marriage brings us face-to-face with the whole Gospel message and the meaning of our lives. It's entitled *Good News* for a very good reason. It's a book about our humanity, and the human drama of our creation, fall, and redemption in Jesus Christ, which truly is *good* news—good news because there's real power in Christ to live the truth.

Do the Church—and yourself—a favor: Read and reread this book. Encourage everyone you know to do the same.

If you want to do something about the "vocations crisis"...you can begin right here.

—Archbishop Charles J. Chaput, O.F.M. CAP.

Introduction

Man cannot live without love. He remains a being that is incomprehensible for himself, his life is senseless, if love is not revealed to him, if he does not encounter love, if he does not experience it and make it his own, if he does not participate intimately in it. This is why Christ the Redeemer "fully reveals Man to himself."[1]

—St. John Paul II

Growing up in the Catholic Church in the 1970s and 1980s, I had plenty of questions about, and objections to, the Church's teachings on sex and marriage. When my hormones kicked in, just about everything I'd been taught about "staying pure" went out the window. Over the next several years, though, my sexual behavior would take its toll on me.

As a freshman in college, I found myself deeply and painfully confused about my own identity as a man. I couldn't deny the fact that I'd brought much of this pain and confusion upon myself through my sexual attitudes and behaviors. The rampant promiscuity of college dorm life only served to magnify the meaninglessness of it all.

The stories of "sexual conquest" that we all shared (and no doubt exaggerated) as freshman guys made me think more and more about the ugliness of which men are capable. For every "conquest" there was a woman on the other end used and discarded. But no one seemed to care.

It all came to a head for me the night I witnessed a date rape in one of the dorms. (This was a Catholic college, by the way.) The experience haunted me: How could a man treat a woman as nothing but a "thing" for his sexual kicks? But the more I asked myself this question in reference to what I'd witnessed, the more I knew I had to direct that same question toward myself.

I've never raped anybody, I thought. *But am I much different from that guy in the way I've treated women in my own thoughts and attitudes? Don't I also use my girlfriend for my sexual kicks?* When I was finally honest with myself, I had to conclude that I wasn't much better than the rapist.

In this time of deep soul searching, I became angry with God. "You gave men these hormones!" I insisted. "They seem to be getting me and everybody else I know in a heck of a lot of trouble. What am I supposed to do with them? I want to know the truth! What's this sex thing all about? What does it mean to be a man?"

That prayer set me on a quest to discover the truth about sex. Christ said, "Seek, and you will find" (Matthew 7:7). So I sought.

To make a long story short, what I ultimately found were the writings of St. John Paul II. Here was a man who rethought and represented the teachings of the Church on sex and marriage with profound insight and great originality. His work set the stage for a new "sexual revolution" that promises to deliver what its precursor couldn't: the true satisfaction of the desire that drives us all—to love and be loved.

In fact, John Paul's contributions to the Church's teachings on sex and marriage are so vast that over two-thirds of what the Catholic Church has ever said on these subjects has come from his pontificate. Yet his work is virtually unknown to the average Catholic. When his insights are given the recognition they deserve, our world will see the restoration of marriage and the family and the building of a true culture of life. This, I believe, will be the new springtime of which he so often spoke.

In the space of a few months I devoured the Holy Father's Theology of the Body[2] his apostolic exhortation On the Christian Family in the Modern World *(Familiaris Consortio),*[3] and his book *Love and Responsibility.*[4] What I read dissected my heart. Somehow, this celibate old pontiff was able to put his finger on the deepest stirrings of my being and help me make sense out of them.

He was able to explain the *whys* behind the *whats* of Catholic teaching in a way that showed the profound beauty of God's reason for creating us male and female in the first place. He radically altered the way I saw myself as a man, the way I looked upon women, the way I understood the Church and God. In short, he changed my view of, well, *everything*. I knew then that I would spend the rest of my life studying this pope's thought and sharing it with others.

Now, as a full-time educator focusing on Church teaching about sex and marriage, I speak to a variety of audiences about these issues on a regular basis. Everywhere I go, people ask sincere, pointed questions about the Church's teaching. They raise issues and objections that weigh heavily on their hearts and intimately affect their own lives and the lives of those they love. Such questions and objections deserve sincere, direct, and thorough responses—responses that address this most intimate area of human life head-on, in a way that helps people make sense of seemingly "arbitrary" or "antiquated" Church teachings.

Inevitably, as I draw from my own experience and what I've learned from St. John Paul II to explain the Church's teaching, people respond: "I went to Catholic schools my whole life and never heard this. Why not?" Others respond in tears: "If I had only known this earlier in my life, perhaps I would have been spared the pain of so many mistakes."

This book was born out of these exchanges. It's a book that people like you have helped me to write. I've gathered together questions and objections from single adults, engaged couples, newly married couples, couples who have been married ten, twenty, even forty or more years; from Catholics, Protestants, and unbelievers; from those who are happily and unhappily married; from those who have suffered the pain of divorce; from those who live homosexual lives, and from those who don't believe they even fit into the world of being male or female. I present them all here and address them one by one.

Following John Paul's lead, chapter one lays the biblical foundations for God's plan for sex and marriage. Subsequent chapters are divided topically and presented in a question-and-answer format. The aim is to be as comprehensive as possible in terms of what people want to know. Even if you have a question that isn't directly addressed, you can gain the tools necessary to arrive at an educated Catholic response.

Some readers might want to look up answers to specific questions for quick reference. That's fine, but keep in mind that each chapter builds on the previous one. To get the full picture, you should proceed chapter by chapter. I'd also strongly recommend taking the time to read the endnotes. Besides references, they often contain helpful information, including additional resources.

It's my heartfelt prayer that, whatever your state and stage in life, this book will help you in your quest to know, understand, live, and experience the beautiful truth about human love. For that's where we find the image of the divine, a foretaste of heaven—the consummate satisfaction of all our most intimate longings.

—Christopher West

1

The Great Mystery

Laying the Foundation

The "great mystery," which is the Church and humanity in Christ, does not exist apart from the "great mystery" expressed in the "one flesh... reality of marriage and the family.[1]

—St. John Paul II

The Church's teaching on sex, gender, and marriage is *good news*. This truth must be emphasized from the start. It's good news because it's the truth about love, and true love is the fulfillment of the human person.

But the Church's teaching on sex, gender, and marriage is also *challenging* news. This is so because the truth about love is always challenging.

When we search out the true meaning of our sexuality, we touch on the core of our being as men and women. We encounter our deepest longings and aspirations and, at the same time, our deepest fears, wounds, selfishness, and sins. Here lies the challenge: We must face the reality of our humanity—the good and the bad—if we are to discover the truth about our sexuality. Inevitably this leads us to the cross. For it is Christ who, by showing us the truth about love, shows us the meaning of life.

"Love one another as I have loved you" (John 15:12). These words of Christ sum up the meaning of life *and* the meaning of human sexuality. At its core, sexual morality is about expressing God's love through our bodies. This is why St. John Paul II can say that if we live according to the truth of our sexuality, we fulfill the very meaning of our being and existence.[2]

The opposite, however, is also true. If we don't live according to the truth of our sexuality, we miss the meaning of our existence altogether. We forfeit true joy, true happiness.

Disputes about sexual morality, then, are not merely about differing ethical perspectives, different interpretations of Scripture, or Church authority versus personal conscience. No, they go much deeper than that. At their root, disputes about sexual morality are disputes about the very meaning of life.

The Church never fails to proclaim that Christ came into the world not only to show us the meaning of life but also to give us the grace to overcome our fears, wounds, selfishness, and sins in order to live life according to that meaning. True love is possible. That's the promise the Church holds out to us in her teachings on sex, gender, and marriage. This is good news. This is great news.

But if this is such "great news," you might ask, why do so many people dispute the Church's teaching? Let's be honest here. People find many points about Catholic teaching to dispute, but if someone has a bone to pick with the Catholic Church, it's almost always related to sex. Whether it's Church teaching about contraception ("C'mon, get with the modern world!"), divorce and remarriage ("How insensitive can you get?"), the ordination of men alone to the priesthood, or homosexuality ("Proof positive that the Church is an oppressor of women and of gays"), such contentions depend finally on disagreements over our ideas about sex.

That's why it's so important that we come to a clear understanding of what God has revealed to us about the nature, meaning, and purpose of human sexuality. While popular opinion holds that a Christian perspective on sex is downright negative, what we actually discover by reflecting on the Scriptures is that sex in God's plan is more awesome than any human being could possibly dream. It reveals a "great mystery" that takes us to the heart of God's plan for the universe.

The Central Place of Sexuality in God's Plan

Sex, then, is by no means a peripheral issue. In fact, St. John Paul II said the call to "spousal love" revealed through our sexuality is "the fundamental component of human existence in the world."[3] It doesn't get more important than that. He even insisted that we can't understand Christianity if we don't understand the truth and meaning of our sexuality.[4]

From beginning to end, the Bible itself is a story about marriage. It begins in the book of Genesis with the marriage of Adam and Eve, and it ends in the book of Revelation with the "wedding of the Lamb"—the marriage of Christ and the Church. Throughout the Old Testament, God's love for his people is described as the love of a husband for his bride. In the New Testament, Christ *embodies* this love. He comes as the heavenly Bridegroom to unite himself forever to his Bride—to us.

So, applying this analogy, we can say that God's plan from all eternity is to "marry" us (see Hosea 2:19). God wanted to reveal this eternal plan to us in a way we couldn't miss, so he stamped an image of it right in our very being as male and female. This means that virtually everything God wants to tell us on earth about who he is, who we are, the meaning of life, the reason he created us, how we are to live and even our ultimate destiny is contained somehow in the truth and meaning of sexuality and marriage. This is important stuff.

Let's take a closer look.

Male and Female: Image of the Trinity

The book of Genesis actually contains two creation accounts. We read in the first account that God created humanity in his image and likeness specifically as male and female (see Genesis 1:27). This means that somehow, in the complementarity of the sexes, we image God. As male and female, we make visible God's invisible mystery.

What is God's invisible mystery? St. John sums it up well: "God is love" (1 John 4:8). We often think of this verse in terms of God's love for us. That's part of its meaning. But even before God's love for us, he is love *in himself*, in the relationship of the three Persons of the Trinity.

God is in himself a life-giving *Communion of Persons*. The Father, from all eternity, is making a gift of himself in love to the Son. (As we read in the Scriptures, Jesus is the "beloved" of the Father; see Matthew 3:17.) And the Son, eternally receiving the gift of the Father, makes a gift of himself back to him. The love between them is so real, so profound, that this love *is* another eternal Person—the Holy Spirit.

Among other things, this is what our being made in the image and likeness of God reveals: We're called to love as God loves, in a life-giving *communion of persons*. And we do this specifically as male and female. The man is disposed in his very being toward making the gift of himself to the woman. And the woman is disposed in her very being toward receiving the gift of the man into herself and giving herself back to him. And the love between them is so real, so profound, that, God willing, it may become another human person.

Thus, sexual intercourse itself is meant to participate in the very life and love of God. Sexual intercourse itself reveals (makes visible) something of the invisible mystery of God.[5] This, of course, does not mean that God is sexual. God is pure Spirit in which there's no place for the difference of the sexes. We must be careful not to misunderstand what's being said. The fact that our sexuality reveals something of the mystery of the Trinity does not mean that the Trinity is sexual. God is not made in humanity's image as male and female, but humanity in God's.[6] God's mystery remains infinitely beyond any human image or analogy. We must always keep this in mind when applying the analogy of sexual love lest we make the serious error of reducing the infinite God to our finite concepts.

That being said, the analogy of faithful, sexual love, while limited, helps us understand God's love in a particularly profound way. To love and be loved as God loves—this is the deepest desire of the human heart. God put it there when he made us in his image. Nothing else can satisfy. Nothing else will fulfill.

This is what we embody as male and female. Sex is so beautiful, so wonderful, so glorious, that it's meant to express God's free, total, faithful, and fruitful love. Another name for this kind of love is marriage.

Yes—sex is meant to express wedding vows. It's where the words of the wedding vows become flesh. That's why sexual intercourse is called the marital embrace.

At the altar, bride and groom commit themselves to each other freely, totally, faithfully, and fruitfully until death—these are the canonical promises they make, the promises of fidelity, indissolubility, and openness to children. Then that night, and throughout their marriage, they enact their commitment. They express with their bodies what they expressed at the altar with their minds and hearts. In doing so, they consummate their marriage. That is, they complete it, perfect it, seal it, renew it.

Marriage: Sacrament of Christ and the Church

Spouses not only image the love of God within the Trinity; they also image the love between God and all humanity, made visible in the love of Christ and the Church. By virtue of their baptisms, the marriage of Christians is a sacrament. That means it's a living sign that truly communicates and participates in the union of Christ and the Church. The marriage vows lived out in the whole of married life and particularly in the spouses' "one flesh" union constitute this living sign.[7]

Paraphrasing St. Paul: For this reason a man will leave father and mother and cling to his bride, and the two shall become one flesh. This is a great mystery, *and it refers to Christ and the Church* (see Ephesians 5:31–32). Christ left his Father in heaven. He left the home of his mother on earth—to give up his *body* for his Bride, so that we might become "one flesh" with him.

Where do we become "one flesh" with Christ? Most specifically in the Eucharist. Again, we use sexual love only as an analogy of God's love. The Eucharist is obviously not a "sexual encounter." But, applying the analogy, the Eucharist is the sacramental consummation of the mystical marriage between Christ and the Church. And, continuing with the analogy, when we receive the body of our heavenly Bridegroom into our own, like a bride we conceive new life in us—God's very own life. As Christ said, "unless you eat the flesh of the Son of man and drink his blood, you have no life in you" (John 6:53).

Since the "one flesh" communion of man and wife foreshadowed the Eucharistic communion of Christ and the Church right from the beginning, St. John Paul II spoke of marriage as the "primordial sacrament." Let's pause for a moment to let this reality sink in. Of all the ways that God chooses to reveal his life and love in the created world, John Paul II said, marriage—enacted and consummated by sexual union—is in a certain way the most fundamental. Christ, of course, is the fullest revelation of God's love in the world. Yet it's marriage—more than anything else—that prepares us to understand the love of Christ.

St. Paul wasn't kidding when he said this is a "great mystery." Could God have made our sexuality any more important than this? Any more beautiful? Any more glorious? God gave us sexual desire itself to be the power to love as he loves, so that we could participate in divine life and fulfill the very meaning of our being and existence.

Sounds great, you say, but it's a far cry from the way sex plays itself out in the experience of real human beings. Yes, it is. The historic abuse of women at the hands of men; the manipulation of men at the hands of women; the tragedy of rape, abuse, and other heinous sex crimes, even against children; AIDS and a host of other sexually transmitted diseases; unwed mothers; "fatherless" children; abortion; adultery; skyrocketing divorce rates; prostitution; sex trafficking; a multibillion-dollar pornography industry; hookup culture; gender confusion; the general cloud of shame and guilt that hangs over sexual matters—all of this paints a very different picture from the one St. Paul and St. John Paul II gave us.

The picture it paints, in fact, is the tragedy of human sinfulness and our fall from God's intention for our sexuality "in the beginning."

Human Sexuality "in the Beginning"

Back to the book of Genesis. While the first creation story gives an objective account of our call to love, the second creation story speaks of our first parents' subjective experience of that call. Adam and Eve represent us all. If we allow the inspired Word to speak to us, we see in their story the inner movements of our own hearts being laid bare. We experience an "echo" of God's original intention deep within us. We sense its beauty, realize how far we've fallen from it, and long for its restoration.

Someone might object: "Hasn't science disproved all that Adam and Eve stuff?" No. The creation stories in Genesis were never intended to be a *scientific* account of how the world was created. Genesis uses figurative language that speaks of much deeper truths about the universe, and our existence in it, than science can ever tell us. To mine the riches of the biblical creation accounts, we have to approach the text as a poet, not as a historian or a scientist.[8]

We read that God created Adam from the dust of the ground and breathed the breath of life into him (see Genesis 2:7).[9] The Hebrew word for "breath" in the original biblical language is also a word for "spirit." And let's remember that the Spirit of God is the very love between the Father and the Son. God is breathing *his love* into the man.

What this means, as we've seen, is that the man is a person called to live in a relationship of love with God. The man, having received the love of God, is called to give himself back to God. He's also called to share the love of God with others (see Matthew 22:37–40). It's stamped in his very being, and he can only fulfill himself by doing so. As the Second Vatican Council put it, "Man, who is the only creature on earth that God created for his own sake, cannot fully find himself except through the sincere gift of himself."[10]

Not Good to Be Alone

This is why the Lord said, "It is not good that the man should be alone; I will make for him a helper fit for him" (Genesis 2:18). That is, God said: "I will make someone he can love." So, the Lord created animals from the dust of the ground and brought them to the man for him to name.

In naming the animals, he realized he was different from them. The animals weren't free to determine their own actions as he was. They weren't called to love in the image of God as he was. We can imagine Adam's reply to God: "Thanks, God, for all these animals. But I can't love a giraffe. I can't give myself to a fruit fly."

So the Lord put the man into a deep sleep and took a rib from his side. Yet again, we lose some things in the English translation. "Deep sleep" might better be translated "ecstasy." *Ecstasy* literally means "to go out of oneself," and Adam's "ecstasy" is that God takes a woman *out of himself*. Furthermore, for Jews *bones* signified the whole human being. The point here is that man and woman share a common humanity. *Both* have God's Spirit within them, which means *both* are called to love in the image of God.[11]

Now imagine Adam's state of mind when he awoke to the sight of the woman. The deepest desire of his heart is to give himself away in love to another person "like himself," and he has just finished naming billions of animals and found no one. So what does he say?

"At last, you are the one! You are bone of my bone and flesh of my flesh" (see Genesis 2:23). That is, "At last, a person like myself that I can love."

How does Adam know that she's the one he can love? Remember that they were naked. It was their *bodies* that revealed the spiritual truth of their persons. In their nakedness they discovered what St. John Paul II called the "spousal meaning of the body," that is, the body's "power to express love: precisely that love in which the human *person becomes a gift* and—through this gift—fulfills the very meaning of his being and existence."[12]

Adam looked at himself; he looked at Eve. He realized this profound reality: "We go together. God made us *for* each other. I can give myself to you, and you can give yourself to me, and we can live in a life-giving communion of love"—the image of God, marriage.

That was the sentiment of sexual desire as God created it and as they experienced it: to make a gift of themselves to each other in the image of God. This is why they were naked and felt no shame (see Genesis 2:25). There's no shame in loving as God loves, only the experience of joy, peace, and a deep knowledge of human goodness.

The Effects of Original Sin

Let's think about this situation for a moment. If the "one flesh" union of marriage is meant to be the fundamental revelation in creation of God's own life and love, and if there's an enemy of God who wants to keep us from experiencing God's life and love, how might he go about keeping us from it? Hmm...let's take a look.

God had told Adam that he was free to eat from any tree in the garden except the "tree of the knowledge of good and evil." If he did, he would die (see Genesis 2:17). In the symbolism of biblical language, here we see God drawing a line that humanity is not free to cross. God alone knows what is best for us. As creatures, we must trust in God's providence and not seek to determine good and evil for ourselves. If we do, we will die.

Here's an analogy. Suppose you just purchased a new car and are pulling into the gas station to fill it up for the first time. The sticker by the gas tank reads "unleaded gas only."

Now, the person that designed the car knows it inside and out. He knows what's best for it. It would be foolish to say, "I don't care what the manufacturer says. I'm stickin' diesel in here." If you did so, you would have some major car troubles.

Just as it is with the car, the only way our lives will "run" the way they're meant to run is if we live according to the Designer's plan. The sticker on the car isn't meant to limit our freedom but to facilitate our freedom in making good choices. It's the same with God's commands. They serve our freedom.

True freedom is not to do whatever I want. True freedom is to do whatever's good, whatever's in keeping with the truth of our humanity. As Jesus said, it's the truth that sets us free (see John 8:32).

But how tempting is the thought of determining for ourselves how we are to live. "I don't care what God says. I don't care that he established a Church to teach the truth. I'm gonna do what *I* want to do." If we recognize this tendency in ourselves, then we recognize that we've inherited original sin.

But why would we ever doubt God's love and provision for us? Why would we ever have eaten from the tree from which God, in his love for us, told us not to eat? Remember: this is just as stupid as putting diesel fuel in an unleaded engine.

Why would we do it? Because, as the *Catechism of the Catholic Church* puts it, "behind the disobedient choice of our first parents lurks a seductive voice, opposed to God, which makes them fall into the death out of envy."[13]

This seductive voice is the Father of Lies, the deceiver, Satan. As a fallen angel, Lucifer is a pure spirit. What do we have that he envies? Bodies. He is envious of the fact that humanity is created in God's own image and likeness and is called *bodily* as male and female to share in divine life. The deceiver hates our bodies and despises God's plan for sex with all his diabolic fury. And his goal is to get us to hate our bodies and despise God's plan as much as he does. So he sets out to convince us that God is against us.

Placing doubt in the woman's mind, the serpent says: "Did God say, 'You shall not eat of any tree of the garden'?... You will not die. For God knows that when you eat of it your eyes will be opened, and you will be like God, knowing good and evil" (Genesis 3:1, 4–5). The implication: God doesn't want you to be like him; God is withholding himself from you; God's plan is not one of love. If you want to be "like God," then you have to reach out and grasp it for yourself.

Now, wait a minute. God had already created them in his image and *likeness* (see Genesis 1:26). Satan's trying to sell them something they already have.

When the woman saw that the fruit was "pleasing to the eye," she took some and ate it. She gave some to her husband, and he ate it. Then their eyes were opened, and they realized they were naked, so they covered themselves (see Genesis 3:6–7).

What's happened here? Before they ate the fruit, they were both naked and felt no shame. Now their experience of nakedness changed. Why?

God, who is Truth, cannot tell a lie. He said that if they ate from the tree they would die. Now, they didn't immediately fall over dead, but they did die spiritually.

It was the Spirit that was given to them as the calling and the power to love. When the Spirit "died" in our first parents, so did their ready ability to love in the image of God as male and female. Absent the Spirit, sexual desire became inverted, self-seeking.

Adam and Eve no longer clearly saw in each other's bodies the reve-lation of God's plan of love. They each now saw the other's body more as a thing to use for their own selfish desires. In this way, the experience of nakedness in the presence of the other—and in the presence of God—became an experience of fear, alienation, shame: "I was afraid, because I was naked; and I hid myself" (Genesis 3:10).

Their shame was connected not so much with the body itself but with the selfish sting of lust now in their hearts. For they still know that since they were created as persons for their own sakes, they were never meant to be looked upon as things for another person's use. So they covered their bodies to protect their own dignity from the other's lustful "look." This is, in fact, a positive function of shame, because it actually serves to protect the "spousal meaning of the body."

Sexual Complementarity Becomes Sexual Discord

The body is the revelation of the person, as John Paul II put it.[14] This means that all our differences as men and women (emotional, mental, spiritual, as well as physical) were created by God to complement each other, to unite us in life-giving ways. Because of sin, however, we often experience these differences as the cause of great tension, conflict, and division. Indeed, history tells the tale of the chaos that original sin has brought into man and woman's relationship.

Initially, Adam received Eve as the true blessing and gift from God that she is. But after sin, he was blaming her for all his problems. He even faulted God, saying, "The woman *you* put here with me—*she* gave me the fruit" (see Genesis 3:12). It's all *her* fault. How often do men, even today, blame and resent women for their own problems?

Furthermore, women throughout history have suffered greatly because of the domination of men. "Your desire shall be for your husband, and he shall rule over you" (Genesis 3:16): This is not God's intention. This is a result of sin. Some men, however, refusing to face their own sinfulness, even try to use various Scripture verses to justify their domination of women (see, for example, chapter three, question 18).

But let's remember that it's a two-way street. Fallen woman's "desire for her husband" has also been a source of real angst for men. While men often dominate and manipulate women for their own gratification, women often use their femininity to control and manipulate men as well. Either way, we end up treating the other not as a person created for his or her own sake but as a thing to be used for our own selfishness.[15] In turn, we make the tragic mistake of calling that "love." We shouldn't be surprised that self-gratification at the expense of others—like diesel fuel in an unleaded-only engine—causes serious "car troubles."

The Redemption of Our Sexuality in Christ

While an echo of God's original intention remains in our hearts, this distorted way of relating has become our lot. Tragically, for many people, it's all they know. They simply accept it as the norm. The *good news* is that Christ came to restore God's original intention of love in the world. Through an ongoing conversion of heart, we can experience the redemption of our sexuality.

This is what Christ was calling us to in the Sermon on the Mount when he said: "Everyone who looks at a woman lustfully has already committed adultery with her in his heart" (Matthew 5:28). Of course, his words apply to men and women equally. As if to emphasize the seriousness of this sin, he immediately added, "If your right eye causes you to sin, pluck it out.... And if your right hand causes you to sin, cut it off.... It is better that you lose one of your members than that your whole body go into hell" (Matthew 5:29–30).

Hell is the absence of God's love. So is lust. That's why it's so serious.

So what are we to do? If we look at the common human experience, it seems that everyone is condemned by Christ's words. That's true. But let's remember, Christ came into the world not to condemn us. He came to save us (see John 3:16–18).

Reflecting on these words of Christ, John Paul II posed the question: "Should we *fear* the severity of [Christ's] words, or rather *have confidence* in their salvific content, in their power?"[16] Their power lies in the fact that the man who utters them is "the Lamb of God, who takes away the sin of the world" (John 1:29).

How does he do it? By making a total, faithful, and fruitful gift of his body to his Bride, the Church, on the cross. And by once again breathing the Spirit upon humanity (see John 20:22).

Paraphrasing John Paul II, sin and death entered human history, in a way, through the very heart of the unity of the first Adam and Eve.[17] Similarly, redemption and new life entered human history through the very heart of the unity of the New Adam and Eve, that is, Christ and the Church. Right after Adam and Eve fell, we have the foretelling of this redemption in a Scripture passage known as the *Protoevangelium* (the first announcement of the Gospel). Speaking to the serpent, God says: "I will put enmity between you and the woman, and between your seed and her seed; he shall bruise your head, and you shall bruise his heel" (Genesis 3:15).

Jesus is the New Adam, the offspring of "the woman" who will deliver the fatal blow to the serpent's head. As the model of the Bride-Church, Mary represents the New Eve.[18] Christ's redemptive "marriage" to the Church is foreshadowed at the wedding feast of Cana (see John 2:1–11) and consummated on the cross at Calvary.[19]

When Mary came to Jesus to tell him that the wedding feast was out of wine, Jesus said, "O woman, what have you to do with me? My hour has not yet come" (John 2:4). Already, Jesus is referring to the hour of his passion.

The water changed to wine at Cana prefigures the blood and water that flow from Christ's side at Calvary (see John 19:34). As figures of baptism and the Eucharist, the blood and water symbolize the very life of God coming from the side of the New Adam as the birth of the New Eve. And like the first Adam, the New Adam calls her by name—"woman" (see Genesis 2:23 and John 19:26).

First Adam and Eve	New Adam and Eve
Adam put into deep sleep	Christ put into "deep sleep" on the cross
Eve comes from his side	Church born of his side in blood and water
Eve is given a message by the angel Lucifer to deny God's life	Mary is given a message by the angel Gabriel to receive God's life
God's life dies within her (us)	God's life is conceived within her (us)
They denied the gift of God's love and were unable to love others	They believed in the gift of God's love and are able to love others
Their union transmitted original sin to all humanity	Their union brings the new life of redemption to all humanity

Creation is, as theologians would say, recapitulated—that is, repeated, summed up—in the work of Christ. Man and woman have been born again. Their perennial love for one another has been recreated. (See the chart above.)

"The woman" at the foot of the cross represents us all, men and women. We are *all* called to be the Bride of Christ.[20] In offering us his body, Christ offers us a "marriage proposal." All we need to do is say yes by offering our bodies—our whole selves—back to him. This is what the sacramental life of the Church is all about.

In fact, the *Catechism* describes baptism as a "nuptial bath."[21] Here, as we unite ourselves with Christ's sacrifice, we're cleansed of our sin by the washing with water through the Word (see Ephesians 5:26). Furthermore, having already been united (or married) to him in baptism, when we receive Christ's body in the Eucharist, we consummate a mystical marriage, and, as stated earlier, we even conceive new life in us—life in the Holy Spirit.

As much as lust blinds man and woman to their own truth and distorts their sexual desires, so much does this new life in the Holy Spirit empower men and women to love one another as they were called to in the beginning. Through the sacraments we can know and experience the transforming power of Christ's love.

This is good news. This is great news. Yes, we've put the wrong gas in our engines and suffered the consequent car troubles. But God doesn't say, "You idiot. I told you so." No! In his infinite mercy he offers us an engine overhaul and all the free unleaded gas we could ever need. He doesn't leave us to wallow in our sin but offers us redemption.

In short, it's okay that we're broken, because there's a remedy. But it is not okay to call our brokenness health. Only by reflecting on God's plan "in the beginning" do we have the proper measure of what health is. When we justify our own sinful attitudes and behaviors by claiming "God created me this way," we actually forfeit his offer to recreate us.

A Question of Faith

It makes sense that, since it was man and woman's turning away from God that distorted their relationship in the first place, restoring the truth and meaning of human sexuality requires a radical *re-turn* to God. Satan convinced us in the beginning that God doesn't love us, that he's withholding himself from us. In order to dispel all doubt, God became one of us and made an everlasting gift of himself to us on the cross.

Each of us, then, needs to ask himself or herself: *Do I believe in God's gift? Do I believe in his infinite love for me?*

Living the truth about our sexuality is thus really a question of faith. Do we believe in the good news of the Gospel? We confess that Christ came to save us from sin and reconcile us to the Father. Yet this may simply rattle off our tongues without much thought.

Ask yourself: *Do I really believe that Christ came to save me from sin? Do I really believe that, with the help of God's grace, it's possible to overcome my weaknesses, selfishness, and lust in order to love others as Christ has loved me? In other words, do I really believe that Christ can redeem me—even my sexuality?*

Resisting the sinful distortions of sexual desire and living in accordance with the truth is a very difficult struggle, even for someone with a solid moral formation. In a sense, this struggle brings us to the heart of the spiritual battle (see Ephesians 6:12) that we must fight as Christians if we are to resist evil—both in the world and in ourselves—and love others as Christ has loved us. Winning this battle takes faith in Christ, dedication, commitment, honesty with ourselves and others, and a willingness to make sacrifices and deny our own selfish desires. But love is not afraid of those things; love *is* those things.

Yes, the Church's teaching about sex is challenging. It's the challenge of the Gospel itself, the challenge to pick up our crosses and follow Christ. Like St. Paul we may carry a particular "thorn" of weakness in our flesh throughout our earthly journey (see 2 Corinthians 12:7). Even so, God's grace is sufficient for us to remain faithful to the beautiful plan that God revealed "in the beginning."

Let's not empty the cross of its power, but let's believe in the Good News. Let's believe that in Christ, true love—that love that is the very meaning of our being and existence—is possible. This is what the Church never ceases to proclaim to every man and woman.

God's Original Plan: The Norm for Sex and Marriage

When questioned about divorce, Christ pointed his followers back to God's original plan. "For your hardness of heart [i.e., sin] Moses allowed you to divorce your wives, but from the beginning [before sin] it was not so" (Matthew 19:8). Because Christ takes away our sin, he is able to restore God's original plan of love as the norm for marriage and all sexual expression.

This means marriage is only marriage, and sex is only sex, to the extent that they participate in God's free, total, faithful, and fruitful love. This norm—God's original plan of love prior to sin—is the proper basis for addressing all the many questions and objections that people are posing today about the Church's teaching on sexual morality and marriage.

2

Who Says?

Church Authority and Other Preliminary Questions

No man is so free as he who is able to renounce his own will and do the will of God.

—Author unknown

People hate being told what to do and what not to do, especially when it comes to sex. Part of this attitude bears witness to our dignity as free human beings. When we're *forced* to do something, we often sense that it violates our dignity.

Yet, another aspect of this attitude bears witness to the reality of original sin. We don't want anyone, not even God, telling us that something we want to do is wrong. We want to determine what is good and evil for ourselves. It's the problem of pride.

Human pride rebels against authority. And when authority is abused, we should protest. But when authority is exercised according to God's own design, if we want to be truly free, then we must obey it. It's the paradox of the Gospel: by dying, we live (see John 12:24); by giving ourselves away we find ourselves (see Matthew 16:25); by obeying the truth we're set free (see John 8:32).

Obedience at its best doesn't stem from force or fear but from love for the true, the good, and the beautiful—love for God. Freedom is not liberation from the external constraint that calls me to what is good. True freedom is liberation from the internal constraint that keeps me from choosing what is good. The truly free person doesn't look upon God's commands as a burden. The truly free person longs to do God's will.

But how do we know God's will, especially with regard to our sexuality? It simply wouldn't make sense for God to hold us accountable to his will if we didn't have a sure way of knowing what it is. In this lies the good news of the Church's teaching: God has revealed his will to us.

With that in mind, let's consider some of the most frequent questions asked about the Church's teaching authority—questions that must be answered before we can deal with what the Church teaches specifically about human sexuality.

1. Who determines what the Church officially teaches? Aren't we all "the Church"?

The Church is united to Christ as a bride to her husband. It's Christ who determines what his Bride teaches. Christ gave authority to some members of the Church to be faithful witnesses of all that he has commanded; this is the role of the Church's Magisterium. This official teaching office is made up of the pope and the bishops throughout the world who are in union with him. When the pope teaches on issues of faith and morals, and when the bishops teach on faith and morals in union with him, they teach in Christ's name and with his authority.

Yes, all baptized Catholics make up the Catholic Church. We are all "one body" in Christ (see 1 Corinthians 12:12). This body, however, has a sacred order to it, a *hierarchy* (*hier-archy* literally means "sacred order"). As St. Paul said, the body of Christ has different members who play different roles (see 1 Corinthians 12). All these different roles are vital to the organic functioning of the body: "The eye cannot say to the hand, 'I have no need of you,' nor again the head to the feet, 'I have no need of you'" (1 Corinthians 12:21). Nor should the eye wish she were a hand, nor the foot wish he were the head.

Those in the Church who teach with the authority of Christ don't claim the task for themselves. They are ordained by God to do so. That's their role within the body. The Magisterium, then, is a tremendous gift to the Church and the world because it gives us a sure way of knowing the teachings of Christ.

2. Where did the Church get the idea of having a "Magisterium" to give official teachings?

Christ founded his Church upon St. Peter, the leader of the apostles. He gave Peter "the keys of the kingdom of heaven" and told him: "Whatever you bind on earth shall be bound in heaven, and whatever you loose on earth shall be loosed in heaven" (see Matthew 16:13–20 for the whole discourse).

In other words, Christ gave St. Peter the authority to represent him on earth, to teach in his name and with his authority. This wasn't because Peter was an impeccable guy, but because Christ would protect him and the other apostles by sending them the Holy Spirit to guide them into "all truth" (see John 16:13).

What Christ promised two thousand years ago continues in our own day. The pope and the bishops are in a direct, traceable line of succession from St. Peter and the other apostles—hence we speak of the one, holy, catholic, and *apostolic* Church. They too are promised the gift of the Holy Spirit to guide the Church into all truth. So as Catholics we believe that when they teach on matters of faith and morals, they do so with the authority of Christ himself.[1]

Led by the pope, the Church is "the pillar and bulwark of the truth" (1 Timothy 3:15). This isn't because of human merit but because the Church remains in the most intimate union with her Bridegroom, Jesus Christ. Jesus said to his apostles, "He who hears you hears me, and he who rejects you rejects me" (Luke 10:16). Thus, the Second Vatican Council can teach that when we receive the teachings of the pope and bishops and live according to them, we are receiving "not the mere word of men, but truly the word of God" (see 1 Thessalonians 2:13).[2]

3. Are you saying the Church actually believes she speaks for God and knows "the truth"? That's so arrogant!

In those circumstances when she authoritatively proclaims teachings on faith and morals, yes, the Church actually believes she does so with a divine authority and has been granted by Christ a share in his own infallibility.[3] That's an amazingly bold claim with which we all must reckon. We can draw only one of two conclusions: Either the Church is extremely arrogant, as you say—or, just maybe, the Church really is Christ's authoritative witness to the truth.

In the end, there's no middle ground. If the Church is who she claims to be, then we will see her as a great blessing from God, and we will want to conform our lives to what she teaches. Even when we may not understand a certain *why* behind a teaching, we will trust that it will come to light in due time. On the other hand, if the Church is extremely arrogant, then we should not even want to be associated with the name *Catholic*.

This is a weighty reality. It confronts us and forces us to choose. We live in a culture that teaches us to avoid such ultimate choices. We prefer to invent both/and scenarios rather than face up to the inescapable either/or realities of life.

In other words, we live in a culture that rejects objective truth. "That may be true for you, but not for me," people say. Or, "Anybody's opinion is just as valid as anyone else's." We've all been affected by these attitudes.

But Jesus taught something very different. He taught that he is the truth (see John 14:6), and he established a Church that he promised would teach the truth (see John 16:13). He invites us to accept that. We are free not to accept it. But it's a terribly weighty decision that we shouldn't take lightly.

Approaching the matter from a purely practical perspective, it only makes sense that Christ would establish a definitive authority on earth to make his will known. Otherwise, interpreting Scripture and determining God's will on issues with eternal consequences would amount to a guessing game. A God-given authority on earth is essential to maintain unity in faith.

If Christ truly gave a divine authority to the Catholic Church, it's not arrogant for her to exercise it. If we're honest, what's arrogant is for us to think we have a better plan than God.

4. How can the Church claim to teach without error? History shows that the Church has made lots of mistakes and done some horrible things. What about Galileo, the Crusades, and the Inquisition?

On the first Sunday of Lent, 2000, St. John Paul II publicly sought God's mercy and forgiveness for the past sins committed by members of the Church. As this gesture so clearly indicates, the Church doesn't claim that all her members and leaders throughout history have never spoken in error or never made mistakes. (As a member of the Church, have you ever made a mistake or spoken in error? Blows that theory...) The charism that protects the Church from error applies to her definitive teachings on matters of *faith* and *morals*.

Certainly members of the Church, including some priests, bishops, and popes, have not always lived according to the teachings of their own faith. They have made mistakes. At times, terrible things have been done in the name of "the Church." Horrible crimes have even been committed by certain corrupt leaders in the Church (one need only think of the sexual abuse cases of certain clergy and the cowardly attempt of certain leaders to cover them up).

Such things are scandalous and there's no difficulty understanding why they can weaken or destroy people's faith in the Church. Yet the fact that the Church has endured so much corruption and is still standing after two thousand years also bears testimony to Christ's words when he founded the Church upon Peter: "The powers of death shall not prevail against [the Church]" (Matthew 16:18).

Why has there been corruption in the Church? First of all because the Church is made up of people such as you and me. As the saying goes, the

Church is not a "hotel for saints," it's a "hospital for sinners." Yes, we're all called to be saints, but we don't reach perfection in this life. Meanwhile, as Christ said, both wheat and weeds will be growing in the Church until the harvest (see Matthew 13:24–30).

But the good news is this: Even when individual members of the Church have been unfaithful, even when in certain times of history the weeds have seemed more plentiful than the wheat, Christ has never abandoned his Bride. While members of the Church have made mistakes, the Church has never erred in those teachings on faith and morals that she has proclaimed in a definitive manner, and she never will. This is God's own promise.

5. With so much corruption and scandal in the Church, why do you keep defending it? How can you even remain Catholic?

I am in no way defending the corruption itself. That is indefensible. But let us not throw out the baby with the bathwater.

One will always be able to find enough folly and corruption in the Church to want to leave (or never enter). But the folly and corruption in the Church is not unique to Catholics. It's found everywhere human beings are found. If I were to leave the Church in response to the folly and corruption within her, I would soon find I've taken that folly and corruption with me— because the potential for it is *in me* (not because I'm Catholic, but because I'm human). No one can escape the human condition.

I stay in the Church because I've come to believe that within her dwells, at the same time, both all the folly and corruption of the human condition *and* the only complete remedy for it. Within the Church we receive a "full access pass" to an infinite mercy and love that has not only "approached" us in our wounded humanity, but come *within us* to heal and restore us. And it's done so not only in some "spiritual" way. Infinite love and mercy have become *incarnate*, manifested *in the flesh*, and the Catholic Church claims to be the continuation in history of that incarnate mystery.

If the Church is Christ's *Body* on earth, we should expect her to be bruised, broken, and blemished, just as he was. But we should also expect her to be headed toward a resurrection "without spot, wrinkle, blemish, or any such thing" (Ephesians 5:27). If it is indeed true that the Church is Christ's Body on earth—bruised, broken, and headed for glory—then I want to be part of that; I want to "graft" my bruised and broken humanity into this "Body" and hang on for the ride: a ride that promises to take me to Infinity… and beyond!

Since I was very young, I've felt a wild, burning, ache inside for "something"…a cry in my chest for the infinite that I didn't put there and that won't let me go. "Through many dangers, toils, and snares," I've come to discover with St. Augustine that the "whole of life" for someone truly living the Catholic faith "is a holy longing." That's our life as Catholics, Augustine insists, "to be trained by longing."[4]

And this means that despite all the widespread impressions to the contrary, *Catholicism is the religion of longing and desire*. It's the religion that *redeems eros* (that mad cry of the heart for infinite love and union, for infinite truth, goodness, and beauty) by directing it to the union of love that alone can satisfy: the eternal "nuptials" of God and humanity, of Christ and the Church. The saints recognized by the Church are those who've had the courage to *feel* the infinite abyss of longing in their souls and in their bodies and to open that longing in "the groanings of prayer" to the One who alone can heal their "wound of love."

I remain Catholic because I want that healing—*I need that healing*—more than oxygen. I remain Catholic because I've come to believe that the heavenly nuptials promised to the Church, the Bride of Christ, are the definitive answer to that cry in my heart for the infinite.

6. What do you mean that Catholicism is the religion of longing and desire? The Catholic Church I grew up in was a religion of rules and regulations!

Tragically, as in your experience, Catholicism is thought far more often to be a "religion of law" than a "religion of longing." I was given the same impression growing up in the Church. If we really want to know what the Church holds out to the world, we have to dig deeper than the faulty impressions we were often given in our upbringings.

The *Catechism of the Catholic Church* is a great place to look for real answers. It doesn't begin with a discussion of law. It begins with a discussion of *desire*:

> The desire for God is written in the human heart, because man is created by God and for God; and God never ceases to draw man to himself. Only in God will he find the truth and happiness he never stops searching for: The dignity of man rests above all on the fact that he is called to communion with God.[5]

Of course, there are "laws" within the Church, but each and every one of them serves only to point our longing in the right direction. As G.K. Chesterton astutely observed, "And the more I considered Christianity, the more I found that while it had established a rule and order, the chief aim of that order was to give room for good things to run wild."[6]

When the Catholic Faith is not properly framed as God's passionate desire for union with us and our quest for the true satisfaction of our deepest longings in union with him, it eventually becomes incomprehensible and even meaningless. More than that, it can even morph into something destructive to our humanity.

In the words of the late Monsignor Lorenzo Albacete, "Religion is either the reasonable quest for the satisfaction of all the original desires of the heart, or it is a dangerous, divisive, harmful waste of time."[7]

7. Doesn't the "infallibility" of the Church apply only in rare pronouncements of the pope?

The Church exercises the charism of infallibility (the inability to err) in two ways. The *extraordinary* way is exercised when the pope makes an *ex cathedra* ("from the chair" of St. Peter) pronouncement.[8] The *ordinary* way is exercised when the Magisterium agrees on a matter of faith or morals as definitively to be held.[9]

It's a common error to think infallibility only applies to *ex cathedra* pronouncements, as if these are the only teachings Catholics "have" to believe. That would mean we wouldn't "have" to believe in the Trinity or the Incarnation or a host of other core beliefs that have never been defined by *ex cathedra* pronouncements. As the *Catechism* makes clear, "The infallibility of the Magisterium...extends to *all* the elements of doctrine, including moral doctrine, without which the saving truths of the faith cannot be preserved, expounded, or observed."[10]

Furthermore, even in those cases when the Magisterium teaches without exercising the charism of infallibility, we are called to adhere to those teachings "with religious assent."[11]

8. The Church should get rid of its hierarchical structure and be more democratic and open to dialogue.

In recent times, the term *hierarchy* has become a bad word. Many seem to think it's somehow synonymous with inequality. But as we noted before, *hierarchy* simply means "sacred order."

To reject hierarchy, then, is not to reject inequality. To reject hierarchy is to reject God's ordering of the universe. Not a good idea. The opposite of hierarchy is not equality but *anarchy*—no order at all, chaos.[12]

Our world today is filled with chaos, and it all stems from rejecting God-given authority. To a large extent, what has been specifically rejected is God's plan for sex and marriage. It's difficult to find even one social evil, one element of societal chaos, that is not in some way related to the breakdown of marriage and the misuse of sex.

The Church is not a democracy. The truth about Christ and what he teaches cannot be determined by popular vote. If God reveals something to be true, it's not open for "dialogue" about whether or not it's really true.

On the other hand, if by dialogue we mean an open discussion about a given teaching with the goal of understanding *why* the Church teaches what she teaches, that's legitimate. But if by dialogue we mean that the Church needs to listen to other opinions with the goal of being willing to change her definitive teaching on faith and morals, that's not legitimate. The Church simply cannot change what the Holy Spirit has revealed to be true. It's not a matter of stubborn unwillingness; it's a matter of *impossibility*.

For example, it makes no sense to "dialogue" about whether or not 2 + 2 = 4. We can "dialogue" about *why* 2 + 2 = 4 with the goal of explaining it for those who don't understand, but we can't hope to change the fact that 2 + 2 = 4.

God does not change for us. We must change for him. How our pride rebels! But until we come to grips with this fundamental reality—that we are *not* God—then we're living an illusion.

9. As a Catholic, am I not allowed to question the Church's teachings? Perhaps the Church is wrong about some things. Do I have to believe everything the Church teaches?

There's nothing wrong when a person growing in his faith poses questions in an earnest quest for truth. That's how we discover what the truth is. No one, then, should be afraid of entertaining "perhaps." Perhaps God doesn't exist. But perhaps he does. Perhaps the Catholic Church is woefully misguided in her teachings. But perhaps her teachings come from God himself. These kinds of questions *must* be entertained.

Those who are afraid to put their beliefs to the test in this way are clinging to an ideology that they fear will not stand up to reality. On the other hand, those who seek the truth have no fear of surrendering their beliefs to reality. Entertaining "perhaps" is the only path to the truth. It's the only path to the surety and freedom of faith.

Faith, however, is a gift that doesn't necessarily come all at once. The Church herself recognizes that "an educational growth process is necessary in order that individual believers...may patiently be led forward arriving at a richer understanding and fuller integration of [Christ's] mystery in their lives."[13]

Still, if the Church is who she claims to be, then the gift of faith will ultimately lead the seeker of truth to embrace all that she teaches. If in the end a person still protests what the Church teaches, then that person doesn't really believe the Catholic Church. At that point it would seem hypocritical to remain Catholic.

"Ask, and it will be given you; seek, and you will find; knock, and it will be opened to you" (Matthew 7:7). Pose every question you've ever had about the Church, entertain every "perhaps" you can think of, but don't be satisfied until you find the answers.[14] The truth is not afraid of your questions. The question is, are you afraid of the truth?

10. Isn't morality a matter of my own conscience?

The Church has always taught that Catholics, like all people, are obligated to follow their own consciences—on issues of sexual morality and every other matter. But there is an even more fundamental obligation to *form* the conscience according to the truth. Conscience is not free to *invent* right and wrong. Conscience is called to discover the truth of what is right and wrong and to submit its judgments to the truth once the truth is found.

While all of us have the basic moral law written in our hearts by God, original sin tends to cloud our judgment. Sometimes our own fallen desires can take us completely off track. This is why the conscientious person sees the Church's moral teachings as a tremendous gift. They're a *sure norm* for forming one's conscience according to the truth.

Too often we use "conscience" to give a morally acceptable veneer to what we wanted to do all along without discerning our behavior in light of objective standards. Think about it: if personal conscience is the autonomous determinant of good and evil, morality becomes whatever *I* want it to be. Who are *we*, then, to tell a rapist or a mass murderer that what he does is evil if *his* conscience says it's okay? There must be objective standards that we're all responsible to follow. Those objective standards are given to us by God and are revealed through the teachings of his Church.

Yet, what is frequently our response when we don't like what his Church teaches? We hide behind our claims of "conscience" and imagine a God who accepts what *we* want. But that's a god who is other than God. That's an idol.

We'll never find peace and true happiness until we embrace God's will for our lives. That's what conversion of heart is all about—and we're *all* in need of it.

11. The Church should stop judging people and imposing her teaching on everybody. We should all be free to make our own choices.

We *are* all free to make our own choices. The Church never *imposes* her teaching. But the Church does boldly and fearlessly *propose* her teaching to the world as the truth of what it means to love. We're free to embrace the Church's proposal or reject it. Love can't be forced on anybody.

While it's true that God alone can judge the human heart, we can and must make moral judgments about certain *behaviors*. The Church would betray God and all humanity if she didn't uphold God's will as the objective standard for all. To condemn a person's *behavior*, however, is not to condemn the *person*, but to call that person to embrace the truth of love.

Love isn't arbitrary. Love isn't whatever makes a person "feel good." Love means following Christ and keeping his commandments (see John 15:10). That is what the Church's teaching is all about. And it's a joy to live, not a burden.

12. Why is there such a widespread notion that the Church is down on sex?

Even the most loyal Catholic must admit that this generally held notion—even if incorrect—is not merely the fancy of illusion. Far too many impressionable young minds have been formed (or mis-formed) by the prudish, scolding tones of a well-intentioned (we pray) but misguided and sexually disintegrated nun or priest. From where comes this general cloud of "sexual negativity" that seems so closely associated in people's minds with the Catholic Church?

To be sure it has much to do with misinterpretation of Church teaching. But we don't do a disservice to the Church by admitting that it also has much to do with the disparaging treatment of sex that has recurred all too often in the works of various historical Christian authors.

The objective person will admit that a deep ambivalence about the body and its functions, particularly its sexual, genital functions, is not a limited Christian phenomenon but a universal human phenomenon.[15] As such, Christian authors, like many others, have not been exempt from the failure to appreciate fully the goodness and beauty of sex. Still, it's important, within the context of this admission, that we not confuse the mind *of* the Church with the minds of the people *in* the Church.

In the face of many attacks, the Church's official teachings have always upheld the inherent goodness of the body and of sexuality. The Church has deemed all contrary systems of thought nothing short of heretical. Unfortunately, until the twentieth century, official pronouncements on the matter have been relatively brief and juridical in nature. As such, they haven't made as lasting an impression on our culture's "historical conscious-ness" as some of the more extensive writings of Catholic thinkers who were heavily influenced by currents of thought alien to the mind of the Church. Thus, despite significant developments of Magisterial teaching on sex and marriage in the last century, the notion that the Church is "down on sex" still lingers.

Regarding Church teaching itself, it seems that misinterpretation of the esteem accorded the celibate vocation, as well as misinterpretation of the Church's strict moral code, have also contributed to the prevailing attitude. Traditionally, those who followed Christ's words and chose to remain cel-ibate "for the sake of the kingdom" (Matthew 19:12) were considered to have chosen the more holy or "higher" path. While there is a proper way of understanding this (as we'll discuss in chapter ten), it has often been misun-derstood to mean that those who do marry and have sex are somehow less holy, or even "unholy."

The sentiment goes like this: If virginity is so good, sex must be so bad. If refraining from sex makes one pure and holy, having sex must make one dirty and unholy.

Yet nothing could be further from the mind of the Church in promoting the celibate vocation. The Church holds this vocation in such high regard precisely because she holds that which is sacrificed for the sake of God—genital sexual expression—in high regard. If sex were something unclean and unholy, offering it as a gift to God would be an act of sacrilege. But since sex is one of the most precious treasures God has given humanity, making a gift of it back to God is one of the most genuine expressions of thanksgiving (*eucharistia*) for such a great gift. The other is receiving it from God's hands and living it as the expression of the marital covenant.

The misinterpretation of the Church's strict moral code is similar. The sentiment goes like this: If the Church says you can't do this and you can't do that—everything that it seems people *want* to do—then the Church *must* think sex is bad, even if she grants the one reluctant exception of "doing it" for the purpose of procreation. This latter belief (that the Church teaches you can only have sex if you want a baby) is a fallacy we'll get to in chapters five and six.

For the present, we must clarify the simple fact that saying, "Handle with care"—or even "Handle with *extreme* care"—is in no way synonymous with saying, "This is bad." In fact, what are those things in life that we handle with the most care? The things that have the most inherent value. It's because sex is so valuable, because it's so precious in the eyes of Christ and his Church, that it must be handled with extreme care.

When we venture into the realm of sex, we are on holy ground. Only those who are properly disposed can handle the mystery.

There's a parallel here with another holy mystery of the Church: the Eucharist. The Church has many "strict" teachings about who can and cannot receive the Eucharist, how it's to be received, and with what spiritual dispositions. It would be absurd to conclude that the Church is therefore "down on the Eucharist." It's no less absurd to conclude that the Church is down on sex because of her strict moral teaching about it.[16]

Historically speaking, God tends to grant the Church what she needs when she needs it. Not until the twentieth century, with its widespread dismissal of long-held sexual mores, did the Church have "need" to deepen her understanding of conjugal love, sex, and marriage beyond her previous brief pronouncements. Hence, as noted before, over two-thirds of what the Catholic Church has ever officially said about sex and marriage has come from Pope St. John Paul II.

Granted, the Church tends to move slowly. But once this pope's profound rethinking of the Church's teaching has been assimilated into the consciousness of the Church, it's sure to dispel once and for all the notion that the Church is down on sex.

13. The Church should stick to religion and keep its nose out of my bedroom.

When the Church speaks about sex she *is* "sticking to religion." Sex is a religious event! According to John Paul II, when we speak of the "great sign" of the sacrament of marriage we are speaking about the entire work of creation and redemption.[17]

Sex plunges us headfirst into the Christian mystery. There's no getting around it: "Do you not know that your bodies are members of Christ?" (1 Corinthians 6:15).

By becoming "one flesh," spouses establish themselves and their family as the *domestic church*, a Church in miniature. Thus the Church isn't intruding into the bedroom. Christian spouses are bringing the Church into the bedroom with them.

Sex is sacred. It's holy—more so than our fallen passions sometimes wish it to be. If we think sex is somehow "better" with God out of the picture, we have it totally backward!

The joy of sex—in all its orgasmic grandeur—is meant to be the joy of loving as God loves. The joy of sex—in all its orgasmic grandeur—is meant to be a foretaste in some way of the joys of heaven: the eternal consummation of the marriage between Christ and the Church. Christ gives us his plan for sex through the Church not to be a "kill-joy" but a "bring-joy."

"If you keep my commandments," he said, "you will abide in my love.... These things I have spoken to you, that my joy may be in you, and that your joy may be full" (John 15:10–11). So if you want the most awesome, joy-filled sex possible, open wide the doors to Christ—including (and especially) the bedroom door.

14. I find it quite ironic that old celibate men seek to dictate sexual moral-ity to others. What do they know about sex?

First of all, as we clarified above, the pope and the bishops don't dictate anything to anybody. They simply witness to what God has revealed with the authority that Christ has given them. We always have the freedom to embrace it or reject it.

Second, the message they speak about sexual morality is not their own, it's God's. God created sex. He knows why he did it, what it's for, how it can bring great joy when it's respected, and how it can bring great misery when it's abused. In God's wisdom (which is often so different from ours) he has entrusted his plan for sex to these "celibate old men." To repeat our earlier illustration, refusing to listen is just as foolish as putting diesel fuel in your car when the manufacturer's sticker says, "unleaded gas only."

Third, anyone who doesn't think celibates can know anything about sex has never entered in to what St. John Paul II has to say about it. As we will explore more in chapter ten, contrary to widespread opinion, Christian celi-bacy is *not* a rejection or negation of sexuality. When authentically lived, it's a vibrant sign of the ultimate purpose and meaning of our sexuality: to point us to eternal union with God, to what Scripture calls the "marriage of the Lamb" (Revelation 19:7). Sexual pleasure in God's plan is meant to be a sign or an icon of our ultimate fulfillment in heaven. But when we treat sexual pleasure as ultimate fulfillment itself, the *icon* becomes an *idol*.

Like the fuel of a rocket, God gave us sexual desire as the power to launch us to the stars. The tragedy is that, with original sin, our rocket engines became inverted. This is why so many of our attempts to find love and fulfillment backfire on us. This is why following our sexual desires as we typically experience them in our fallen humanity eventually causes us to crash and burn. The good news I learned from St. John Paul II is that Christ came into the world not to condemn those with inverted rocket engines. He came to redirect our rocket engines to the stars!

Those who live Christian celibacy in an authentic way are pointing the rest of us to the stars. They're aiming all of their desires for ultimate love and fulfillment toward the *real thing*—union with God. As such, they become authentic witnesses to the deepest meaning of human sexuality—*if* we have the courage to listen.

15. Why is the Church so obsessed with sex?

Questions like this usually refer to the Church's keen interest in upholding sexual morality. To be sure, the Church does feel an urgent need to uphold the truth about sex. Why? For all the reasons we've noted about how important the issue of sex really is.

Sexuality is not just something biological but concerns the "innermost being of the human person."[18] To the extent that our understanding of sexuality is skewed, so is our understanding of *ourselves*. Think how intertwined sex is with the mystery of life. Without sex there would be no life.

The deepest truth about sexuality actually reveals the deepest truth about life. It's this: we are called through the gift of God's grace to share in God's life by loving as he loves—and this call is stamped into our very bodies as male and female; it's stamped into our sexuality. Paraphrasing John Paul II, rediscovery of the spousal meaning of the body always means rediscovery of the meaning of the whole of existence, the meaning of life.[19] *That's* why it's such an urgent matter.

The sexual urge taps into the most powerful drives and desires of the human heart. Depending on how they're directed, these drives and desires have the power for great good or great evil. In short, as created by God, the sexual urge was given to us as a "love instinct" that leads to life. But when it's cut off from the source of love and life (God), it tends to become a "lust instinct" that leads to death.

Sexual attitudes and behaviors, then, have the power to orient not only individuals but entire nations and societies toward respect for life—or toward its utter disregard. To be sure, when lust is woven into the fabric of a society, that society can be nothing but a "culture of death."

Sound exaggerated? Our nation alone murders over four thousand preborn babies *every day* in order to satisfy its lusts. And that's only the beginning.

Disordered sexuality is the "Pandora's box" that unleashes a host of societal evils: from the poverty of "fatherless" families and the staggering proliferation of sexually transmitted diseases (some fatal, such as AIDS), to the newborns found in dumpsters and increased violence among teens—all these can be traced to the breakdown of the sexual mores that hold the family intact as the fundamental cell of society. As sexual attitudes and behaviors go, so goes marriage. As marriage goes, so goes the family. As the family goes, so goes society. Paraphrasing John Paul II once again: Human life, its dignity and its balance, depends at every moment of history and at every point on the globe on the proper ordering of love between the sexes.[20]

We will never build a civilization of love and a culture of life unless we first live according to the truth of our sexuality. If the Church is "obsessed" with sex, it's because she's "obsessed" with upholding the dignity and balance of human life and the plan of God for humanity that our sexuality is meant to reveal.

3

What Are You Saying "I Do" To?

The Basics of Marriage in the Church

There are people who try to ridicule, or even to deny, the idea of a faithful bond which lasts a lifetime. These people—you can be very sure—do not know what love is. [1]

—St. John Paul II

I'll never forget November 18, 1995, nor the sight on that day of my bride processing down the aisle. She was glowing, radiant with feminine beauty. As I stood there by the altar, waiting to receive her, our eyes met and filled with tears. This was the moment. In the presence of God, the parish priest, and all our family and closest friends, we were giving our whole lives, unconditionally, to each other.

Throughout our engagement, strange as this may seem to some, there was perhaps nothing we'd discussed more than the Church's vision of marriage. We knew what the Church was holding out to us as the nature and meaning of this sacrament, and we desired it with all our hearts.

In my work over the years preparing engaged couples for marriage, I've been confronted with how few of them really understand what it is they're saying "I do" to. Marriage isn't whatever two people want it to be. For a relationship to be truly marital, it must conform to God's plan for marriage as *he* created it to be.

The questions and objections of this chapter cover "the basics" of marriage in the Church, including issues surrounding divorce and annulments and some contested Scripture passages. Since much confusion and resistance to the Church's teaching about sex stem from a misunderstanding of the meaning of marriage, this chapter will provide the necessary context for the discussion of sexual morality in the chapters that follow.

1. What exactly is marriage in the eyes of the Catholic Church?

We'll start with a basic definition paraphrasing a teaching from Vatican II and canon law, and then explain each of its points:

> Marriage is the intimate, exclusive, indissoluble communion of life and love entered by man and woman at the design of the Creator for the purposes of their own good and the procreation and education of children; this covenant between baptized persons has been raised by Christ the Lord to the dignity of a sacrament.[2]

Intimate communion of life and love. Marriage is the closest and most intimate of human friendships. It involves the sharing of the whole of a person's life with his or her spouse. Marriage calls for mutual self-surrender so intimate and complete that the two spouses become "one flesh," yet without losing their uniqueness as persons.

Exclusive. As a mutual gift of two persons to each other, this intimate union excludes such union with anyone else. It demands the total fidelity of the spouses. This exclusivity is essential for the good of the couple's children as well.

Indissoluble. Husband and wife are not joined by passing emotion or mere erotic inclination, which, selfishly pursued, fade quickly away.[3] They're joined by God in an unbreakable bond of love through the firm and irrevocable act of their own consent. For the baptized, this bond is sealed by the Holy Spirit and, once consummated, becomes absolutely indissoluble.[4] Thus, the Church does not so much teach that divorce is *wrong* but that divorce—in the sense of ending a valid marriage—is *impossible*, regardless of the civil status of a marriage.

Entered by man and woman. The fact that multiple governments around the world now claim that members of the same sex are able to marry only serves to underscore how widespread the confusion has become about the nature, meaning, and requirements of marital love. We've become blind in the modern world to the significance of the sexual difference. Still, when personal or social agendas are put aside, any objective person can recognize that there is something that a man and woman are designed to do together that two men or two women simply cannot do. That *something* (the ability to engage in the act designed by God to generate new life) is the very essence of what marriage *is*. When we understand this we also understand why those who cannot engage in this act cannot marry (see chapter eight for further discussion).

At the design of the creator. God is the Author of marriage. He inscribed the call to marriage in our very being by creating us as male and female.

Marriage is governed by his laws, faithfully transmitted by his Bride, the Church. For marriage to be what it's intended to be, it must conform to these laws. Human beings, therefore, are not free to change the meaning and purposes of marriage.

For the purposes of their own good. "It is not good that the man should be alone" (Genesis 2:18). Thus, it's for their own good, for their benefit, enrichment, and ultimately their salvation, that a man and woman join their lives in the covenant of marriage. Marriage is the most basic (but not the only) expression of the vocation to love that all men and women have as persons made in God's image.

And the procreation and education of children. The fathers of Vatican II declared: "By their very nature, the institution of marriage itself and conjugal love are ordained for the procreation and education of children and find in them their ultimate crown."[5] Children are not added on to marriage and conjugal love, but spring from the very heart of the spouses' mutual self-giving, as its fruit and fulfillment. Intentional exclusion of children, then, contradicts the very nature and purpose of marriage.

Covenant. Marriage is not only a contract between a man and a woman, but a sacred covenant. God created marriage to image and participate in his own covenant with his people. Thus, the marital covenant calls spouses to share in the *free, total, faithful,* and *fruitful* love of God. Contrary to some trends in thought, the Church's recent emphasis on marriage as a covenant does not exclude the idea that marriage is also a contract. It's true that a covenant goes beyond the rights and responsibilities guaranteed by some contracts and provides a stronger, more sacred framework for marriage, but canon law still purposely uses both terms to describe marriage.[6]

The dignity of a sacrament. By virtue of their baptisms, the marriage of Christian spouses is an efficacious sign of the union between Christ and the Church, and as such is a means of grace (see the next question for a more thorough discussion). The marriage of two unbaptized persons, or of one baptized person and one unbaptized person, is considered by the Church a "good and natural" marriage, but not a sacrament.

2. What makes a marriage a sacrament?

The simple answer is baptism. As St. John Paul II said, "Indeed, by means of baptism man and woman are definitively placed within...the spousal covenant of Christ and the Church. And it is because of this indestructible insertion that [marriage] is elevated and assumed into the spousal charity of Christ, sustained and enriched by his redeeming power."[7]

Still, of all the seven sacraments (baptism, confirmation, Eucharist, reconciliation, anointing of the sick, holy orders, and marriage), marriage seems, at first glance, the most unlike a sacrament. Marriage isn't unique to Christians, after all, but is found in all cultures and all religions. So what makes such a universally common reality a Christian sacrament? To provide a more thorough answer to this question, we first need to understand better what sacraments are.

If you had religion classes in your childhood, you may remember being taught that a sacrament is "an outward sign instituted by Christ to give grace."[8] For most people this textbook definition fails to capture how wonderful and profound the sacraments really are. Through these "visible signs instituted by Christ" we actually encounter the *eternal* God in the *temporal* world and become sharers in his divine life. Through the sacraments, we are called to experience what the early Christians called "divinization"—participation in God's very own life and nature.

An infinite abyss separates Creator and creature. The wonder of the sacraments is that they bridge this infinite gap. Sacraments are where heaven and earth "kiss," where God and humanity become one *in the flesh*.

God is invisible. Sacraments allow us to see him under the veil of visible things. God is intangible. Sacraments allow us to touch him. God is incommunicable. Sacraments are our communion with him.

This communion of God and humanity is a living reality in the person of Jesus Christ. Thus the sacramental life of the Church flows directly from the dynamism of the Incarnation, the mystery of the Word made flesh, God made Man. In Christ, God has forever wed himself to our flesh and impregnated the material world with his saving power. Indeed, as Tertullian, an early Christian writer, declared: "The flesh has become the hinge of salvation."[9]

In contrast to authentic sacramental spirituality, there is a widespread but gravely mistaken notion of spirituality that tends to devalue the physical world (especially the human body), view it with suspicion, or at times even treat it with contempt. Catholicism, however, is a deeply *sensual* religion. That's to say, it's in and through *the body* (sensually) and the "stuff" of the physical world that we encounter the divine.

God doesn't communicate himself to us by some sort of spiritual osmosis. Rather he meets us where we are as earthly, bodily creatures. This is the great gift of the sacraments.

We truly become sharers in divine life through bathing *the body* with water (baptism); through anointing *the body* with oil and the laying on of *hands* (confirmation, holy orders, anointing of the sick); through confessing with our *lips* and receiving the *spoken* words of absolution (reconciliation); through *eating* and *drinking* the *Body* and *Blood* of Christ (Eucharist); and yes, through the lifelong joining of a man and a woman in "one *flesh*" (marriage).

The marital embrace itself is meant to be an encounter with Christ and a sharing in divine life. Through sexual intercourse, the spouses *enact* their sacrament. It's where the words of the wedding vows become flesh, and, as such, together with the whole of married life, sexual intercourse becomes the visible sign of the sacrament of marriage. As St. John Paul II said: "The sacrament, as a visible sign, is constituted with man, inasmuch as he is a 'body,' through his 'visible' masculinity and femininity. The body, in fact, and only the body, is capable of making visible what is invisible: the spiritual and the divine. It has been created to transfer into the visible reality of the world the mystery hidden from eternity in God, and thus be a sign of it."[10]

Here it is in plain English: God created our bodies as male and female to be a sign in the world that reveals his own eternal mystery, and this happens most specifically when husband and wife unite their bodies in "one flesh."[11] What is this mystery hidden in God from all eternity? In a nutshell (as if it were possible to put God in a nutshell), it's God's Trinitarian life and his amazing plan for us to share in this life through Christ as members of the Church. *This* is what marriage symbolizes and reveals.

Sacraments are *efficacious* signs, which means they truly communicate what they symbolize. So the love of husband and wife is not merely a metaphor that indicates the love of Christ and the Church. For the baptized, it's a *real* participation in that love. This is a "great mystery," as St. Paul says (or as some translations say, this is a "great sacrament"—see Ephesians 5:32).

Because all the sacraments are meant to draw us more deeply into the marriage of Christ and the Church, St. John Paul II described marriage as the "prototype," in some sense, of all the sacraments.[12] As the *Catechism* says, "The entire Christian life bears the mark of the spousal love of Christ and the Church. Already Baptism...is a nuptial mystery; it is so to speak the nuptial bath which precedes the wedding feast, the Eucharist."[13]

Since the union of spouses provides a window for understanding the whole of the Christian life, John Paul II said that marriage, inasmuch as it points us to Christ's union with the Church, provides "the foundation of the whole sacramental order." *This* is what makes marriage a sacrament. It is the original revelation in the created world of the eternal mystery of God.

3. I always thought the Christian life was something spiritual. I never even thought about the role our bodies play in the sacraments. How do you reconcile this emphasis on the body with what the Bible says about living "by the Spirit" and not "by the flesh"?

St. Paul says we should "live by the Spirit" and not "gratify the desires of the flesh. For the flesh has desires against the Spirit, and the Spirit against the flesh" (Galatians 5:16–17). Elsewhere he admonishes us to "live according to the Spirit" because "those who are in the flesh cannot please God" (see Romans 8:4–8).

These verses do *not* mean, as many have tragically concluded, that St. Paul condemns the body or thinks of it as an inherent obstacle to the "spiritual" life. Christian spirituality is based on Christ, the Word made *flesh*. This means Christian spirituality is always and only an *incarnational spirituality*. The goal, as St. Paul himself insists, is not to reject our bodies, but to open them to divine life: "If the Spirit of the one who raised Jesus from the dead dwells in you, the one who raised Christ from the dead will give life to your mortal bodies also, through his Spirit that dwells in you" (Romans 8:11).

The modern world tends to put matter and spirit in fundamental opposition largely because of the philosophy of Rene Descartes. His famous dictum, "I think, therefore I am," introduced an insidious rupture into our understanding of the world that we often project onto the authors of Scripture. Catholic scholar Peter Kreeft explains:

> Pre-Cartesian cultures did not divide reality into two mutually exclusive categories of purely immaterial spirit and purely nonspiritual matter. Rather, they saw all matter as in-formed, in-breathed by spirit.... Descartes initiates "angelism" when he says, "My whole essence is in thought alone." Matter and spirit now become "two clear and distinct ideas." ...This is *our* common sense; we have inherited these categories, like nonremovable contact lenses, from Descartes, and it is impossible for us to understand pre-Cartesian thinkers while we wear them. Thus we are constantly reading our modern categories... into the authors of the Bible.[14]

In Paul's terminology "the flesh" refers to the whole person (body and soul) cut off from God's "in-spiration"—cut off from God's life-giving Spirit. It refers to a person dominated by vice. And, in this sense, as Christ himself asserted, "the flesh is of no avail" (John 6:63). The person who opens himself authentically to life "according to the Spirit," however, does *not* reject his body; it's his body that becomes the very dwelling place of the Spirit. "Do you not know that your body is a temple of the Holy Spirit within you, whom you have from God?... Therefore glorify God in your body" (1 Corinthians 6:19–20).

We glorify God in our bodies precisely by welcoming his Spirit into our entire body-soul personality and allowing the Spirit to guide what we do with our bodies. In this way, life in the Spirit becomes at one and the same time "the redemption of our bodies" (Romans 8:23).

Understanding and embracing this essential unity of body and soul, of matter and spirit, is critical if we are to understand properly not only *what* the Catholic Church teaches about sex and marriage but, more importantly, *why*. Indeed, as we will see more clearly throughout this book, virtually every contemporary objection to Catholic teaching on sex, gender, and marriage is rooted in the modern world's ruptured understanding of body and soul. Conversely, if we remain unflinching in holding body and soul in their proper unity, *everything* the Catholic Church teaches about sex, gender, and marriage will fall logically and beautifully into place.

4. The Church's teaching against divorce leaves some women in abusive relationships with no escape.

In the case of an abusive relationship, the Church readily recognizes the need of spouses to separate and even, if necessary, obtain a civil divorce. Still, such a decree would not *end* a valid marriage. Death alone ends marriage.

5. If the Church believes marriage is "until death do you part," why are there so many annulments?

There's a great deal of confusion today about annulments. An annulment (properly referred to as a "declaration of nullity") is not a "Catholic version of divorce." A divorce declares that you were once married but now you are no longer. A declaration of nullity is an official statement by the Church that a *valid marriage never existed in the first place.*

The Church is consistent with her own teaching on the permanence of marriage and in granting declarations of nullity. Valid, consummated, sacramental marriages can never be dissolved under any circumstance. But if it turns out that, despite all appearances, a couple was never validly married, then their relationship has no binding force.

Why are so many annulments granted today? It's not outside the realm of possibility that at times the system is abused. On the other hand, the number of annulments granted today may well be an accurate reflection of the number of couples who do not enter marriage validly. First of all, tribunals in the United States report that one-fourth to one-third of all annulments granted are due to "lack of form." This means large numbers of baptized Catholics are getting married *outside the Catholic Church*. If they do this without a dispensation, their marriage is null from the start (see next question).

Furthermore, people who approach the Church for marriage today have been raised in a culture that not only has lost a support structure for marriage but also very loudly, incessantly, and convincingly promotes values that are *antithetical* to marriage. The effects of this culture on people's ability to enter marriage validly should not be underestimated.

6. What makes a marriage valid?

Marriage is brought about by the legitimately manifested consent (vows) of a properly qualified bride and groom. Among other things, this means that the bride and groom are the ministers of the sacrament of marriage. Although people typically say Fr. So-and-so married us, that's incorrect. Fr. So-and-so hasn't married anybody—he's a celibate. The priest (or deacon) only serves as an official witness for the Church.[15]

This is an important point. Marriage is not something that simply "happens" to the couple by virtue of getting dressed up and going through the motions of a wedding ceremony. Marriage only "happens" if bride and groom minister it to each other.

If they don't, they aren't married, even if they went through the motions. Of course, if a Catholic couple has had a wedding ceremony in accordance with the teaching of the Church, we're always to assume they did minister the sacrament to each other. The Church always assumes the validity of a marriage unless proven otherwise.

But back to the question: What makes a marriage valid? Providing a comprehensive response is the task of an entire book, and several of those have been written.[16] It's only possible to provide a general overview here.

In order for the marriage of Catholics to be validly established, spouses must: (1) not have any impediments to marriage; (2) follow the proper form of the sacrament; (3) have the proper capacity to exchange consent and do so freely and unconditionally; and (4) consent to what the Church intends by marriage, that is: *fidelity, indissolubility,* and *openness to children.* Let's look at each of these aspects individually.

Spouses must not have any impediments to marriage. Impediments are prohibitions to marriage originating from divine or natural law and Church law. There are twelve:[17]

• *Age.* A man under age sixteen, and a woman under age fourteen, cannot marry validly. (Keep in mind we're dealing with a universal Church.

While marrying at these ages wouldn't be recommended in most developed countries, in some cultures it's common. Notice also that these ages indicate the age of sexual maturity, indicating the nature of the marital relationship.)

• *Impotence.* Definitive and perpetual inability to engage in that act designed by God for the generation of new life (sexual intercourse).

• *Previous bond.* Preexistence of a valid marriage to someone else.

• *Disparity of cult.* When a baptized Catholic attempts to marry an unbaptized person (though a dispensation from this impediment can be granted in certain cases).

• *Sacred orders.* Persons bound by holy orders—that is, deacons,[18] priests, and bishops—cannot marry.

• *Perpetual vows of chastity.* Public vows of celibacy taken in a religious institute (that is, an institute of religious brothers or sisters).

• *Abduction.* When a person has been abducted for the purpose of marriage.

• *Crime.* When a previous spouse has been murdered in order to "free" someone to marry.

• *Consanguinity.* Blood relationships including anyone closer than second cousins.

• *Affinity.* In-law relationships in the direct line. (For example, a stepfather could not marry his stepdaughter, but a man could marry his deceased wife's sister.)

• *Public propriety.* When an unmarried person cohabiting with someone else wishes to enter marriage with a close relative in the direct line of the person with whom he or she has been living. (For example, a woman living with a man cannot marry either his father or his son.)

• *Adoption.* Family relationships established by adoption to the degree mentioned above.

Spouses must follow the proper form of the sacrament.[19] This requires the presence of an official witness (usually a priest or deacon) who receives their consent in the name of the Church and two other witnesses (usually the "best man" and the "maid or matron of honor"), who are also present for the exchange of vows. Thus baptized Catholics who marry outside the Church (for example, in a civil ceremony or in another denomination) do so invalidly. If a Catholic wishes to marry a non-Catholic and has sufficient reason to hold the ceremony in a non-Catholic setting, a dispensation from the form can be granted.

Spouses must have the capacity to exchange consent and do so freely and uncon- ditionally.[20] A person must be psychologically capable of understanding what the marriage commitment entails and must be capable of committing to it. Thus, serious maladies of a psychological nature can invalidate a person's consent. Further, if consent is offered under fear or duress it is not valid. Thus, there is no such thing as a "shotgun wedding." Nor can couples place *any* conditions on their consent—that is, they can't be thinking, "I'll only stay married *if....*" Consent must assume that "come what may, we are married forever."

Spouses must consent to what the Church intends by marriage, that is, fidelity, indissolubility, and openness to children. It is essentially to these three promises that bride and groom say "I do." These promises are so much a part of what marriage *is* that if either bride or groom withholds consent to any of them, they are not truly married.

7. What does it mean to withhold consent from these promises?

Withholding consent involves a concrete act of the will that's contrary to any of these promises. It means that at the time of consent, when the person's lips said "I do," his or her will said "I don't." This is to be distinguished from butterflies, questions and even minor doubts. These are normal enough and don't necessarily call into question the sincerity of a person's consent. A closer look at each of these promises will help us understand to what couples must consent.

Fidelity. Marriage by its very nature demands faithfulness of heart, mind, and action to your one and only spouse. If a bride and groom don't commit themselves to such fidelity, they are not committing to marriage. There is no such thing as an "open marriage," for example. The very term is self- contradictory. It's important to clarify, however, that subsequent failings in this area do not, in themselves, invalidate a marriage, so long as both spouses sincerely committed to fidelity at the time of consent.

Indissolubility. Marriage establishes an unbreakable, lifelong bond between the spouses. If this isn't what bride and groom intend to establish, then they don't intend to establish a marriage. Marriage is all or nothing. This means there's no such thing as a "trial marriage," in which a man and a woman "just see" if it works out. Like "open marriage," the very term is self-contradictory. Once a valid marriage has been consummated, the bond that God establishes between the spouses can be broken only by death.

Openness to children. Children flow directly from the very nature of married love to such a degree that if a couple has absolutely no intention of having children and *positively* excludes them from their relationship, then their relationship is not one of marriage. The "child-free by choice marriage," becoming more popular today, is also self-contradictory.

8. What if a couple just doesn't think they'd make good parents? Are you saying the Church won't let them get married?

It's not that the Church won't "let" them get married. It's that such a couple doesn't actually *want* to get married. They want to have a sexual relationship that intentionally excludes children, and it's assumed they will do so by intentionally sterilizing their acts of intercourse. Whatever kind of relationship this is, it's not marriage.

Marriage, as part of its definition, is a sexual relationship in which spouses are open to the possibility that God may bless them with children. Spouses commit themselves never *intentionally* to sterilize their acts of intercourse. If a couple refuses ever to engage in noncontracepted intercourse (that is, an act of intercourse that's open to children), then they don't want to commit to marriage. This is how an intention against the good of children is to be understood.

If we truly understand what the marriage commitment *is*, then people who don't think they would make good parents must also admit they would not make good spouses. The self-sacrificial love that's necessary to be a good mother or father is the same kind of love that's necessary to be a good husband or wife. This is often difficult to understand for people raised in developed countries. A widespread "contraceptive mentality" has afforded members of our culture the illusion that children are a superfluous, optional "add-on" to a sexually active relationship. But such a mentality is utterly incompatible with a Catholic faith perspective.

9. What if a couple is unable to have children?

Marriage retains its intrinsic goodness even without children, so long as they're not positively excluded. Thus, unintended infertility is *not* an impediment to marriage.

This condition is often confused with the impediment of impotence. Impotence isn't an impediment to marriage because such a couple can't have children. It's an impediment because they can't have sexual intercourse. Whether a child *does* or *does not* come from sexual intercourse is up to God. If *he* chooses not to bring a child forth from the spouses' union, their marriage is no less valid because of it.

10. I can't believe how unfeeling it is for the Church to withhold the sacrament of marriage from people who are impotent. Sex isn't everything in marriage.

Of all the impediments to marriage, this is the one that seems to trouble people the most. So it's worth taking some time to explain.

It's certainly true to say and important to understand that sex isn't everything in marriage (see question 12 below). But its possibility is so essential to what marriage *is* that if there's absolutely no chance of sexual intercourse ever happening, there's no possibility of marriage ever happening. To clarify, it has to be *definitive* and *perpetual* impotence. This, we must realize, is extremely rare.

It's important not to let our sympathies cloud sound reasoning. For example, when people learn about this impediment, they'll often think of the sufferings of veterans wounded in war who can't function sexually. Indeed, this is a sad situation that's worthy of our sympathy.

But it doesn't change the objective truth of the matter. Sympathy for the blind, for example, shouldn't lead the state to issue blind people driver's licenses. It's a sad situation, but blind people *can't* do what driving requires. Similarly, definitively impotent people can't do what marriage requires. Jesus himself confirms this when he speaks of the inability of "eunuchs" (people unable to have sex) to marry (see Matthew 19:12).

This impediment isn't unreasonable but is actually very sensible. Think about it. What is it that a man and a woman pledge to share with one another that makes their relationship one of marriage rather than, say, just a nice friendship? What is it that a husband and a wife share with one another that is so unique and intrinsic to *their* relationship that it would be a violation of the very meaning of marriage to share it with someone else?

What exactly is it that makes marriage an "intimate, exclusive, indissoluble joining of man and woman's lives for their own good and the procreation and education of children"? Sexual intercourse. Sexual intercourse is the defining element of marital love. This doesn't mean marriage can be reduced *merely* to sexual intercourse (no more than driving a car can be reduced *merely* to seeing). But dispense with its possibility, and you no longer have marriage.

We must recognize the influence of the prevailing culture in the difficulty that people have with this impediment. The sexual revolution untethered sex from its social and psychological moorings. Thus for the typical modern mind, sex no longer expresses the marriage commitment. It just expresses some vague sort of desire for pleasure and intimacy, or worse, just a desire for selfish gratification.

The assumptions here are faulty: Sure, married people have sex, but so do lots of other people, and there's nothing wrong with that, right? So, if a couple couldn't have sex for some reason, what bearing would that have on their desire to get married? From the perspective of the modern mind-set, none. But from the perspective of the true meaning of sex and marriage, it would have direct bearing, so much so that marriage would be *impossible*.

Here's a silly analogy that may help clarify things. You can't reduce chocolate chip cookies merely to chocolate chips, but without the chocolate chips, you no longer have chocolate chip cookies. Chocolate chips are what define this type of cookie. There are other kinds of cookies, but if they don't have chocolate chips, they can't honestly be called chocolate chip cookies.

Similarly, without the *possibility* of sexual intercourse, you can't honestly call the love that a man and woman share "marriage." It doesn't mean they're incapable of love. It just means they're incapable of that unique kind of love called *marital* love.

There are many kinds of love, just like there are many kinds of cookies. Two people may very much want to make chocolate chip cookies, but if by some misfortune they have no possibility of acquiring chocolate chips, the plain reality is they're unable to make chocolate chip cookies. They'll have to make some other kind of cookies.

Applying this banal analogy: If by some tragedy a couple is definitively and perpetually unable to express the defining element of marriage, then the reality is that their love (while it may be a very beautiful, lasting, and intimate love) cannot be the unique and specific love that makes a marriage. No amount of sentiment or sympathy for individual situations—as understandable as such feelings are—can change this reality.

11. Marriage is just as much a spiritual union as a physical one. So what if you can't have sex?

This is certainly true, but the two realities (physical and spiritual) cannot be separated without falling into a serious error about human identity. Recall our earlier reflection on the "angelism" introduced by Rene Descartes (see question 3 above). By positing human identity in "thought," Descartes unwittingly led the modern world into new form of an ancient heresy called Gnosticism.

Gnosticism is a death-dealing system of thought that involves a rupture of body and soul, positing human identity in spirit and salvation in the soul's deliverance from the "grossness" of matter through secret knowledge (*gnosis* means "knowledge"). It's death-dealing because that's precisely what death *is*: the separation of body and soul.

The truth is that human identity is found in the marriage of flesh and spirit. The soul is not an "immaterial self" housed in a non-spiritual body. Rather, the soul is what makes the body what it is: not just *a* body, but *some-body*. We're not persons "in" a body; we're *body-persons*.

This is why Christ doesn't offer salvation *from* the body, but salvation *of* the body. After death, the soul remains in an unnatural state while it awaits the resurrection of the body at the end of time. Then the souls in heaven will become, once again, *fully human* as body-persons (just as Christ and his Blessed Mother are now in heaven body and soul).

Because of this profound spiritual and physical unity of the human person, it's incorrect to make a sharp distinction between "physical" and "spiritual" love in human beings. What we do with our bodies we do with our souls, and what we do with our souls we can only do through our existence as body-persons. Human love is manifested through the human body, through our masculine and feminine selves.

Even our emotions (not that we can reduce love to mere emotion) and our prayers are communicated through the body. As St. John Paul II said, any attempt to break the personal unity of soul and body "strikes at God's creation itself at the level of the deepest interaction of nature and person."[21]

This profound spiritual and physical unity in humanity is the very principle of the Church's sacramental life—including the sacrament of marriage. For even God, who is pure Spirit, took on a body in order to show human beings his love and win the redemption of our bodies: "And the Word became flesh" (John 1:14). *All* sacraments are *bodily, physical* realities.

It's in and through their bodies that husband and wife express the love that's unique to the sacrament of marriage. Their "one flesh" union (or at least its possibility) is no more dispensable to the sacrament of marriage than bread and wine are to the Eucharist or water is to baptism. It's in and through these physical realities that the spiritual realities proper to each of these sacraments are communicated. Without the physical reality of the sacrament, there simply is no sacrament.

12. We were already married for several years when my husband had a work-related accident that made sexual intercourse very difficult if not impossible from that point forward. Are you saying we no longer have a sacrament because we can't have sex?

No. When you exchanged vows your sacramental bond was established (the Church uses the word *ratified* at this point). And when you expressed those vows in sexual intercourse, your sacramental bond was sealed. From that point on your marriage became a ratified and consummated sacrament in the Church.

A couple's sexual life goes through various phases and stages throughout the course of marriage. Sometimes for reasons out of a couple's control (age, health, injury, etc.) sexual union can become difficult, painful, or even impossible. This, indeed, can be trying, but it in no way invalidates a sacrament that had already been validly established.

Sexual union plays the critical role of bringing the marriage bond to its highest expression and completion. But, technically speaking, that only needs to happen once for the marriage to be consummated. Suppose you had consummated your marriage on the wedding night and your husband's injury happened the next day. That one act of sexual union, as the lived expression of your vows, bound you to one another "in good times and bad, sickness and health, for richer or poorer, till death do you part." This is what the dignity of the person and the dignity of the marriage bond demands. This is what a human person is worth!

I have nothing but reverence and sympathy for the sufferings this has brought to your marriage. This has become your path, a particularly painful one, of living out your vows, of witnessing to the dignity of the person, of the marriage commitment, and of the real possibility of being faithful to the demands of love in severely trying circumstances. Thanks be to God that the grace of the sacrament *empowers* couples to fulfill those demands. Cry out for that grace. Allow your questions and sufferings to become a prayer that opens you to that grace.

Of course, medical attention may be of some assistance here. There is nothing wrong, in itself, for instance, with making use of drugs or medical procedures designed to help a couple enjoy the marital embrace when it would be otherwise difficult, painful, or impossible.

13. My parents were married for more than twenty-five years, with five kids, but even they were granted an annulment by the Church. How can the Church all of a sudden say after so much time that my parents' marriage never existed? Doesn't this make me an "illegitimate child"?

First, a clarification about "legitimacy." This is a term used by various legal systems throughout the world to ensure a child's paternity. (It's usually quite obvious who the mother is.) From a faith perspective, however, God is the Father of us all. So, regardless of the circumstances of conception, there is really no such thing as an "illegitimate child" in God's eyes.

An annulment, then, does *not* make the children of that relationship illegitimate. This is a common misunderstanding that needs unambiguous clarification. Furthermore, a declaration of nullity from the Church does not affect the state's legal recognition of the paternity of the children. Even legally speaking, the children remain "legitimate."

A declaration of nullity does not and cannot erase your parents' relationship. They obviously were together for many years. They had good times and bad. They conceived and raised children. None of this is "wiped away." It's certainly difficult to come to terms with the fact that on the day of the wedding, something prevented your parents from entering marriage validly. But, again, it's important not to let sentiment cloud sound reasoning.

Sound reasoning recognizes that marriage is not something that just "happens" to a couple by going through the motions of a wedding. Some things—many things—can prevent couples from entering marriage validly. While most invalid marriages are determined to be such within the early years of the relationship, it's not impossible for a couple to live together for many years and raise a family, only later to discover after a thorough tribunal investigation that their marriage was not entered validly.

Children of marriages that have been declared null by the Church should never despair. It's God's very nature to bring good out of all situations. In fact, such children are perhaps the greatest good that God brings out of marriages that are later proven invalid.

14. My sister (a Catholic) wants to marry a Protestant who is divorced, but her priest said he would need to apply for an annulment, and if he didn't get one, they couldn't get married. Why does the Church make even Protestants go through the annulment process?

Since only Catholics are bound to observe the Catholic form of marriage, the Church recognizes the marriages of all non-Catholics and assumes they are valid unions unless proven otherwise. She even recognizes the marriage of two baptized Protestants as a sacrament, even if they themselves don't believe marriage is a sacrament and even if the wedding took place in the presence of a justice of the peace. Thus your sister can't marry a man who is already validly married to someone else.

According to Christ's own words, that would be committing adultery (see Luke 16:18). Civil divorce never changes one's actual marital status in the eyes of the Church, whether Catholic or not.

If they would like to pursue the matter, however, he is free to apply for a declaration of nullity to see whether his first marriage was valid. (Close to 20 percent of annulment cases actually deal with non-Catholics.) If it's determined that it wasn't valid, your sister would then be free to marry him.

But keep in mind, annulments are never a sure thing. It has to be proven with moral certainty that on the day of the wedding some defect prevented the couple from entering marriage validly. It would be wrong for your sister even to consider marriage unless and until an annulment were granted.

15. Why doesn't the Church get with the times and admit that some marriages just don't work out?

It's obvious to everyone, including the Church, that some marriages "don't work out." As mentioned earlier, in serious circumstances the Church even encourages separation of "bed and board." But this is very different from accepting divorce.

It's hard to overestimate the importance that the Church places on defending the permanence of marriage. History tells the tale of entire nations separating from the Catholic Church because of disputes over this point.

Why is the Church so obstinate? Because marriage is where human and divine love "kiss." To diminish in any way the permanence of married love is to diminish the permanence of God's love. As a sacrament, marriage is a true participation in the love of Christ for his Bride, the Church.

If we truly understand this, to admit divorce is to say in the same breath that Christ has left the Church. *Impossible!* Christ will never, ever abandon his Bride. This is what's at stake.

But we're not God, people say. How can we love as Christ loves?

On our own we cannot. But "with God all things are possible" (Matthew 19:26). It's no coincidence that these words of Christ from the Gospel of Matthew appear shortly after Christ's teaching on the permanence of marriage (see Matthew 19:1–11). When Christ's disciples learned what the permanence of marriage demanded of them, they thought it would be better not to marry at all (see Matthew 19:10). Jesus responded, "Not all men can receive this precept, but only those to whom it is given" (Matthew 19:11).

To whom is this teaching on the permanence of marriage given? To men and women who remain slaves to their weaknesses? No! To men and women who have been given the power to love as Christ loves through the Holy Spirit!

This is the good news of the Gospel. Christ's love has been poured into our hearts through the Holy Spirit (see Romans 5:5). This means husbands and wives *can* learn to love one another as Christ loves. It doesn't mean it's easy. It takes ongoing willingness to grow, to mature, and to allow our hearts to be purified of selfishness and egoism.

What's at stake in the permanence of marriage is really a question of faith. Do we believe in the saving power of Christ's death and resurrection in our lives, or do we believe we are only left to our weaknesses, failings, and sinfulness?

To admit the possibility of divorce is to say that Christ cannot save us from our fallen humanity. Woe to the Church if she were ever to say such a thing. The permanence of marriage is an objective reality to which the Church must bear witness if she is to tell the truth.

16. Didn't even Jesus say divorce was acceptable in the case of adultery?

This is commonly referred to as the "exception clause." It appears in Matthew 5:32 and 19:9, where Jesus prohibits divorce except in the case of *porneia*. This Greek word is sometimes translated as "unchastity," "impurity," "lewd conduct," or—less accurately—"adultery." Many biblical scholars believe the exception clause refers to marriages that were not true marriages because they were within the forbidden degrees of blood relationship (see Leviticus 18:6–16). Thus it would be expected that Christians who found themselves in these incestuous relationships would "divorce."

The exception clause does not appear in the parallel passages of Luke 16:18 or Mark 10:11–12. First Corinthians 7:10–11 also expresses the prohibition against divorce as an unconditional command from the Lord for his followers. This is the way the Church, as the authority that Christ instituted to speak on such matters, has always understood it.

It simply would make no sense for Christ to teach that people could divorce if one or the other spouse committed adultery. All spouses would need do, then, if they wanted a divorce, would be to go out and have an affair. The commonly held interpretation of *porneia* is much more plausible.

17. My brother is a good Catholic who loves his new wife and loves God. But because he wasn't granted an annulment of his first marriage, he can't receive Communion. He feels left out and unappreciated by the Church. Why is the Catholic Church so harsh and insensitive about these things? Other churches welcome people no matter what.

Christ's love is welcoming of all. If the Church fails to show her members the love of Christ, she has failed indeed. So, too, we must admit, if the Church fails to challenge her members to live the love of Christ, she has failed indeed.

There's a certain tension here. Christ's love is unconditionally welcoming of sinners, but in his love for us he is uncompromising with our sin. As with the woman caught in adultery, he does not condemn us. But he calls us to sin no more (see John 8:10–11).

Welcoming a person can never mean welcoming that person's objectively wrong choices. Christ said, "Whoever divorces his wife and marries another, commits adultery against her" (Mark 10:11). Thus, if your brother's ("first") marriage was valid, by living in a sexually active relationship with someone else, he's actually committing adultery against his ("first") wife.

Christ, our heavenly Bridegroom, shows us what sexual union means by making an everlasting gift of his body to us (his Bride) on the cross, which we receive sacramentally in the Eucharist. The sexual union of husband and wife participates in Christ's Eucharistic self-giving. Yet the sexual union of two people who aren't married is a direct contradiction of the Eucharistic love of Christ. This is even more so when one or both of the sexual partners is married to someone else.

For this reason, a Catholic person who persists in engaging in intercourse with someone, when in reality he or she is married to someone else, is not able to receive Communion. Objectively speaking, such a person is living in direct contradiction to what the Eucharist means. In the Eucharist, we consummate a mystical marriage with Christ. In it, Christ gives himself to us completely, and we give ourselves to him completely, pledging total faithfulness to him. If we don't intend to be faithful to Christ's teachings, then it would be hypocritical to receive the Eucharist.

It's very important to distinguish here between willfully persisting in an objective "state of sin" and struggling with resisting sin. Being faithful to Christ is difficult. For every human being it's a struggle.

By no means is the Eucharist only for those who are "perfect." If that were the case, no one could go to Communion. But at the very least, in receiving the Eucharist we are telling Christ that we're willing to struggle to live according to his will, resisting all that is contrary to it.

Will we fail at times? Certainly. Such is the fallen human condition. And that's why Christ graciously provides us with the sacrament of reconciliation.

18. Every time I hear that Scripture verse that says, "Wives, be subject to your husbands," the hair stands up on the back of my neck. Why should I listen to what the Bible says about marriage when it's so demeaning toward women?

The verse you're referring to is Ephesians 5:22. If it makes the hair on the back of your neck stand up, I want to affirm your response. Why? Because you probably think the passage means something like: "Wives are doormats who must surrender to their husbands' domination." If that's what you think it means, then I'd be concerned if it didn't make the hair on the back of your neck stand up.

Nevertheless, that's *not* what the verse means. When we look at this verse in the context of the whole passage (Ephesians 5:21–33), the context flips the typical interpretation on its head. Unfortunately, as soon as people hear this one verse, they tune out the rest of what St. Paul says.

While we must admit that some men throughout history have pointed to this Scripture verse to justify their fallen desire to dominate women, St. Paul is in no way justifying such an attitude. He knows it to be a result of sin (see Genesis 3:16), which is why in this passage he's actually restoring God's original plan before sin. He does so by pointing out what marriage was all about in the first place. It was meant to foreshadow the marriage of Christ and the Church. St. Paul simply draws out the implications of this analogy.

He starts by calling both husbands and wives to *be subject to one another* "out of reverence for Christ" (v. 21)—out of reverence for the "great mystery" that spouses participate in by imaging Christ's union with the Church. In the analogy, the husband represents Christ, and the wife represents the Church. So, he says, as the Church is subject to Christ, so should wives also be subject to their husbands (see v. 24).

Another translation uses the word *submission*. I like to explain this word as follows. *Sub* means "under," and *mission* means "to be sent forth with the authority to perform a specific service." Wives, then, are called to put themselves "under" the "mission" of their husbands.

What's the mission of the husband? "Husbands, love your wives, as Christ loved the Church and gave himself up for her" (v. 25). How did Christ love the Church? He died for her. Christ said he came "not to be served but to serve," and to lay down his life for his Bride (Matthew 20:28).

What, then, does it mean for a wife to "submit" to her husband? It means let your husband serve you. Put yourself under his mission to love you as Christ loved the Church. As St. John Paul II said: "The wife's 'submission' to the husband, understood in the context of the whole of Ephesians 5:22–23, means above all 'the experiencing of love.' This is all the more so, because this 'submission' refers to the image of the submission of the Church to Christ, which certainly consists in experiencing his love."[22]

What woman would not want to receive this kind of love from her husband? What woman would not want to be subject to her husband if he truly took his mission seriously to love her as Christ loved the Church? So often it's husbands who want their wives to take this Scripture passage to heart. I think it's we men who need to take it to heart first.

19. Didn't Jesus say there's no marriage after the resurrection? Why not? Does this mean my wife and I won't be together in heaven?

In chapter 22 of the Gospel of Matthew (see also Mark 12 and Luke 20), the Sadducees, a group of Jews who didn't believe in the resurrection of the dead, came to Jesus with a scenario that they thought would corner him into denying the resurrection as well. A man had a wife, and he died. One of his brothers married her to give his deceased brother offspring, but he died too. This happened again and again until seven brothers had all been married to the same woman in succession. The Sadducees then asked Christ whose wife she would be in the resurrection.

Christ responded, "You are wrong, because you know neither the scriptures nor the power of God. For in the resurrection, they neither marry nor are given in marriage" (vv. 29–30).

For many this saying of Christ strikes a sour note. Why? Because we know neither the Scriptures nor the power of God. If we did, we would rejoice in these words. Christ's statement is not a devaluation of marriage; rather, it points to the ultimate purpose and meaning of this wonderful sacrament.

Marriage in this life is meant to point us to heaven, where, for all eternity, we will celebrate the "marriage of the Lamb" (Revelation 19:7), the marriage of Christ and the Church. This is the deepest desire of the human heart—to live in the eternal bliss of what the saints call "nuptial union" with the Lord.[23] As wonderful as marriage can be in this life, it's only a sign, a foretaste, a *sacrament* of this joy to come. Earthly marriage is simply preparation for heavenly marriage.

It's the same with all the sacraments. They prepare us for heaven. There are no sacraments in heaven, because they all will have come to fruition. Human beings will no longer need signs to point them *to* heaven when they are *in* heaven.

Think of it in terms of road signs. If your destination is Denver, Colorado, then once you arrive you no longer need a sign to point you there.

Will you be with your spouse in heaven? Of course, if you both accept Christ's marriage proposal and live in fidelity to him in this life. In fact, every member of the human race who accepts the invitation to the heavenly wedding feast will be in the most intimate possible communion with every-one else.

This is what we call the "communion of saints." In heaven, all that separates and divides us on earth will be done away with. We'll all live in a heavenly *communion of persons* as the one Bride of Christ. And as the one Bride of Christ, we'll live in the ecstatic bliss of consummated union with our Bridegroom, Christ the Lord. We will *know* God and see him as he is, face-to-face (see 1 Corinthians 13:12). As the *Catechism* says, the Church "longs to be united with Christ, her Bridegroom, in the glory of heaven" where she "will rejoice one day with [her] Beloved, in a happiness and rapture that can never end."[24]

4

What to Do Before "I Do"

Chastity Outside of Marriage

The person who does not decide to love forever will find it very difficult to really love for even one day.[1]

—St. John Paul II

Now it's time to address some of the "nitty-gritties" of sexual morality. While this chapter will focus on the questions and objections of unmarried people, we'll also address various themes that are just as pertinent to those who are married. So if you're hitched, don't just skip to the next chapter—there's something here for you as well.

Speaking of "do's" and "don'ts" is unavoidable in any discussion about morality. But it's important not to misconstrue such discussion as a *minimalist* approach to following Christ. We shouldn't be seeking how much we can "get away with" before being guilty of doing something wrong.

If this is our perspective, we'll be unable to see the Church's teaching as the good news that it is. Instead, we'll view it with suspicion. We'll see it as an arbitrary moral code that bans the things we *really* want to do. We'll see Church teaching as a burden imposed from outside that's difficult, if not impossible, to live up to. This sentiment is virtually inevitable unless we encounter the person of Christ in a life-transforming way.

When our hearts are open to Christ's transforming love, we are not seeking to "get away" with anything. Rather, we are seeking what it means to follow Christ as the model of love and self-giving. With this disposition, we don't see the Church's teaching as an imposition, but recognize it for what it is—the truth about love that God has written in our very being.

When Christ is desired for who he is, his Church's teachings aren't viewed with suspicion or seen as something to *live up to*. Rather, they're trusted as the standard never to *fall below* if one is seeking true love, true joy, true fulfillment. In that light, we should approach these important issues with a prayer:

> *Lord Jesus, help me to see that the moral teachings of your Church are not impersonal and imposed standards of an arbitrary moral code, but are truly your own design written in my heart as a man (woman) through which I discover the meaning of life and love. Soften my heart to receive and live the truth that sets me free. Amen.*

1. What does chastity mean?

Chastity comes from the Latin word *castus* which means "pure." Sadly, sexual purity is often confused with *puritanism*—a fearful, repressive approach to all things sexual. As a result, the word *chastity* itself tends to have negative connotations and needs to be rehabilitated.

Purity, properly understood, is something altogether positive. Think of pure gold. Wouldn't you prefer that to impure gold? Chastity is the virtue that results from allowing the fire of God's love to purify our sexual desires, thoughts, and behaviors from the selfish sting of egoism and lust, like fire purifies precious metal from dross. Through this purification, chastity orders all of our sexual desires, thoughts, and behaviors toward the truth of authentic love.

This means chastity is not primarily a *no* to illicit sex. Chastity is first and foremost a great *yes* to the true meaning of sex, to the goodness of being created as male and female in the image of God. Chastity isn't repressive. It's totally liberating.

Our culture talks a big line about sexual freedom. But what does the culture mean by that? "Do whatever you want, whenever you want, without ever saying no." Is a person who cannot say no to his sexual desires free? Or is such a person in chains? Take a closer look. What our culture promotes as sexual freedom actually leads to sexual addiction.

Freedom is not liberty to indulge our compulsions. It's liberation from the compulsion to indulge. Only such a person is free to be a gift to others. Chastity affords precisely that freedom—the freedom to be a gift, the freedom to love. This takes discipline, to be sure, but it's like the discipline of an athlete that enables him or her to excel in sport, or the discipline of a musician that enables him or her to make beautiful music.

2. Why shouldn't two consenting adults be able to have sex?

Two consenting adults are *able* to have sex. The question is this: Is it *good* for them to do so? What are people saying to each other by having sex? Is it in keeping with the true meaning of sex? Is it in keeping with the dignity of the person? Is it honest? Is it loving? We'll address those questions throughout this chapter. For now, let me offer a few preliminary observations.

When the first edition of this book came out in the year 2000, sex had already been severed from marriage, but there was still a general connection in most people's minds between sex and love. Today, the hookup culture has almost completely erased the notion that love need have anything to do with sex. As one college student put it, "In the past, it would be—let me take you on a date, let me get to know you a little bit before we take it any further. Versus now, now you get a girl's number and it's [all about having] sex." He continued, "Sex is nothing. Sex doesn't mean anything anymore. Sex is just pleasure." [2]

"Our generation has given up on love. It's easier to find a f*** buddy than a boyfriend," observed one female college student on the beach during spring break. "Love is not real," another insisted. "It's like this fictitious thing that society invented so you can have sex with someone." [3]

While it would be hard to find a more depressing and pessimistic evaluation of human relationships, I do believe this young cynic is on to something. If she's saying, "Look, if you're only in it for the pleasure, don't whitewash what you're doing with fictions of love," then, on this point, she's in full agreement with John Paul II. What we often call love, he insisted, amounts to little more than two people using each other—the exact opposite of love. [4]

However, whereas this young woman capitulates to a vision of sex without any hope of love, the Church insists that, even if lust and egoism incline us to use one another, there is always the possibility of passing over from lust to authentic self-giving love. And in all she teaches about sex, including her teaching on saving sex for marriage, the Church is holding out this hope to the world: love *is* real; love *is* possible; you're not crazy to desire to be loved for who you really are; you're not crazy to want to be loved forever; believe in real love and don't settle for less!

3. So you're saying sex is supposed to express love. Okay, but what difference does a marriage certificate really make, anyway?

Yes, sex is meant to express love. But love is not arbitrary. Love is not whatever I want it to be. Love is not simply warm feelings for another person. Love can't simply be equated with sexual attraction toward, nor sexual desire for, another person. Love is not something that "happens" to people. Love is a decision to uphold the good of another no matter the cost to myself.

I don't say this to downplay the role of emotions and attractions. As St. John Paul II said, these are the "raw material" of love. But it's a mistake to regard the raw material as the "finished form."[5] A person must allow grace to shape and form the raw material into a free choice for the good of the beloved. Of course, this concept is foreign to our popular culture. A scene from an old Robert Redford movie *The Horse Whisperer* illustrates what I mean.

When a stressed-out, unhappily married city woman realizes she has "fallen in love" with a laid-back, divorced cowboy, she declares, "I didn't want this to happen." Proof-positive that whatever feelings she had for said cowboy weren't feelings of love.

By definition, love always *chooses freely* to sacrifice oneself for the good of the beloved. Sexual love chooses freely to make a total, faithful, and fruitful gift of self to the beloved. Sexual intercourse speaks this language—the language of God's love. This is the language of the marriage bond, the language of wedding vows. Anything less is a counterfeit for what our hearts truly desire.

Language is meant to convey truth. It's an abuse of language to convey lies, and it can never be loving to do so. The "language" of the body is also meant to convey truth. St. John Paul II actually speaks of the "prophetism of the body." The body is "prophetic" because it speaks the language of God, which is love.

But we must be careful to distinguish between true and false prophets.[6] People who are having sex but haven't made the marriage commitment are "false prophets." They're saying something with their bodies that isn't true. While their bodies are saying, "I am yours freely, totally, faithfully, fruitfully, forever," their wills are saying something else. In short, they're lying to one another.

"When did you stop caring?" asks Cameron Diaz's character of Tom Cruise's in the psychological thriller *Vanilla Sky*. "Caring about what?" he wonders. "About the consequences of the promises that you've made," she retorts. "You've been inside me," she reminds him. "That *means* something!" Then she demands, "Don't you know that when you sleep with someone your body makes a promise whether you do or not!?"

Wow. Sometimes even Hollywood gets it right.

The point is this: sex is meant to be a sharing of one's very self at the most profound, vulnerable, and intimate levels. It's possible to go through the motions of sex and *not* share one's self at that level, but that's a compartmentalization of the person that ruptures the body and soul. And that's the very definition of death: the separation of body and soul. If sex is to be an exposure not just of one's body but of one's most intimate self—in other words, if sex is to be experienced in such a way that it does *not* rupture body and soul—then it warrants the promise: "I will never leave you; I will never forsake you." That's what the totally naked human heart demands. And that promise is called *marriage*.

Kim Biddle, an award-winning social worker who's dedicated her life to serving the sexually wounded, speaks pointedly to this yearning to be loved in our entirety, body and soul:

> I think in the heart of a woman, we want to be seen as truly beautiful, someone to be treasured and lifted up. And we're hoping, constantly hoping, that someone will *not* exploit, not degrade, but treasure who we are, who we *really* are. And that's at the heart of *all* of us. We all need to be *known*, to have human connection, to be seen and to still be loved in that place. If we're keeping parts hidden, or just displaying one thing, or compartmentalizing our life, it's preventing us from being liberated in who we are in our fullness. There needs to be a resurgence in our culture that values humanity, that values a man and that values a woman for their entirety—mind, body, and soul.[7]

To value a person in his or her entirety demands that we learn how to speak the language of the body honestly, so that what we say with our bodies expresses the truth about love. A couple who understands this and desires it will naturally want to refrain from speaking falsehoods to each other through the language of their bodies. They understand the language of sexual intimacy as an expression of wedding vows and will want to reserve that language until they have *already made* those vows.

So what difference does a marriage certificate make? In itself, not much. It's just a piece of paper. But such a piece of paper indicates that God has established the marriage bond between the spouses. And that bond makes every difference in the world.

When a bride and groom stand at the altar and declare their consent before the Church, it's not merely a formal recognition of something that already exists between them. At the moment they give their consent, bride and groom are changed. They *become* right then and there (and only right then and there) *husband* and *wife*. What did not exist five minutes before does exist now—a marital bond sealed by the Holy Spirit that, once consummated, can never be dissolved by anything but death.

Sexual intercourse is the expression of *this* bond. It's the visible sign of this invisible reality. If this bond doesn't exist between a man and a woman, sexual intercourse between them is void of its *raison d'être*. Regardless of how much passion, feeling, and sentiment may be involved, such acts of intercourse can never be acts that truly honor the dignity of the person, and acts that do not honor the dignity of the person cannot be called acts of love.

A couple who is regularly engaging in sex before they marry, and sees nothing wrong with it, demonstrates that they don't understand the meaning of sex and marriage. Such a couple will most likely fail to comprehend the significance of the marriage bond altogether. They'll tend to reduce the change in their relationship to a piece of paper—a "marriage certificate"— and continue having sex as they always did.

The fact that the couple is now married does not automatically make their sexual union what it's supposed to be. Sex is only what it's supposed to be if it expresses the commitment to free, total, faithful, and fruitful self-giving. There are many married couples who have plenty of sex that actually violates their own wedding vows. The fact that it's happening after the wedding has taken place doesn't make it okay.

Instead of framing the discussion in terms of *premarital* sex versus *postmarital* sex, it's much more accurate to speak of *nonmarital* sex versus *marital* sex. It's impossible for unmarried people to have marital sex. They have no marriage bond to express, no wedding vows to renew. On the other hand, while the existence of a marriage bond is no *guarantee* that sex will always be marital, it is an absolute prerequisite for the possibility.

4. I went to Catholic schools for twelve years and never heard this. Why not?

This is a typical response to lectures I give around the world. The answer's complex, but the simple version is that many of the Church's educators have themselves been deceived to one degree or another by the prevailing mentality. It's fairly common for teachers who openly dissent from Church teaching to hold prominent positions in Catholic seminaries, colleges, and universities. The same problem exists in many Catholic high schools, grade schools, and parish-based religious education programs.

It's not an alarmist claim to say that there is a crisis within Catholic education. In response to this crisis, God has blessed the Church in modern times with a pope and a saint who did more to uphold and explain the Church's teaching on sex than any other pope or saint in history. John Paul II brought to the Church a vision never before articulated about the dignity and meaning of the human body and of sexual union. Although it may seem as if few are listening, I believe it's only a matter of time before his astounding insights become part of the fabric of the Catholic community, and, from there spread out into society as a whole.

George Weigel confirms this view in his biography of John Paul II. He describes the pope's Theology of the Body as a *"theological time bomb* set to go off with dramatic consequences, sometime in the third millennium of the Church. When that happens," he continues, "perhaps in the twenty-first century, the theology of the body may well be seen as a critical moment not only in Catholic theology, but in the history of modern thought."[8]

I myself am frustrated by the fact that I didn't learn about the richness and sensibleness of the Church's teaching when I was growing up, despite twelve years of Catholic education. For the most part, the message was simply, "Don't do it." So what did I do? The exact opposite, of course.

Had I been taught how wonderful and beautiful the Catholic vision of sex and marriage actually is, perhaps I would have thought it something worth holding out for. Perhaps I would have been spared the pain I inflicted on myself and others. But when I speak of a God who can forgive, heal, and restore us, it's not just a theory to me. I'm a very broken man who has encountered a very merciful God. The healing we need calls us on a lifelong journey, but it is the most hope-filled adventure that this life has to offer.

5. How can I regain this understanding of sex if I've already blown it?

In light of the redemption that Christ has won for us, nothing is completely "blown." Nothing we've ever done could possibly be more powerful than the cross of Christ. When Christ died, he took all our fallen humanity with him, and he rose from the dead so that we too could live a new life (see Romans 6:4).

Jesus became sin so that we might become the righteousness of God (see 2 Corinthians 5:21). This means there's always the possibility of "renewing our minds" (see Romans12:2). There's always the possibility of conversion. There's always the possibility, no matter how deep in the pit we may be, of turning around, walking toward the light, and experiencing new life.

If I may paraphrase St. Paul's words to the Romans: I appeal to you, in view of God's mercy, to offer your sexuality as a living sacrifice, whole and entire to God. You need not conform any longer to the pattern of this world, but you can be transformed by the renewing of your mind. Then you will understand and desire God's will for your sexuality—his good, pleasing, and perfect will (see Romans 12:1–2). And his will truly is the path to the happiness we desire. Every other promise of happiness is an illusion.

Yes, Christ's teachings are difficult. We should never underestimate that difficulty. How many among us, by our own strength, are able to love our enemies? I have a hard enough time trying to love my friends. How many among us, by our own strength, are able *never* to lust in our hearts?

It seems there's a fundamental dilemma here. Christ holds out his will only for us to realize that we can't live up to it. And how does Christ respond? "With men this is impossible, but with God all things are possible" (Matthew 19:26). Let's pray:

> *Lord, please help me. Give me the grace to trust you with my whole self—all that I am, body and soul. I give you my hopes and fears, my achievements and failings, my strengths and weaknesses, my sins, my longings, my desires—especially, right now, my sexual sins, longings, and desires. I lay them all at your feet. Help me to be the man (woman) you've created me to be. Renew my mind that I might see the great gift of sex and marriage as you've created them to be. I know I cannot live your will on my own, but I trust you to make up what I am lacking. Amen.*

6. We're getting married in two months. We know we're already committed to one another and we're already sexually active. What's the big difference between us having sex now and us having sex then?

That's precisely the problem: Unless you have a change of heart, there will be no difference. What you're doing in bed right now is *not* a renewal of wedding vows; it's *not* the marital embrace. As such, you've actually been training yourselves in a non-marital (hence, dishonest) approach to sex. A change of heart is, of course, possible. But without it, you will bring that same non-marital thinking and behaving right into your bedroom even after you're married.

Sexual intercourse is the visible (physical) expression of the invisible (spiritual) marriage bond. It's where the words of the wedding vows become flesh. It's an integral part of the sign of the sacrament of marriage that, for Catholics, only comes about when bride and groom have exchanged valid consent in the presence of a priest or deacon and two witnesses. It's not merely an expression of a feeling in your hearts that you're "already committed."

That feeling is understandable. I remember how committed I felt to Wendy when we were engaged. It's true to say that at some level engaged couples are "already committed."

Committed to what? To getting married. Otherwise, they wouldn't be planning a wedding. Yet engaged couples must also recognize *they're not yet married*. Otherwise, they wouldn't be planning a wedding.

Despite how committed I felt to Wendy when we were engaged, she wasn't my wife until the Holy Spirit established the marriage bond between us. That didn't happen when I proposed to her and she said yes. It didn't happen when we met with our priest to discuss wedding dates and marriage preparation. It didn't happen when we booked the reception site and sent out our invitations. It didn't happen at the rehearsal in the Church the night before.

All these were clear indications that we were committed to getting married. But it wasn't an absolute or irrevocable commitment. We were both free to back out at any time up until the moment we exchanged consent at the altar. At that moment, the Holy Spirit established the marriage bond between us. When we consummated our marriage, we knew that we were sealing and completing the spiritual bond established between us earlier that day.

That's the joy of sacramental sex. Hold out for the real thing. Even though you've already had sex, there's no reason you can't stop now. Go to confession (if you're Catholic), and wait until your physical union is an honest expression of the spiritual bond of marriage. This is one of the *best* things you can do to prepare for this wonderful sacrament.

7. My soon-to-be fiancé and I both have parents who divorced, so we decided to move in together to see if we're compatible before making any serious commitment. In our situation, that seemed like the smart thing to do. Why does the Church teach that we're "living in sin"?

At first glance, there seems a certain logic to the idea of "trying it out" before making the serious, permanent commitment of marriage. But precisely because marriage is a permanent commitment, it's not something you can "try." In fact, the internal dispositions a couple acquire by "trying it out" reveal that living together, rather than preparing you for marriage, is more likely to prepare you for divorce.[9]

This phenomenon can only be fully understood within the broader context of the widespread abandonment of Christian teaching on the meaning of sex. A cohabiting couple is "living in sin" not so much because they live under the same roof, but because it most often means they have made a public commitment to engage in sex outside of marriage. While sharing a common life in the same residence before marriage raises additional issues, the core problem is a misunderstanding and misuse of sex.

For most of us, society has robbed us of the tools to understand and embrace the true meaning of sex. We grow up in a world that has almost completely severed the inherent, God-given connection between sexual union and marriage. To many, the idea that a couple would marry as virgins seems archaic. In fact, it's not uncommon for both husband and wife to have already had multiple sexual partners before meeting each other.

None of this is outside the reach of Christ's redeeming, healing love. Yet, if this issue is left unaddressed, a couple who enters marriage having already engaged in sex with each other or with other people will inevitably face difficulties, perhaps totally unaware that the pain they're experiencing stems from the wounds of illicit sex. It's no coincidence that the dramatic rise in the divorce rate has coincided with the dramatic rise in sexual activity outside of marriage. I offer the following as some plausible reasons for the connection:

• Indulging in a sexual relationship which is dissoluble, uncommitted to lifelong fidelity, and closed to life[10] cannot prepare a couple to embrace a sexual relationship (marriage) that demands indissolubility, lifelong fidelity, and openness to life. By consistently choosing such behavior, the couple is demonstrating that they are, in fact, *ill-prepared* for the commitment of marriage because they've been psychologically trained in its opposite.

• Authentic love is ready to sacrifice everything for the good of the beloved. Above all, it never entices another to do evil. To engage in gravely disordered kinds of behavior and encourage one's beloved to do so as well manifests an attitude seriously opposed to authentic love. At the very least, it manifests a blatant ignorance of the meaning and demands of that love, which must be the foundation of the sacrament of marriage.

• Here's an eye-opener. If you're having sex with your intended, there's one thing you know about each other: You are both willing to have sex with someone you're not married to. Is that going to change when you get married? The failure to respect the inherent connection between sex and wedding vows *before* marriage doesn't bode well for ensuring that connection *after* marriage. Adultery is obviously not inevitable for those who have premarital sex, but it stands to reason that it's more likely. Adultery is, of course, one of the main causes of divorce.

• Premarital sexual activity establishes a pattern of self-indulgence that fosters the very vices (lust, pride, selfishness, dishonesty, distrust, sloth, and more) that serve to undermine—and if not addressed, destroy—the healthy relationship of a husband and wife.

• The love required for the sacrament of marriage demands a profound purity, humility, selflessness, honesty, trust, and willingness to sacrifice that can be established *only* by embracing the virtue of chastity—that is, lived respect for the truth and meaning of sexuality outside *and within* marriage.

• Sexual intimacy clouds a couple's judgment of their relationship, preventing them from reaching the objective assessment essential to discerning an authentic vocation to marriage.

• By their choices, cohabiting couples and those that are otherwise sexually active deprive themselves of the fullness of God's grace in their lives. Without this grace it's impossible for a man and woman to love one another as they're called to—in imitation of Christ.

All these factors contribute to the disintegration of men and women as individuals and of any relationship they share. If left unaddressed, the attempt to establish a marriage on such patterns of relating is akin to building a house on sand (see Matthew 7:26). But this shouldn't be cause for despair.

It doesn't matter how long a list of sins we have in our lives. Christ came not to condemn us but to save us. Christ can forgive us. Christ can restore us. Christ can heal our wounds. Christ can teach us how to love. But only if we let him.

So if you're truly serious about staying out of the divorce courts, turn to Christ and seek the grace that he will freely give you to live according to the truth of sex and marriage *now*. There's no better guarantee of a successful marriage than to train yourself in the virtues that are necessary for a successful marriage ahead of time. It's never too late to start. Go for it!

8. My boyfriend and I are very much in love and very attracted to each other. We haven't gone "all the way," but we find it hard to know where the line is. Is there a line?

When I was in Catholic school, I had a religion teacher draw a line along a scale of physical behaviors and say, "If you cross this, you've sinned." I'm not trying to discount the need for such physical "lines," but they often fail to do justice to the complexity of human hearts.

It's in our hearts that we experience the battle between love and lust. It's in our hearts that we decide which force within us will hold sway in our actions. So before the line is drawn along the scale of physical behaviors, it must be drawn in our hearts. This line applies to *everyone* in *every* situation and in *every* romantic relationship—married, engaged, or dating.

In his pre-papal book *Love and Responsibility*, St. John Paul II spoke of the moral principle that should guide all human behavior. He called it the *personalistic norm*. Stated negatively, it says that persons have such great dignity that never, under any circumstance, is it acceptable to *use* a person merely as a means to an end. Stated positively, the *personalistic norm* says that the only proper response to another person is that of *love*.

In this understanding, the opposite of love is not so much hatred. It's *use*. Here lies the battle for purity in physical manifestations of affection. We must resist every impulse in us that tends to treat other people as a means to our own selfish gratification, so that we can learn to love others for their own sake.[11]

Again, this points to the need for a deep conversion of heart. Without the perspective of God's plan in the beginning and our redemption in Christ, almost all we know are the distortions that sin has caused in us. We consider it completely "normal" to use others for our own physical or emotional pleasure, so much so that we often call it "love." Our society fosters this attitude, shamelessly encouraging it at every turn.

This is the very essence of the distortions that occur in man and woman's relationship.[12] If we are ever to discover and experience true love, we must take up the battle in our hearts with lust, with any desire to use people for our own gratification. This is a long and exacting work, and no one can ever consider the battle won once and for all. It demands a renewed effort at every stage of our lives and can only be accomplished through the help of God's grace.[13]

Physical manifestations of affection, no matter where they fall on the scale—from holding hands and kissing to sexual intercourse—are meant to be outward signs that express genuine inward realities. When outward signs do express genuine inward realities, there's a corresponding physical and emotional satisfaction, from the tender comfort of a gentle touch to the explosive intensity of orgasm in intercourse.

These joys are God-given. They're some of the joys promised by Christ when he calls us to love as he loves, so that his joy might be in us and our joy might be complete (see John 15:11). Thus, those who are sincerely seeking to love as Christ loves, and express that sincerity in a manifestation of affection appropriate to the state of their relationship, should receive the joy that flows from that expression as a gift from God.

We cross the line in the heart, however, when we seek that physical and emotional satisfaction as an end in itself—when we treat another person, not as a person created for his or her own sake, but as a means to our own selfish ends. This can happen all too easily, even if we don't cross the line on the scale of physical behaviors.

For example, a married couple isn't "crossing the line" when they have intercourse. It's appropriate to their relationship. But if a married couple is having intercourse *merely* because "it feels good" and not because each wants to say what intercourse means ("I am yours freely, totally, faithfully, and, yes, I am open to children"), they've crossed the line in the heart. Similarly, a dating couple is not crossing the line of physical behaviors by embracing or kissing. But if a dating couple is embracing or kissing *merely* because "it feels good" and not because they want to say what these expressions mean, they've crossed the line in the heart.

Admittedly, the meaning of an embrace or a kiss is not as universal or God-given as sexual intercourse. At a minimum, however, these behaviors mean (or should mean), "I respect you deeply as a person, I have tender affection for you, and I want to speak to you of your goodness." They should never be the expression of a desire to "get something" from the other for one's own ends. They should instead be expressions of a disinterested desire to affirm the other person for his or her own sake and to be affirmed in the same way.

Discerning the inner movements of our hearts can be confusing and difficult. Because of our own fallenness, we'll inevitably recognize elements of self-seeking mixed in with otherwise genuine desires of love. This acknowledgment shouldn't stifle expressions of affection. Instead, it should lead to their ever-purer realization.

Such genuineness in expressions of affection—from the first gesture of a touch to sexual intercourse in marriage—is only possible as we surrender our whole selves as sexual beings, as men and women, to the transforming love of Christ. Without such surrender, we'll inevitably be stuck to one degree or another in a habit of using others, and for lack of knowledge of anything else, we'll make the tragic mistake of calling that "love."

9. I think I understand, but aren't there still physical lines that shouldn't be crossed?

Yes. But any attempt to draw them should not be an excuse to avoid the battle in our own hearts. Such avoidance is all too easy if we're relying solely on external lines. If we fight the interior battle honestly and courageously, our hearts will *know* the line not to cross and will not want to cross it, for our own good and the good of our beloved. That being said, I offer the following "lines" on the physical scale only as a way to help you honestly assess your own heart.

One obvious example of a line not to cross for an unmarried couple is sexual intercourse. If a couple were to claim that they had made an honest and courageous assessment of their hearts and then had come to the conclusion that they could engage in intercourse as a genuine expression of their relationship, they'd be fooling themselves. It's true that they could experience some elements of love in intercourse. There always remains an echo of truth even in our distorted expressions of love. But it's not true that the act itself would be an act of love. In fact, it could not avoid being an act of use instead.

Similarly, physical behaviors that aim to arouse the body in preparation for intercourse (fondling each other's genitals or breasts, and even some kinds of extended kissing and embracing) are not appropriate expressions of affection for the unmarried. When there is simply no moral possibility of consummated love, it is, in fact, unloving intentionally to arouse someone to the point of physical craving for intercourse. If we must talk about physical lines in order to keep our hearts honest, we can say this: if either the man or woman is brought to the verge of climax, or has reached climax, or is aroused to the point of being tempted to masturbate, such a couple "crossed the line" *a long time before* and is in serious need of examining their hearts and their motives.

As the expression goes, it's foolish (read: wrong, unloving, inappropriate) to start the engine if you can't drive the car. A person brought to climax or tempted to masturbate has not only started the engine but has spent a long time revving it as well.

We're speaking here not just about a need to modify our behavior to fit some arbitrary moral code. We're speaking about the need of a deep transformation of our hearts from "loving" as the world "loves" to loving as Christ loves. Underneath all our distorted sexual expressions, there is something genuine that men and women are seeking. They're seeking love, physical closeness, intimacy, joy, and pleasure—in a word, happiness.

But how many (myself included) can attest to the emptiness, guilt, isolation, and despair that follow an illicit sexual experience? How many fail to find what they're truly looking for? We'll search in vain for happiness until we realize that what we're looking for can only be found in the One who created us.

God gave us sexual passion and desire—believe it or not—to point us to him. Lust and its satisfaction are a pale counterfeit for the true passion of love and the peace that floods the soul upon its discovery. If, through an ongoing conversion of heart, we surrender our lusts to Christ and allow him to transform them, we'll come to experience sexual desire more and more as the desire to love as he loves. As all our expressions of affection become more Christlike, we begin to discover what we failed to find previously.

Then, the simplest manifestation of affection—whether a look, a touch, or a gentle kiss—is more joyous and fulfilling than the most intense illicit sexual "encounter." Why? Because it's genuine. It's real. It's honest. It's true to what's appropriate in the given stage of the relationship.

It's not seeking to *get* anything. It's seeking to give and *affirm*. It's not interested merely in its own satisfaction. It's interested in loving the person for his or her own sake, and receiving the same love in return.

Such freedom and genuineness come at a high price—the price of the cross of Christ. Lust, pride, self-seeking, all must die in us if we're to rise to love: true love, pure love, the love for which we're all incessantly searching. The alternative to taking up our cross and following Christ (see Matthew 10:38) is the desperate attempt to camouflage the void and disappointment in our souls by the fleeting pleasure of mutually exploitative orgasms. Only the most hardened heart can continue to feign solace in the "afterglow" of such an experience.

10. Isn't there some kind of difference between dating and engaged couples with regard to chastity?

As the *Catechism* states: "Those who are *engaged to marry* are called to live chastity in continence.... They should reserve for marriage the expressions of affection that belong to married love."[14] Still, it's right to recognize a degree of intimacy appropriate for engaged couples that isn't appropriate for those who are merely "dating."

Remember that physical manifestations of affection are meant to be outward signs that express inward realities. There's an inward reality present in the hearts of the engaged that isn't present in the hearts of those who are dating. As Fr. Paul Quay suggests in his insightful book *The Christian Meaning of Human Sexuality*: "Those who are engaged, since they are committed to each other, even though not yet fully, have sufficient reason to manifest their love, even by prolonged kissing and embracing...provided, of course, that this leads neither of them into sin [using the other for selfish gratification, for example], provided they do not get themselves violently overwrought [to the point of climax or temptation to masturbate, for example], and provided the engagement does not go on forever."[15]

His counsel is clearly not given as a license to "push the envelope." It assumes a mature Christian commitment and an experience of the freedom to which we're called in Christ Jesus (see Galatians 5:1). This is the freedom to love, to see what is good, true, and beautiful, and to desire it with all one's heart.

Such freedom *always* chooses the good of others, rejecting any temptation to violate that good. An engaged couple who knows this mature level of freedom is able to express their affection for one another without fear that one would ever *use* the other for his or her own gratification, without fear that one would ever push the envelope in order to see how much more he or she can "get."

To any doubter, I can say from experience that this type of freedom is truly possible. It calls, of course, for open and honest communication. It calls for care, as St. Paul cautioned, never to use our freedom to indulge the cravings of our fallen nature (see Galatians 5:13). And while it's certainly true that we should never underestimate our weaknesses (conversion is ongoing), we should also never underestimate the power of the cross to set us free.

Unfortunately, we've been trained to think of ourselves as animals without control. So in order to stay chaste, some couples think it necessary never to be alone for any extended time before they get married. The fear is that if they *were* alone they wouldn't be able to say no to sex. This isn't freedom. Let's not take up again a yoke of slavery (see Galatians 5:1).

Certainly, if a couple knows they'd do something wrong if they were alone, then they shouldn't be alone. (In traditional Catholic language, it's called "avoiding the near occasion of sin.") Those who make the sacrifices necessary to avoid temptations are to be commended. But if the only thing that kept a couple from having sex before they got married was the fact that they didn't have the opportunity, what does that say about the desire of their hearts? Do they *truly* desire the good? Are they truly *free*?

Freedom is essential to authentic marital love. If an engaged couple isn't capable of expressing their affection in ways that are genuine, true, and *free* (in a word, chaste), things won't automatically change when they get married. Without this freedom—which can only be achieved by experiencing the ever-deepening redemption of our sexuality in Christ—sexual activity will remain, at some level, exploitative, even if the couple doing it is married. Let's pray:

> *Lord Jesus, come into my deepest self. Transform my sexual desires into those of love. Make me chaste. Grant me a living experience of the freedom for which you died to set me free. Amen.*

11. Does the Church really teach that masturbation is wrong? What about adolescents who are just experimenting?

Yes. Masturbation is always an objective disorder (see the next question for a further discussion of *why* it's wrong). Nevertheless, subjective responsibility for masturbation can be lessened by immaturity, the force of habit, conditions of anxiety, or other psychological factors.[16]

It's perfectly natural for adolescents to be curious about their maturing bodies. And the novelty of hormone surges can be a powerful temptation to experiment with masturbation. This is understandable. But it doesn't change the objective fact that masturbation is a disorder. It's not in keeping with our great dignity as men and women who are called to love as God loves.

While those stuck in a habit of masturbation must be shown compassion, it's a service to no one to water down the truth. By doing so, we only keep people in their chains. Christ has redeemed us. This means it's truly possible to live according to the full truth of our sexuality.

12. Most psychologists speak of masturbation as a normal, healthy thing. They even indicate that it's unhealthy *not* to masturbate. Why doesn't the Church just get with it?

We must realize that without the perspective of God's plan in the beginning, and without understanding that Christ came into the world to restore that plan, we'll inevitably be looking at our experience of sexual desire through the lens of our fallen humanity. From *this* perspective, masturbation does seem like a "normal" and even "healthy" thing.

It's "normal" to be sexually aroused, right? It's "normal" to want to "relieve" sexual tension, right? If you have an itch, you don't just let it drive you crazy—you scratch it, right? In fact, only the oddball would choose to endure the itch without scratching it, right? So it could actually be "unhealthy" to let sexual tension build up without "relieving" it, right?

There's a certain logic here. In fact, it's virtually impossible to understand why masturbation is wrong within this paradigm. What's needed—not just to understand the masturbation issue but in order to understand the truth of sexuality and, in turn, the true meaning of love and life—is a complete paradigm shift.

We've inherited a worldview (modern rationalism) that's closed in on itself. We're all a bunch of *omphaloskeptics* (a fancy word for "navel-gazers"). We cannot see beyond the physical and visible to the spiritual and invisible. We can't see beyond the temporal and immanent to the eternal and transcendent.

We look at the stars and, rather than pondering the expansive grandeur of the Creator, we reduce the universe to mathematical equations. We
encounter another body, and rather than seeing the revelation of a person
made in the image and likeness of God, we see a *thing* to use and consume
for our own gratification. We encounter the deep waters of sexual desire, and
rather than seeing our call to share in the divine mystery by swimming in the
pure waters of life-giving love with an "other," we dive headfirst into our
own shallow, stagnant swamp and get stuck in the sludge of self-indulgent
isolation.

As we've noted, sex is symbolic. It's meant to be an efficacious sign of
God's free, total, faithful, fruitful love. It's meant to be a human participation
in the divine Communion of Persons. Yes, sex is meant to point us beyond
the stars to Ultimate Reality—God.

Masturbation, however easy a habit it is to fall into, only throws us back
on ourselves. It exemplifies a worldview devoid of the transcendent *otherness*
of God. It symbolizes self-pity, fear of abandoning oneself to another, and the
utter sterility of isolation.

It's the antithetical expression of our call to image God in a life-giving
communion of persons. Masturbation epitomizes the inversion of sexual
desire caused by original sin. What is it but self-seeking, self-gratifying sexual indulgence?

Such behavior speaks very pointedly about a person's concept of his or
her own sexuality and, in turn, about his or her whole person. It speaks of
an anxiety toward self and others, an inner frustration with the truth of one's
own being, and an unwillingness or inability to make a sincere gift of self to
another. The fantasy life that often accompanies masturbation speaks of a
dissatisfaction with and withdrawal from reality.

If one who struggles with masturbation is ever to enter marriage lovingly and fruitfully, it's utterly essential that he or she overcome this habit
through perseverance, prayer, the sacraments, God's grace, and perhaps
the guidance of a wise spiritual director. Why? If one's sexual impulse is
conditioned by self-indulgence rather than self-giving, and if the pleasure of
orgasm is divorced in one's mind from the risk of loving an "other" and the
responsibility of fertility, then merely standing at an altar and pronouncing
vows will do little if anything to undo that condition.

Those who have been trained by a habit of masturbation will simply
transfer their self-indulgent impulse onto their spouse. They'll have sex with
a fantasy rather than with the real person they married. Is that love? Can that
ever be an expression of the marriage bond and a renewal of wedding vows?

Psychologists who promote masturbation, and those who accept their advice, have been deceived. Let's cry out to God for the grace to pierce through our fears, our anxieties, our inner frustrations. Let's endure the pain of allowing God to reverse our inversions.

Only then will we know the true joy and satisfaction we're looking for. It's not self-satisfaction we're looking for. It's the satisfaction of sacrificing all in the risk of love. It's the satisfaction of holding out for the real thing—the encounter with an "other" that's meant to prepare us for the ultimate encounter with the Ultimate Other: God.

13. What am I supposed to do with all my sexual feelings and desires if I can't have sex and I'm not supposed to masturbate? Sometimes I feel as if I'm going to explode.

This is a good place to address the difference between the repression of sexual desire and its redemption. Most people who are trying to live a chaste life fall into the mistake of "stuffing" their sexual feelings or trying to ignore them by sweeping them under the rug. The problem is, they keep coming back, and usually with more force than they had in the first place.

Sexual feelings and desires are extremely powerful. Repressing them is *not* the answer. In order to know true freedom and put our sexuality at the service of authentic love, we must experience the redemption of our sexuality. Our sexual desires need to be transformed in Christ so that we can experience them as God intended in the beginning (see chapter one).

Because of the rupture between body and soul caused by original sin, we've all inherited disordered sexual desires.[17] They can be difficult, if not seemingly impossible at times, to control. So we need to ask ourselves: Am I in control of my sexual desires, or are they in control of me? If they're in control of us, then we're not free.

We also need to ask ourselves: What's the sentiment or character of these desires? Are they at the service of authentic love, or are they simply a desire for selfish gratification?

When sexual feelings, desires, and temptations present themselves, as they inevitably do, instead of trying to ignore them or "stuff" them by pushing them down and under, we need to bring them up and out. Not up and out in the sense of indulging them, but up and out and into the hands of Christ our Redeemer. You might simply say a prayer such as this:

Lord Jesus, I give to you my sexual desires. Please undo in me what sin has done so that I might know freedom in this area and experience sexual desire as you intend. Amen.

The more we invite Christ into our passions and desires and allow him to purify them, the more we find we're able to exercise proper control of them. And we begin more and more to experience our sexuality, not as the desire for selfish gratification but as the desire to give ourselves away in imitation of Christ. This is what redemption is all about.

But it's not easy. To be sure, it can be an intense spiritual battle (see Ephesians 6:12). Allowing Christ to purify us involves a real death to our disordered passions. It involves being crucified with Christ so that we might be raised with him to a new life (see Romans 6)—a new life in which we find ourselves more and more able to love as he loves, which is what the call of our sexuality is all about.

In fact, as powerfully as the fallen sex drive leads us toward selfish gratification at the expense of others, even more powerfully does God want the redeemed sex drive to lead us toward the freedom of loving others as Christ loves us. Sexual desire is meant to lead us to the fulfillment of the Gospel. This is why St. John Paul II described the sexual urge as "a vector of aspiration along which [our] whole existence develops and perfects itself from within."[18]

True love and true freedom are possible. But we don't arrive at them overnight. It can be a long and difficult road. Nevertheless, paraphrasing John Paul II, Christ calls us to learn with perseverance and consistency the true meaning of sex. He calls us to understand the inner movements of our hearts so that we can distinguish between what, on the one hand, constitutes sexual attraction as God intended it and what, on the other hand, bears only the sign of lust. And although these different movements of the heart can, within certain limits, be confused with one another, Christ calls us to discern the difference. Again, this is difficult, but as John Paul II adds, "this task *can* be carried out and that it is truly worthy of man."[19]

So what do you do with all your sexual desires and feelings? Give them to Christ and allow him to work this miracle of redemption in you. The only thing that will explode is your concept of sex. In God's plan it's more awesome than we as fallen human beings could possibly imagine.

Another important thing to remember: This redemption isn't just for those who don't have a "legitimate outlet" for their sexual desires. It's for everyone, married people included. Marriage in no way legitimizes spouses' using one another just to "relieve" their disordered sexual desires. They too must experience the redemption of their sexuality if their lovemaking is to be just that—making *love* and not making *lust*.

Here are some additional prayers you may find helpful as you seek to grow day by day in the true freedom of the redemption of your sexuality.

A Prayer for Purity of Heart

Lord, you have created me in your image and likeness as a man (woman). Help me to accept and receive my sexuality as a gift from you. You have inscribed in my very being, in my sexuality, the call to love as you love, in sincere self-giving, and you have made the "one flesh" union of man and woman in marriage a sign of your own life and love in the world. Grant me the grace always to resist the many lies that continually assail the truth and meaning of this great gift of sexuality. Grant me purity of heart so that I might see the image of your glory in the beauty of others, and one day see you face to face. Amen.

A Prayer in a Moment of Temptation to Lust

This is a woman (man) made in the image and likeness of God, never to be looked upon as an object for my gratification. Lord Jesus, grant me the grace to see the image of your glory in the beauty of this woman (man), and order my sexual desires toward the truth of love. I renounce any tendency within me to use others for my own pleasure, and I unite my sufferings with yours on the cross. Amen.

14. Should I feel guilty if I have wet dreams?

No, because there is no moral fault involved here. Ejaculating involuntarily in your sleep is of a different nature altogether from intentionally stimulating yourself to orgasm.

15. What's the big deal with pornography?

Let's be clear on this point from the start: The problem with pornography is *not* the fact that it shows naked bodies. The Sistine Chapel shows naked bodies. The problem with pornography is *the manner* in which it shows naked bodies. It shows them with the explicit intention of inciting lust, reducing the human person to an object to be used. While this is clearly the intention of pornographers, it is clearly *not* the intention of artists like Michelangelo.

Such artists use their skill to portray the naked body in a way that can help us see the true beauty and dignity of the human person, of our being created male and female in the image of God. In fact, to underscore this pure vision of the body, as part of the restoration project of the Sistine Chapel, St. John Paul II called for the removal of several loincloths that prudish clerics had had painted over Michelangelo's original nudes. He then described the restored chapel as *"the sanctuary of the theology of the human body."*[20]

What's the big deal with pornography? The worst evils are the corruption of the greatest goods. Since the human body and sexual love represent some of the greatest goods, pornography is one of the worst evils. But we'll never recognize it as such if we're stuck only in our fallen perspective and our lustful desires. From this vantage point, easy access to an unlimited supply of porn seems like a boon since it allows me to gratify my lusts whenever I so desire. However, if we recognize even the faintest echo in our hearts of God's original plan for the body and sex, we'll see that pornography epitomizes how far we have fallen from that plan.

If we're ever to discover true love, true joy, true happiness, we must rediscover the "spousal meaning of the body" and live according to it (see chapter one). We must die to our lusts and experience the redemption of our bodies in Christ. This is not a minor point of the Gospel message; it's not merely an appendix to the Gospel message. The redemption of the body "is, in fact, the perspective of the whole Gospel, of the whole teaching, even more, of the whole mission of Christ."[21]

What's the big deal with pornography? It's an anti-Gospel message that robs us of the very meaning of life by fostering precisely those distortions of our sexual desires that we must struggle *against* in order to discover true love.

No amount of rationalization, no number of excuses that "it's normal" or that "everyone does it" can change what pornography is and what it does to the way we think of one another and the way we think of ourselves: we come to view the body as some*thing* to be used rather than as some*one* to be loved in the image of God. In turn, we come to measure our own "worth" based on whether and to what degree we can incite someone else's lusts.

What's the big deal with pornography? It trains us in everything that is antithetical to God's plan for human life and married love. Indeed, those who view pornography, so long as they remain in its clutches, have incapacitated themselves to see and to love others authentically. So long as they remain in its clutches, they have incapacitated themselves to enter and live marriage honestly, fruitfully, and faithfully because they've blinded themselves to the full truth and dignity of the human person.

From this perspective, the problem with pornography is not that it reveals too much of the person, but that it reveals far too little. This is why pornography can never satisfy the desires of our hearts. We have a God-given thirst to know the full truth of who we truly are as persons made in God's image. We have a God-given thirst to know the true meaning of our bodies and the deep mystery of sexuality. We have a God-given thirst to behold perfect beauty and experience perfect love in and through our bodies. Taking that thirst to pornography is like drinking salt water. There's a semblance of satisfaction at first, but it makes us terribly ill and only increases our thirst for the very thing that's sickening us.

So where should we take that thirst? Here's the good news of the Gospel: perfect Love and perfect Beauty *have* been revealed in the human body. It's called the Incarnation! It's called Christmas! "In the fullness of time, God sent his son, born of a woman" (Galatians 4:4). It is in Mary and in Jesus that we see the full glory and dignity of masculinity and femininity manifested. I'm not talking about the caricatures of Jesus and Mary that we see so often in overly sentimental religious art. I'm talking about the real, living, breathing mystery of the New Adam and the New Eve that we can encounter through an authentic life of prayer and a lively participation in the sacraments.

Mary fully illuminates the theology of a woman's body and Jesus that of a man's. In Mary, a woman's body has literally become the dwelling place of the Most High God—heaven on earth! Every woman shares in some way in this incomparable dignity and calling. Every woman's body is a sign of heaven on earth. And, oh, how lovely is your dwelling place, Lord, mighty God (see Psalm 84:1)!

Continue unfolding this astounding mystery and it's not difficult to recognize that the theology of a man's body can be described as a call to enter the gates of heaven, to surrender himself there in a life-giving outpouring of love. In this way, the man images the eternal life-givingness of God as Father, and Christ is the perfection of this image. He not only enters the "earthly heaven" (Mary's womb) at the moment of his virginal conception. Through his bodily ascension he also enters heaven itself in order to pour out the life-giving Spirit of the Father's love on all humanity (see Hebrews 9:11, 24).

As we've been unfolding from the start of this book, human sexuality symbolizes heavenly and divine realities. This holy, sacred, glorious mystery is not only being mocked, but desecrated—often violently and horrifically—by pornography. For lack of knowledge of the eternal glories revealed through our sexuality, we are taking the longing of our hearts to these diabolical distortions. Whether we realize it or not, we are looking for union with God, but we've put an idol in its place. Claiming to be wise, we've become fools, as St. Paul says. We've exchanged the glory of God for an image of mortal man. So God handed us over to our own lustful desires, for the degradation of our bodies (see Romans 1:22–24).

There's nothing degrading or impure about our sexuality as God created it "in the beginning." However, there are dark forces at work that continually aim to pornify what is pure. The good news of our redemption is this: there are infinitely more powerful forces at work that aim to purify what has been porned. Let us tap into those forces of purification! Let us pray for the virtue of purity, which John Paul II described as the glory of God revealed through our bodies as men and women.[22] "Blessed are the pure in heart, for they shall see God" (Matthew 5:8)—in and through the human body. And seeing that mystery, they become sensitive to anything that degrades it.

If you're stuck in a habit of viewing pornography, or if you've been exposed to pornography at any time in your life and are seeking to undo its effects, and/or if you're in a relationship with someone who views pornography, please seek help.[23] You'll find that there is hope, and the journey of healing can begin.

5

"I Do"-ing It

Chastity within Marriage

All married life is a gift; but this becomes most evident when the spouses, in giving themselves to each other in love, bring about that encounter which makes them "one flesh." [1]

—St. John Paul II

If you're married—or are getting married soon, or would someday like to be married—you need to answer each of the following questions:

- Do you intend to be faithful to your wedding vows?
- No matter how difficult it may be to remain faithful, do you *still* intend to be faithful to your wedding vows?
- No matter how much you may have to challenge your own ways of thinking and acting to remain faithful, do you *still* intend to be faithful to your wedding vows?
- No matter how much sacrifice is necessary, no matter how much you may need to call upon God's grace to remain faithful, do you *still* intend to be faithful to your wedding vows?

I trust that you answered *yes* to all these questions. They aren't asking anything more of you than what you've already committed to, or plan on committing to someday, at the altar—to live your vows honestly and truly in good times and bad, through thick and thin, no matter what the cost, until death. Two more questions:

- How healthy do you think a marriage would be in which the spouses were regularly unfaithful to their wedding vows, and thus continually demonstrated their lack of commitment to them?
- Conversely, how healthy do you think a marriage would be in which the spouses regularly renewed their vows to one another, and every time they did so, strengthened their commitment to them?

One of the main points of this book so far has been to demonstrate that sex is only sex to the extent that it participates in the "I do" of wedding vows. (You may want to review chapter three for a discussion of what you're saying "I do" to.) Anything less is a reduction of the fullness of love we long for and deserve as men and women made in the image and likeness of God. This chapter is devoted to explaining what fidelity to the wedding vows means, practically speaking, in the sexual relationship of spouses. Then the following two chapters continue the discussion.

No doubt fidelity to the demands of marital love is challenging. As John Paul II wrote, "If Christian marriage can be compared to a very high mountain which puts the couple in the immediate neighborhood of God, we must recognize that to climb this mountain takes a great deal of time and effort. But," he asked, "would this be reason to destroy or lower the mountain?"[2]

If you find what you're reading about in this book challenging, my challenge is to *let it challenge you*. Have the moral courage to be faithful to the demands of love no matter what the cost, no matter what the difficulty, no matter what the sacrifice. Have the courage to stand firm on the *yes* with which, I assume, you responded to the above questions. And have the courage to be consistent no matter where that consistency takes you.

See it through. Don't duck. Don't bow out. Don't look for excuses. Don't try to rationalize. Allow yourself to feel the agony of accepting the demands of love. And allow yourself to recognize that, in and of yourself, you (like every human being) don't have what it takes to fulfill those demands. But what is impossible for us as human beings is made possible by God's lavish grace and mercy, if we would but open ourselves to it.

1. Why do married couples need the virtue of chastity when the wait is over?

It's a common but mistaken notion that the Church calls people to be chaste *until* marriage. But if we really understand what the virtue of chastity is, we'll recognize that such a statement implies that married people don't need to love each other. Chastity is not the same thing as abstinence. As we've noted earlier, chastity is the virtue that frees all our sexual thoughts, desires, and behaviors from self-seeking and orders them toward the truth of authentic love. So if spouses are truly to love one another, the virtue of chastity isn't an option—it's an absolute requirement.

Everyone is called to be chaste because everyone is called to love. The way chastity is expressed, of course, depends upon a person's state in life. For the unmarried person, it *does* mean abstinence from sex, because that's what authentic love calls for among the unmarried.

For the married person, however, it means that all sexual expression must be an honest expression of the marriage commitment. Any type of behavior that would contradict the free, total, faithful, and potentially fruitful self-giving to which the spouses commit at the altar would be an affront to the very meaning of sex. In other words, it would be a violation of chastity.

2. I've been married sixteen years and never thought about chastity *within* marriage, or about sex as a renewal of our wedding vows. What does chastity within marriage mean, practically speaking?

Regardless of how old you are or how long you've been married, it's never too late to grow in your understanding and your living out of the true meaning of sex. We have a patient, merciful God who wants to draw us ever closer in a spousal relationship with himself. For married couples, growing in the true sacramental nature of their sexual relationship is one of the main ways they grow closer to God, as well as to each other.

The effort to make sex a true union of persons, a true sacrament of God's love (rather than just a means of selfish gratification), presents what St. John Paul II called "the internal problem of every marriage."[3] It's much like the sacrament of love we find in the Eucharist. This act, too, according to the analogy, is the consummation of a marriage, our marriage with Christ. If we receive Christ's Body worthily, it becomes the very source (in union with baptism) of divine life, holiness, and joy in our lives. If we don't receive Christ's Body worthily, we eat and drink our own condemnation because we're mocking what the Eucharist is (see 1 Corinthians 11:27–29). We're going through the motions, but we don't *mean* what we're saying.

Similarly, if husband and wife receive each other's bodies worthily in their sexual relationship, their sexual union becomes a source of life, holiness, and joy in their marriage. But if spouses are just going through the motions and don't *mean* what they're saying—or worse yet, are in some way trying to *cancel* what the act means—then sexual union becomes the source of a fundamental disquiet in their marriage that, over time, will serve subtly (or not so subtly) to eat away at their relationship from the inside out. Again, it's no coincidence that the dramatic rise in the divorce rate in our country has coincided with the widespread abandonment of the Christian sexual ethic. So it's hard to overestimate how important the virtue of chastity is to a marriage.

How do you live it, practically speaking? To answer this question, we need to take a look at each of the elements of the marriage commitment. A valid marriage must be (1) free, (2) total, (3) faithful, and (4) open to children. These are the commitments that spouses are meant to renew when they have sex. Let's look at each.

Free. Any way that a husband or wife might manipulate or coerce a spouse to have sexual relations would be a violation of the freedom of their union. A clear example would be "marital rape." Yet we're not talking only about such an extreme situation. The true freedom of love is also violated when spouses use sex as a tool in their relationship for some other end.

Perhaps sex is employed to gain power or control in the relationship. Perhaps it's offered as a "reward" for something else or withheld as a "punishment." None of this kind of behavior says, "I want to give myself to you freely to affirm your goodness and our marriage commitment."

Freedom is also violated, or you might say is nonexistent, when sex is engaged in merely as a response to a compulsive "need" for gratification. Freedom means there is a choice before you to which you can say yes or no. If you can't say no, your yes is emptied of its meaning. We're called to gain increasing self-mastery so that our passions don't control us, but we control them.

Total. The climax of the sexual act shouts loudly and clearly, "Take me. I'm totally yours. I'm holding nothing back." That ecstatic moment reflects the unreserved surrender of our persons and the unreserved receptivity of the other. To the degree that we knowingly and intentionally withhold any integral part of ourselves from our spouse in the sexual act, we cannot speak of a *total* self-giving.

Perhaps one spouse is emotionally distant from or cold toward the other. Perhaps both spouses are deliberately refusing to be transparent and vulnerable with each other. Perhaps they're not giving themselves to each other in climax at all. Such is the case when one or the other spouse intentionally seeks orgasm apart from the act of normal intercourse.

The acts by which spouses prepare each other for genital intercourse (foreplay)—so long as they are performed lovingly and not lustfully—are honorable and good. But stimulating each other's genitals to the point of climax apart from an act of normal intercourse is nothing other than mutual masturbation. There's no gift of self, no marital communion taking place at all. Nor are such acts open to conception.

An important point of clarification is needed. Since it's the male orgasm that's inherently linked with the possibility of new life, the husband must never *intentionally* ejaculate outside of his wife's vagina (unintended ejaculation involves no moral fault). Since the female orgasm, however, isn't necessarily linked to the possibility of conception, so long as it takes place within the overall context of an act of intercourse, it need not, in any absolute sense, be during actual penetration.

Although it's more easily said than done, in an ideal world we can imagine that the spouses' orgasms would always happen simultaneously. In fact, St. John Paul II, in his pre-papal reflections on the matter, exhorted husbands to learn how to control their own orgasms in order to bring their wives to climax with them. Doing so with altruistic motives, he said, was a husbandly virtue at the service of marital harmony.[4] That being said, if the wife, despite their sincere efforts, was unable to climax during penetration, it may well be the loving thing for the husband to stimulate her to climax thereafter (if she so desired). In this case, such stimulation is not inherently masturbatory since it is within the context of a completed act of intercourse. Nor would it be masturbatory for the wife, in this same context, to assist her husband in helping her reach climax.

Faithful. Spouses must be faithful to each other not only in action but also in thought. For example, fantasizing about someone else while engaging in sexual relations with your spouse would be a blatant violation of fidelity. Right at the moment when spouses should be expressing their unyielding fidelity to each other, they would actually be committing "adultery in their heart" (see Matthew 5:28) with someone else.

This is one of the reasons that the use of pornography is so devastating to a marriage. It does nothing but feed and foster this type of infidelity.

Open to children. In the 1968 encyclical *Humanae Vitae*, St. Pope Paul VI reaffirmed the constant teaching of the Catholic Church that "each and every marriage act must remain open to the transmission of life." Perhaps a better way to understand this statement is that spouses must never do anything of their *own will* to close any act of intercourse to the transmission of life.

Yes, this means that use of any and all methods of contraception is a direct violation of a couple's wedding vows. This is perhaps the most contested and misunderstood teaching of the Catholic Church. For that reason, the entirety of chapter six will be devoted to clarifying it.

3. Are you saying that the only time you have sex with your wife is when you want to have a baby?

No. I'm saying that the only time I have sex with my wife is when we want to renew our marriage commitment. It's a myth that the Church teaches sex is *only* for babies, or that the only justifiable reason to have sex is when you want a baby. Some thinkers within the Church (such as St. Augustine) did mistakenly give this impression.

Furthermore, the long-standing formulation that procreation is the "primary end" of sexual union has often been misunderstood to mean procreation is the *only* end, or the only *good* end, of sexual union. But this has never been the official teaching of the Church. In fact, St. John Paul II said that if the *only* reason you're having sex with your spouse is because you want a baby, then you may be in danger of using your spouse as a means to an end, rather than loving your spouse as a person.[5]

I remember very clearly that the priest asked my bride and me at the altar if we would receive children lovingly from God, to which we individually responded, "I will." So fidelity to our vows demands that we never *intentionally impede* the possibility of pregnancy when we choose to express those vows through intercourse. In other words, while it's not necessary (and, in fact, could be unloving) to resolve that "we are having sex in order to have a baby," we must, in order to be faithful to our wedding vows, say: "In having sex, we know that we could have a baby, and we are willing to receive that baby lovingly from God." As St. John Paul II has concluded, "That approach alone is compatible with love and makes it possible to share the experience of love."[6] (Chapter six will provide a detailed discussion of this issue.)

4. Someone told me the Church teaches that oral sex is wrong even for married couples. Is that true?

It seems there are many troubled consciences out there looking for sound guidance on this issue. I'd even guess that the first thing many readers did when they got this book was look up this question. (If you're one of them, be sure to read the rest of the book to understand better the context of this answer.)

So, what does the Church teach? You're not going to find an official Magisterial statement addressing this issue directly. But the principles we've already outlined in this book enable us to draw sound conclusions.

There's nothing about our genitals that singles them out as being "unkissable" as part of a husband and wife's intimate affection and foreplay to intercourse. The term "oral sex," however, most often refers to acts in which orgasm is sought and achieved *apart* from an act of intercourse. Indeed, many people consider such behavior a desirable *alternative* to normal intercourse. And, yes, this is wrong, even for married couples—though the clarification made above regarding female orgasm is applicable here as well: Mutual climax (or at least climax during penetration) remains a worthy goal, but it's not inherently wrong if the wife climaxes as a result of oral stimulation, so long as it's within the context of a completed act of intercourse.

Oral copulation (that is, to the point of ejaculation) is simply *not* marital. It effects no *communion of persons* between the spouses. It's the consummation of nothing. It involves a severance of orgasm from the responsibility of fertility. It fosters a husband's tendency to seek pleasure apart from sacrifice and to objectify his wife. For these reasons, it does not and cannot symbolize and participate in the free, total, faithful, and fruitful love of God. It does not and cannot symbolize the marriage bond or renew a couple's vows.

Furthermore, while there's nothing wrong *per se* with oral-genital affection, such expressions require a great degree of delicacy and reverence if they are to be a real affirmation of the person and not slide into a selfish pursuit of pleasure. As with all marital intimacies, we need a genuine purity of heart here if we are to recognize the difference between intimately and lovingly affirming the goodness of each other's bodies (and receiving that affirmation) and merely seeking to gratify base desire at each other's expense. As the saying goes, "from the sublime to the ridiculous is but a step." Spouses must always be sensitive to how easily they could take that step if they are to avoid it.[7]

Of course, it should go without mentioning that pressure exerted on a spouse to perform or experience acts with which he or she is uncomfortable—even when they're not objectively wrong—would indicate a serious lack of respect for that spouse.

5. What about anal sex?

Again, a husband should never intentionally ejaculate anywhere but in his wife's vagina. What then are we to say about anal penetration as a form of foreplay to normal intercourse?

Some might conclude based on a legalistic application of the "so long as it leads to intercourse" principle that anything goes when it comes to foreplay. But spouses who truly love each other aren't looking to get away with as much as possible before "breaking the rules." They're looking to symbolize and renew their marriage commitment as sincerely as possible. And here, appealing to an observation of St. John Paul II, "discernment of good and evil inscribed in human conscience can turn out to be deeper and more correct than the content of a legal norm."[8]

Beyond the "legal norm" of ensuring that ejaculation takes place during the act of natural intercourse, we must ask several other questions to evaluate the morality of sexual acts. For example: What is the intention of the spouses in such behavior? What kinds of thoughts and attitudes does this behavior generate in their minds and hearts? Why would someone want to do this? What desire does such behavior purport to satisfy? Is it a good desire? Am I harming myself or my spouse in any way (physically, emotionally, spiritually, or psychologically)? Is this act an affirmation of the other person's goodness and dignity or a degradation? What does this act symbolize?

I am aware that some trusted moral manuals of the past proposed that, under certain conditions, anal penetration could be an acceptable form of foreplay to marital intercourse. Nonetheless, I think their conclusions are in need of serious reconsideration.[9] This is a behavior that seems to stem much more from the disorder of lust than from a genuinely loving desire to symbolize and renew the marriage commitment. Its "desirability" by an increasing number of people today also seems to be the direct result of having one's sexual interests warped by exposure to the evils of pornography.

For these reasons alone (not to mention various health, hygienic, and aesthetic considerations), I would maintain that those who want to justify such behavior as a "loving" form of foreplay to the marital embrace are in need of a more honest and thorough examination of conscience.

6. This all sounds so mechanical, as if expressing love were just about plumbing and the insertion of body parts into the proper orifice.

If we have a split view of the body and soul—one that sees the spiritual element of our humanity as the "real person" and the body as just a "shell"—then, yes, what we've been discussing seems rather mechanical. Such a dualistic view of the human person logically concludes that "love" is expressed on a purely "spiritual level" and need not be bothered by the proper placement of certain body parts. The logic is sound, but it's based on a Gnostic view of the human person (see chapter three, question 11), a view that is absolutely irreconcilable with Christian anthropology.

As we noted in previous chapters, the body is the revelation of the person. We're not persons *in* a body. We're body-persons. The body *expresses* the soul. It makes visible the invisible.

What we do with our bodies we do with *ourselves*. What we do with our bodies reveals the sentiments of our hearts. What we do with our bodies can determine whether we're expressing genuine love or merely an imitation of it.

From this perspective, we're not just talking about mechanics—making sure you put body parts in the right place. We're talking about a husband and wife who, through the integrity of their bodies and souls, are loving each other as God loves—in a life-giving communion of persons. We're talking about husband and wife expressing their marriage commitment and becoming a sacramental sign of Christ's union with the Church.

How does this happen? Precisely through that gift of self by which the spouses become "one flesh." To be specific, only the inseminating union of genitals performed in a "human manner" in which the possibility of a new life is always left in the hands of the Creator consummates a marriage.[10]

When we properly understand the indivisibility of body and soul—that the body expresses the innermost truth of the person—we understand that this union of genitals is not merely a union of body parts. It's the means by which two body-persons image God by becoming *one* in a life-giving communion.

There's something in the average person that rises up against this teaching. There certainly was in me when I first heard it. *What's the big deal with seeking orgasm apart from intercourse, so long as it's with my own wife?* I thought.

But then another question came to mind. Why would I *want* to seek orgasm apart from normal intercourse with my wife? Looking for honest answers in my own heart, I had to conclude that I wanted the pleasure of orgasm apart from any risk of becoming a father. There was simply no other substantial reason.

It's Christ who teaches us what love is. True love involves abandonment to the will of the Father. It involves willingness to accept a lifetime of responsibility.

True love involves risk. It involves sacrifice, pain—in a word, suffering. If we don't think so, we haven't spent much time looking at a crucifix. This is the heavenly Bridegroom giving up his body for his Bride. And this is the model for authentic marital love (see Ephesians 5:25).

What's our typical reaction? "No! I don't want to. I want the pleasure without the responsibility, without the risk, without the suffering." I came to see very clearly that I resisted the Church's teaching because it "cornered" me into accepting the cross of Christ—as it should.

I once heard a bishop explain that marriage involves four rings: the engagement ring, two wedding rings, and "suffer-ring." As Fr. Paul Quay says, "It is just this link between true love and suffering that is rejected by sexual sin."[11] The honest person cannot fail to see the truth of this statement. If we reject the cross of Christ, if we refuse to take the risk of loving as Christ loves, we will still eventually end up with what we resisted—suffering. But the suffering that comes from resisting the cross is fruitless, empty, and despairing, while the suffering that comes from embracing the cross leads to the joy of the resurrection, the joy of love and the hope of everlasting life.

> *O God, have mercy. Have mercy on me for the ways that I resist the pain of your cross. Help me to stop running from you. Help me to stop resisting the risk and the responsibility of love. Give me the grace to embrace your cross in my own life. Give me the grace to love my spouse as you love yours, the Church. I trust you to give me strength in my weakness. Amen.*

7. Is the "missionary position" the only acceptable way for Catholics to have sex? How boring!

For readers who are unfamiliar with the term, the "missionary position" refers to intercourse in which the husband is on top of his wife, while she's on her back facing him. Stories vary, but it seems it was so named because missionaries promoted this as the "proper" position among native peoples they evangelized, discouraging other positions as impersonal and animal-like.

While no position for intercourse is wrong in and of itself, still (if the story is accurate) those missionaries had a point. It's telling, for example, that people speak of rear-entry intercourse as doing it "doggy-style." Such descriptions betray a less-than-personal approach to sex. It doesn't mean this position is inherently wrong, but uniting face-to-face can't help but promote the personal character of the spouses' union.

If you remember our discussion of the book of Genesis, Adam discovered his difference from the animals specifically in his *sexuality*—his call to love through the body. But what was the first result of original sin? Adam and Eve hid from each other and from God.

Whatever it was they did, it was something below their dignity as human beings. In some sense, they stooped to the level of animals. Husband and wife should do everything possible in their sexual relationship to promote a truly personal and intimate union between them rather than stooping to the level of merely satisfying instinct as animals do.

I once heard it said that intimacy means "into-me-see." If husband and wife are afraid to show their faces to each other during sex, then something's off. They should be able to look deeply into each other's eyes right at that most vulnerable moment—yes, right at the moment of climax—and rejoice in the mystery of *knowing* one another so intimately. Every person is an inexhaustible mystery. If sex is approached with the goal of coming to *know* the inexhaustible mystery of your spouse ever more fully (as Adam *knew* his wife, Eve—see Genesis 4:1), *boring* will not be a word you use to describe your sex life.

8. What's wrong with trying to spice up your sex life with a little variety?

Candlelight, making a nice atmosphere, wearing an attractive nightgown, variety in location and position, can certainly add to the overall experience. Few would deny that. But truly "good" sex has nothing *essential* to do with these things.

The most fulfilling sex possible comes when husband and wife unconditionally surrender themselves to each other—and receive each other—in a completely naked and honest revelation of their *persons*. If sex is not delving into the inexhaustible mystery of the other *person*, the "partners" in the exchange will inevitably grow bored. The way society trains us to think about sex breeds such boredom. Hence there are thousands of "sex manuals" on the market today intended to help couples spice up their sex life.

For the most part, these manuals offer suggestions that, if followed, would make what transpires in the marital bedroom resemble something found in the warped world of pornography rather than help a couple experience and participate in the "great mystery" of divine love. If a husband has to have his wife dress up like a porn star in order to be "turned on"; if a couple continually has to seek new and ever more contorted positions in order to avoid boredom; if spouses must become mere actors role-playing the script of one or the other's fantasy life in order to "perform"; if a couple is continually looking for new "techniques" to maximize physical pleasure instead of ever more loving ways to solidify marital union, then something is seriously amiss.[12]

If you really want "good sex," start by inviting God—who *is* love—to be with you. (Don't worry; God won't blush. He created sex.) Keep the lights on. Consciously renew your wedding vows with the language of your bodies. Mean what you say, and say what you mean.

Take the risk of surrendering your whole self *unconditionally* to your spouse. Receive your spouse *unconditionally*. As you do, look deeply and steadily into each other's eyes and thank God for the joy you know in being made in his image as you explode in the ecstasy of a true communion of persons.

Here "ecstasy" won't always mean sheer bliss and excitement. *Ecstasy* literally means "to go out of oneself"—and we can add: to go out of oneself *toward* and *for* the other, for the true good of the other, whatever the cost for myself. This means the ecstasy of marital love will be the fruit of embracing a certain agony.

Marital love entails a willingness to carry one another through life's joys *and* trials. The intimacy of the marriage bed will inevitably open up our fears, our hurts, our weaknesses, our sins, and our insecurities. But authentic love is not afraid of such things. In fact, the "strength of such a love emerges most clearly," St. John Paul II tells us, "when the beloved person stumbles, when his or her weaknesses or even sins come into the open. One who truly loves does not then withdraw his love, but loves all the more, loves in full consciousness of the other's shortcomings and faults.... For the person as such never loses its essential value."[13]

However, when love is based only on maximizing the pleasure the other person can give me, that "love" will last only as long as the pleasure. When the other person's faults, shortcomings, and sins are revealed—which inevitably happens and inevitably causes me to suffer—the shoddy foundation of our love is also revealed, and the illusion of love bursts like a bubble.[14] Only when love reaches the value of the person, which is inexhaustible, does it have a foundation that lasts forever.

And that's the goal spouses should have in the marriage bed: not merely to "spice things up," but to create their own unique "culture" of sexual relations that fosters authentic and mutual self-disclosure, acceptance, blessing, and affirmation at the deepest level of the truth and dignity of the other person.

I like to say a woman's heart is like a deep ocean, and the mission of her husband is to go deep sea diving. A man's heart is like a deep cave, and the mission of his wife is to go spelunking (cave exploring). The marriage bed is a privileged place for this deep heart exploring. Of course, we need to learn how to open our depths to one another, and how to enter those depths in one another, which is a lifelong journey. Those who embark on it together will come to marvel at the endless treasures to be discovered in ever new depths of the other's heart.

9. Doing things the moral way sure does seem to take away the spontaneity. Why can't even married couples just go with the passion of the moment?

We've spoken a lot about the need for a total paradigm shift in order to understand the truth and meaning of sex—about the need to look to God's plan in the beginning, the disordering of our passions caused by original sin, and the redemption of our sexuality in Christ. If a husband and wife spontaneously follow their disordered passions, their love for each other will be overshadowed by self-seeking. They will inevitably end up using each other.

The Church's teaching does confront *this* kind of spontaneity, as it should. But at the same time, Christ calls us to a different, much more fulfilling kind of spontaneity, a spontaneity that in as much as we've made the concerted effort to train ourselves in the truth of love. Through the ongoing appropriation of our redemption in Christ, the very character of our sexual desires is transformed.

The more we've experienced this transformation, the more the desire to make a sincere gift of ourselves will well up within us—and with an intensity much more refined and noble than mere lust can ever rouse. Couples *should* follow the passion of such a movement—with joy and utter abandon. For in doing so, they'll abandon themselves spontaneously according to the demands of love.

I once heard it explained this way: An untrained person can "spontaneously" bang away on a piano keyboard with the satisfaction of having made some noise. But in the end, that's all it is—meaningless noise. On the other hand, when a concert pianist "spontaneously" tickles the keys, he produces sounds of beauty capable of lifting the soul to the heavens and beyond. But as we all know, behind the beauty of the music is a lifetime of self-discipline and training, a lifetime of concerted effort in perfecting his skill.

The effort needed to "make beautiful music" spontaneously through sexual union is no less demanding. Becoming a "professional lover" takes a lifetime and involves a lot of that "fourth ring." But the joy that it brings is so magnificent, the "meaningless noise" of mutually exploitative orgasms can't even be compared to it.

10. This all seems so heavy. Can't sex just be fun?

Sex *is* heavy. Like nothing else, it forces us to deal with the primordial "stuff" of life. The way we understand, think about, and live our sexuality has weighty consequences, indeed, eternal consequences.

Because sex is literally the most creative force in the visible world (there's nothing greater than the power to cooperate with God in creating human life), when misused, it's also the most destructive. Sex confronts us with the most basic and powerful yearnings of our soul and forces us to grapple with the disparity between our highest aspirations and our basest inclinations. It forces us to choose between good and evil, between love and all that is opposed to love, between serving God and others and simply serving ourselves.

St. John Paul II goes so far as to say that sexual union is a "test of life-or-death." When spouses become one flesh, he observes, "they must find themselves in the situation in which *the powers of good and evil fight against each other*."[15]

Holy Moses! This really *is* heavy.

But there's a delightful paradox here. When we stop trying to run from how heavy it really is and instead choose to embrace the eternal magnitude of its importance, it no longer *weighs* on us. We experience what Christ meant when he said, "Take my yoke upon you...and you will find rest for your souls. For my yoke is easy, and my burden is light" (Matthew 11:29–30).

Living the truth about sex is intensely joyous. There simply is nothing that compares to the satisfaction of living in accord with the image in which we're made. There simply is nothing that compares to the joy of a husband and wife who embrace the truth—with all its risks, with all its ramifications, with all its sacrifices and responsibilities—when they embrace each other in the intimacy of their union.

Despite what the media encourages us to think, sex is not meant for our entertainment. Our genitals are not sex toys. They are the revelation of our call to enter the greatest adventure life has to offer: learning, really and truly, what it means to love in the image of God. To be sure, that adventure is full of "fun," but in the end, I don't think that word does justice to what sex in the divine plan is meant to be. It's not merely a cliché to say that true, honest sex is meant to be a little taste of heaven on earth. As the *Catechism* observes, "In the joys of their love [God gives spouses] here on earth a foretaste of the wedding feast of the Lamb."[16]

If you want the greatest sex life possible, then give your sex, your life, and your sex life to Jesus Christ. If that sounds strange or makes you feel uncomfortable, then you've been overly influenced by too many people who have little to no clue about the meaning of life, the meaning of sex, and the meaning of Christ's mission in the world.

11. I've been married almost thirteen years. I know sex is supposed to be good, even holy, but it still makes me feel dirty. What's wrong with me?

You're not alone. This rift between knowledge of how sex should be and how it's actually experienced is quite common, even among those who are striving to live the truth. Head knowledge is not enough by itself to undo the deep-seated and often unconscious attitudes we have inherited or otherwise acquired that distort the truth about sex.

We need to go to their source and, with the help of God's grace, uproot them. Most often we'll find that the way we think and feel about sex as adults has much to do with the impressions we were given about our bodies and sex while growing up—from our parents, from siblings, from neighborhood friends, from exposure to pornography, from the media, from sexual experiences.

I'll often ask how many people in the audiences I speak to experienced open, honest, healthy, regular conversations about the beauty and splendor of God's plan for sex while growing up. I get about a 1 to 2 percent response. This is tragic.

Children have a driving curiosity to know about their bodies, and about sex, even from an early age. If this curiosity is not properly directed and met in healthy and appropriate ways through open, honest, age-appropriate discussion in the home, sex typically becomes a big, dark, hidden taboo and children seek to satisfy their curiosity in covert, distorted ways.

Speaking from my own experience growing up, I can still remember the first time I was exposed to pornography. I was about six or seven. I can conjure up those images in my mind to this day.

I remember kids telling "snake in the garden" and "Johnny Deeper" jokes that I didn't get. I remember a babysitter exposing himself to my brother and me and encouraging us to expose ourselves to him. I remember all kinds of lewd comments from older guys about girls and their body parts.

I remember "experimenting" with kids from the neighborhood and watching boys grabbing and probing girls through their swimsuits in the public pool. I remember being shocked and mesmerized when an older kid told me in full detail what he did with a girl in his class. And I can still remember virtually everything he said.

These were my first impressions of sex. They affected me deeply. And this all happened before I reached puberty. I had no idea what to do with myself when my hormones really kicked in. A steady diet of pornography, masturbation, and adolescent "making out" sufficed until I started a four-year, sexually active dating relationship at age sixteen.

Why do I tell you all this? Because chances are you have similar memories from childhood and adolescence. Somebody needs to take the risk of talking about them. If we don't face the negative experiences that have formed us, we'll never be able to live in the freedom of the truth and to experience sex as it's meant to be.

Painful memories and wounds from distorted ways of thinking and relating don't just go away when you get married. Even people who really want to experience sex as God intends it are not uncommonly haunted by flashbacks of past sexual experiences right at the moment they're making love with their spouses. Many times people who have been exposed to pornography have those images parade through their minds at the least desirable moments: in times of prayer, at Mass (even while going to Communion), and while making love.

Here's the good news: *Christ, the Son of God, is real.* He really became one of us. He really died for us and rose from the dead. He really came to restore God's original plan of life and love in our hearts. He really wants to lead us on a journey of healing and redemption. It's not an easy journey, but it is full of the hope that does not disappoint (see Romans 5:5).

My recommendation would be to look back into your own life. How did you first learn about sex? What were your impressions of your body as you went through puberty? Did others make fun of you? Were you ever exposed to pornography? Were you ever mistreated or abused sexually? Did you masturbate? Were you promiscuous as a teenager?

How did these experiences affect you? The purpose of such a reflection is not simply to dig up old dirt. The purpose is to bring the light of Christ into the dark places of our lives so that he can heal us.[17]

I remember at one point in my life writing on a piece of paper every sexual experience I'd ever had—all the junk that I had long tried to forget but couldn't—and going to a trusted priest to confess it. Afterward I lit the paper and watched it go up in flames. It was a true moment of healing for me and a real turning point in my life.

Furthermore, when Wendy and I arrived at the point in our relationship that we knew we would marry, I asked her forgiveness for not saving myself for her. What does that have to do with her, you ask? We're meant for sexual union with our spouse alone. Sex with others—even if it's long before you meet your spouse—is basically committing adultery "in advance." If we're brave enough to peel away all the layers of excuses we make for ourselves, we know this to be true.

There's a reason people are haunted by their pasts. There's a reason people feel uneasy at class reunions when they stand there with their spouse and see people they had sex with as teenagers. Those experiences were not supposed to happen.

Praise God that he forgives. Praise God that he restores. Praise God that he heals.

Don't sweep the past under the rug as if it were no big deal. Give it all to Christ and let it die with him on the cross. Seek the forgiveness of your spouse if you were unfaithful in advance.

If you have flashbacks of past experiences, give them to Christ. Memories may remain, but Christ can remove their sting and teach you to use them as an opportunity to pray for the people you wronged and to forgive them for wronging you. This is the road to healing. This is the road, not only to knowing that sex is meant to be good and holy, but actually to *experiencing* it as such.

For many, like myself, it's a long road. It's a painful road. But it's not nearly as painful as the alternative. Where else can we go, Lord? You have the words of eternal life (see John 6:68).

> *Lord, you know me. Nothing about my life is hidden from you. You know all those things in my life that have drawn me away from the truth of your plan for my sexuality. Whether these were wrongs that I committed or wrongs committed against me, I give them all to you. Light of Christ, shine in the darkness. Truth of Christ, dispel all the lies. Death of Christ, take all my sins. Resurrection of Christ, re-create me to know, live, and experience the goodness and holiness of my sexuality. Amen.*

12. My mother said that when she was first married, a priest told her that she was obligated to "submit" to her husband's sexual needs upon request. What's up with that?

I don't doubt that your mother was told such a thing. The Church has long been fighting to correct errors that stem from misinterpreting St. Paul's admonition for wives to "submit to their husbands" (see chapter three, question 18). This is one such misinterpretation, and a very serious one at that. It all but blesses a man's disordered desire to use his wife for his own sexual gratification.

It has *never* been the teaching of the Church that husbands are free to use their wives. On the contrary, it has been the constant teaching of the Church that husbands are called to love their wives as Christ loved the Church (see Ephesians 5:25). This includes what they do in the bedroom.

While they may not clearly recognize it, many wives experience a deep resentment toward their husbands that stems from being treated as a means to an orgasm. (Let's not think the proverbial "headache" is without cause.) Such hedonism on the part of the husband often produces a dreadful cycle: the husband desires sex for selfish purposes; his wife resists being used; the husband complains all the more that his wife doesn't "put out"; his wife withdraws all the more in the face of his complaints and demands. This problem is further compounded by the fact that most men will point the finger of blame at their wives, when the lion's share of the problem may well be their own.

That said, women also have their own disorders and dysfunctions to deal with that deeply wound men. I've spoken to countless husbands over the years who have been belittled and even emasculated by the manipulations and selfishness of their wives in withholding sex or demanding it in disordered ways. Oh, the havoc sin has wrought on the original harmony of the sexual relationship!

The balance of genuine love in intercourse must be maintained by husband *and* wife. Hence, before casting blame on the other, both spouses must have the humility and courage to look into their own hearts to see how their personal brokenness may be contributing to frustrations and tensions in their sexual relationship. Still, as St. John Paul II put it, "a special responsibility" rests with the husband in this regard "as if it depended more on him whether the balance is kept or violated or even—if it has already been violated—reestablished."[18]

Husbands, if your wife consistently resists your sexual advances, the solution is not to demand she submit to your requests. This can only create bitterness and resentment. Instead, have the courage to examine your own heart and motives. Is your desire for sex a desire to make a gift of yourself to your bride and renew your marriage commitment? Or is it more of a desire to "relieve" yourself at her expense?

We must all, husbands and wives, undergo a thorough purification of our desires if we are to find the joy and harmony we long for in the marriage bed.

13. Didn't the Church used to teach that one of the specific purposes of marriage was the relief of sexual tension?

Traditional formulations of the Church taught that there are three ends of marriage: the primary end of *procreation*, the secondary end of *mutual help between spouses*, and the third end of *remedy for concupiscence*.[19] The Latin *remedium concupiscentiae* is translated by some as the "relief of concupiscence." This has led some to claim that marriage somehow provides a legitimate outlet for "relieving" sexual tension in the sense of *indulging* concupiscent desire.

Concupiscence, however, refers to our *disordered* sexual desires. By itself, concupiscence only leads toward the *use* of others for the sake of selfish gratification.[20] Marriage does not make this "okay."

Quite the contrary. The grace of the sacrament of marriage, if we're open to it, provides a *remedy* for concupiscence. That is, it provides us with the power to experience a transformation in the very character of our sexual desires, so that such desires lead to love and not merely to "relieving" ourselves as if we were scratching an itch. This understanding of the third end of marriage alone does justice to the dignity of the person.

We *know* that we're not meant to be used, especially by the ones who claim to love us the most. Far too many marriages lie in ruins because of the general mistrust, suspicion, and conflict between spouses that stem from treating sex as merely an opportunity to "relieve concupiscence."

14. Doesn't St. Paul justify relieving sexual tension when he says it's better to have sex in marriage than to burn with desire?

The passage you're referring to is actually directed to unmarried people whom St. Paul is advising to choose the celibate vocation. He says, "But if they cannot exercise self-control, they should marry. For it is better to marry than to be aflame with passion" (1 Corinthians 7:9).

First, "being aflame" here refers to the disordering of our passions. It refers to lust, not to the fire of authentic love. Without getting involved in a thorough exegesis of St. Paul's words, we must understand that no Scripture verse stands alone. All verses and passages of Scripture must be interpreted in light of the rest of the Bible. When St. Paul talks about marrying, he's talking about the moral order. He's talking about husbands loving their wives "as Christ loved the Church," as he says in his Letter to the Ephesians (5:25). As much as love is better than lust, marriage is better than being "aflame with passion."[21]

Allow me to clarify another point. The "relief" of sexual tension is not wrong or bad in and of itself. God made sexual union to be an experience of heightened tension and climactic relief. Sharing the joy of this as husband and wife is an integral part of the sacramental symbol of married love. A "crisis in love" only arises when a spouse seeks that relief as *an end in itself* and treats his spouse as merely a *means to that end*.

15. Isn't there a fine line sometimes between love and self-seeking? It's not always easy to tell what my real motives are.

While at times we must admit it's quite clear whether we're being motivated by genuine love or by self-seeking, at other times it can be less so. We all have mixed motives. But recognizing them shouldn't be a source of discouragement. It's actually the first step in coming to a more mature evaluation of the inner movements of our hearts.

I certainly don't hold myself out as one who loves his wife perfectly in this regard. I can only say from my own experience that the more I expose my heart to the light of Christ, the more I'm able to discern the purity, or lack thereof, of my motives. The human heart is a battlefield between love and lust. While the battle lessens the more we mature in the truth of God's plan for our sexuality, it never ceases entirely in this life.

The goal is simply to let the power of love hold sway over the pull of lust. Yes, at times the two can be confused. But with Christ's help we can acquire the courage necessary to be honest enough with ourselves to discern the difference.

6

"I Do...Not"

Contraception

I call heaven and earth to witness against you this day, that I have set before you life and death, blessing and curse; therefore choose life. [1]
—The Word of the Lord

I was seventeen years old and had been dating my girlfriend for about five months. She called me one Saturday afternoon to tell me her parents were going out for the evening. Tonight was the night.

On the way to her house, I stopped at a drugstore and, for the first time in my life, bought a box of condoms. As I placed the box on the cashier's counter, something inside me sank. Somehow, I knew I was making a concrete decision to separate myself from God.

Not that I had been a saint up to that point. If I even had a relationship with God, it was hanging on by only a thread. But right then and there—in a Thrift Drug on Columbia Avenue in Lancaster, Pennsylvania—as I paid for those condoms, I severed the thread.

As I explained in the introduction, my unchaste behavior caught up with me in my college years, and I eventually came to agree with what the Church taught about sex—*except* on the issue of contraception. I had given up sex before marriage, but I thought when I got married I should be able to have sex with my wife whenever I wanted (without having to worry about raising fifteen kids). Besides, I thought, what was the difference between contraception and natural family planning if both are used to avoid pregnancy?

The more I grew in my faith as a Catholic, the more this issue became a real stumbling block. After all, one of the hallmarks of a Catholic is to believe and profess *all* that the Church believes and professes. Converts to the Church must specifically and publicly profess that they do. Cradle Catholics, on the other hand, can too easily fall into the hypocrisy of believing only what's comfortable. I knew that if I didn't come to terms with the "blasted" teaching, it would be more honest of me to be a Protestant (since I was already protesting what the Church taught). So I sought answers.

My search eventually led me to a book called *Catholic Sexual Ethics.*[2] It was the first thing I had ever read that sensibly explained the Church's teaching. Again, something inside me sank. The Church had proved me wrong on so many things that I did *not* want to surrender my final "reserve." It took some more investigation, prayer, and humility before the scales fell off my eyes completely. Looking back, I marvel at how the issue that once severed my relationship with God (and the Church) was the same issue that brought me back—the *whole* way back.

Embracing this teaching changed the way I see, well, *everything.* The Church's teaching against contraception is where the rubber hits the road (pun intended). On this point we face a dramatic, though often undetected, clash between the forces of good and evil, between the fundamental human decision to love or not to love, to choose life or oppose it. Indeed, the entire Christian sexual ethic—everything discussed in this book—either stands or falls on this point. This is where spouses either choose to communicate God's life and love to each other and the world or choose to communicate, well, something else.

This is also *the* point of departure between Catholicism and popular culture. While our culture teaches that using contraception is the *responsible* thing to do, that it makes for better marriages and a better society, the Catholic Church stands as the lone voice saying it's *always* wrong and terribly damaging to marriage and society. Either popular culture has "lost its noggin," or the Catholic Church has.

If it's the Church that's gone batty, who'd want to be Catholic? On the other hand, if the Church is right, the modern promoters of contraception may well have pulled off the biggest snow job in history.

Lord, please help me, as I read this chapter, to open my heart to the full truth of your plan for sex and marriage. I don't want to be blinded by my pride. I don't want to be deceived by my own desires. I want to live the truth. Only the truth. Please, Lord, if it's true that contraception is against your will, give me the grace to accept it, whatever the ramifications in my own life. I trust in you. Amen.

1. What in God's name could possibly be wrong with contraception?

Astute readers will recognize that everything we've discussed up to this point has paved the way to providing an adequate answer to this question.

I'll begin answering it by once again stating the thesis of this book, and then posing a question of my own:

Sex is only what it's meant to be to the extent that it participates in the "I do" of wedding vows. Is it ever permissible for a married couple to violate their wedding vows?

We can rant and rave and resist all we like, but an integral part of that "I do" is *openness to children*. Someone might respond: "A couple can be 'open to children' over the course of their marriage without *each* and *every* act of intercourse needing to be." But that makes as much sense as saying: "A couple can be 'faithful' to each other over the course of their marriage without *each* and *every* act of intercourse needing to be with each other." If we can recognize the inconsistency in claiming a commitment to fidelity...*but not always,* we should be able to recognize the inconsistency of claiming a commitment to being open to children...*but not always.*

Looking for a way out of the dilemma posed by this logic? You have a few choices:

Option 1: You can claim that sex doesn't have to participate in the "I do" of wedding vows at all. Okay, then the logical conclusion is that it doesn't have to be between people who have exchanged wedding vows at all. In this view, sex has no real meaning whatsoever, other than the exchange, or even solitary experience, of physical pleasure.

This opens the door to the justification of any and every means to orgasm, whether by oneself, between two people, between any number of people (whether this is with the opposite sex or the same sex would be superfluous), or even with animals. This, unfortunately, is the way much of our contracepting culture already thinks.

Option 2: You can change the definition of marriage to exclude "openness to children" as an integral part of the commitment. Okay, then *we* become the authors of marriage, rather than God, and the definition of marriage becomes completely arbitrary.

You want to have a "dissoluble marriage" just in case it doesn't work out? Sure, we can do that. You want to have an "open marriage" just in case you get bored with each other? Sure, we can do that. You want to "marry" your same-sex lover? Sure, we can do that.

After all, if marriage isn't intrinsically linked with procreation, why need it be between a man and a woman? This too is the way most of our contracepting culture already thinks.

Option 3: You can claim that "openness to children" is part of the marriage commitment, but you need not always be faithful to it. We already discussed where this leads. It means you need not always be faithful to the commitments of fidelity or indissolubility, either. And this too is the way much of our contracepting culture already thinks.

As we will begin to unfold in this chapter, continuing into the next few, the modern breakdown of marriage and family life and the widespread sexual chaos and gender confusion in which the modern world is now immersed simply cannot be understood without taking a hard look at the game-changing role contraception has played. That's what we will seek to do.

There is no avoiding the fact that an *intentionally sterilized* act of intercourse fundamentally changes the meaning of the act. The "I do" of wedding vows becomes an "I do...not."

This "I do not" affects not only the commitment to being open to children. A closer look reveals that it also affects freedom, totality, and fidelity as well. Let's take a look at each of these again through the lens of contracepted intercourse.

Freedom. This truth may strike you as odd at first, but give it some time to sink in: *contraception was not invented to prevent pregnancy.* There already existed a perfectly safe, infallibly reliable way of doing that; it's called abstinence. Upon deeper reflection, it becomes clear that contraception was invented *to indulge sexual instinct.* As the saying goes, necessity is the mother of invention. The necessity that mothered contraception was our "need" for sex.

"Sexual freedom," in the popular sense, means the license to have sex without ever having to say no (this is exactly what contraception affords). But only those who can say no to sex (only those who can abstain) demonstrate that when they say yes, they do so *freely.* Contraception, promoted in the name of "sexual freedom," actually fosters self-imposed slavery. It creates a culture of people unable to say no to their hormones.

Totality. As we noted in the last chapter, to the degree that we knowingly and intentionally reserve any part of ourselves from our spouse in the sexual act, we cannot speak of a *total* self-giving. This includes our fertility. Contracepted intercourse contradicts the language of self-giving love by saying, "I give you all of myself *except* my fertility. I receive all that you are *except* your fertility."

The choice to withhold one's fertility during intercourse, or to refuse to receive it as a gift in one's spouse, is a contradiction of the deepest essence of conjugal love right at the moment when it should find its most sincere expression. Precisely at marriage's "moment of truth," the truth is exchanged for a lie.[3]

Fidelity. Being faithful to one's spouse does not only mean refraining from adultery (in deed or in fantasy). It means living what you promised at the altar through thick and thin, no matter how difficult, no matter how challenging, no matter how much sacrifice is required. Couples who succumb to sterilizing their acts of intercourse have consciously or unconsciously decided that fidelity to their vows is too demanding. Consciously or unconsciously, they choose to be unfaithful to the promises they made at the altar.

Wedding vows are the expression of God's love on earth. When spouses contradict their vows through the language of their bodies, they contradict the very meaning of life—our call to image God by loving as he loves. So what in God's name could be wrong with contraception? It's precisely in *God's name*, in his nature as a life-giving Communion of Persons (the Trinity), that we find the most profound answer.

As we discussed in the first chapter, the Holy Spirit—as the very love shared between the Father and the Son—points, in some sense, to the fruitfulness of marital intercourse. I once gave a presentation at which a woman asked: "What if I want to have sex with my husband, but we don't want the Holy Spirit there?" I was taken aback. This is *precisely* why the Church teaches that contraception is wrong, because this is *precisely* what a couple is saying when they contracept: "We don't want the Holy Spirit here."

Who's the Holy Spirit? *The Lord and Giver of Life* who proceeds from the Father and the Son. He is the very love and life of God!

When we understand the prophetic and sacramental meaning of sexual union, the serious *contra*diction of *contra*ception becomes clear. Sex is meant to proclaim to the world that God is life-giving love. An intentionally sterilized act of intercourse proclaims the opposite: God *is not* life-giving love. Contraception turns sexual union from a prophetic act into a form of blasphemy.

Furthermore, if the husband is to be a true symbol of Christ in the "one flesh" union, then he must speak the language of Christ: "This is my body which is given for you" (Luke 22:19). But a contracepted act of intercourse declares: "This is my body *not* given for you." In this sense, the contracepting husband acts not as Christ but as an "anti-Christ."

And if the wife is to be a true symbol of the Church in the "one flesh" union, then she must speak the language of the Church (as modeled by Mary): "Let it be done unto me according to your word" (Luke 1:38). But a contracepted act of intercourse declares: "Let it *not* be done to me according to your word." In this sense, the contracepting wife acts not as the Church but as an "anti-Church."

An intentionally sterilized act of intercourse, then, rather than being an efficacious sign of Christ's union with the Church, is an efficacious *countersign* of this union (an anti-sacrament). Contraception turns sexual union from sacrament to sacrilege.

Perhaps you're beginning to see that much more is at stake in this issue than people typically realize.

2. Are you saying couples who use contraception don't love each other?

They may love each other in many authentic ways. But despite any accompanying amount of sentiment, emotion, and feeling, an act of contracepted intercourse can never be an act of authentic love.

Love is not arbitrary. Love is not whatever we want it to be. Love is not merely an intense feeling or the sharing of pleasure. Love is to live according to the image in which we're made. Love is to give ourselves away freely, totally, faithfully, and fruitfully in imitation of Christ. Contracepted intercourse contradicts all of this.

3. So what the heck is a couple supposed to do, just have twelve kids? Gimme a break!

Let's think about it. Suppose there is a couple who has internalized what it means to renew their vows through intercourse and are determined never to violate those vows (as every married couple should be). Suppose also they have a just reason to space their children, or even not to have another baby at all. (We'll discuss what constitute "just reasons" in a subsequent question.) What could they possibly do that would not violate their vows?

Chances are you're doing it right now. They could abstain from sex.

If they are to speak the truth with their bodies, every time a couple chooses to have sex they must speak the "I do" of their vows. But couples aren't always obligated to have sex. In fact, throughout the course of a marriage there are many occasions when a couple might want to renew their vows through intercourse, but have a serious reason not to. In fact, love may well demand abstinence.

Perhaps one or the other spouse is sick. Perhaps the wife just gave birth. Perhaps the couple is staying at the in-laws and there are thin walls. Or perhaps they have a good reason not to have another baby. These are all good reasons *not* to have sex, even if they may *want* to.

Human dignity and the meaning of sexual intercourse reveal that the only acceptable birth control is *self-control*. Think about it: Why do people spay or neuter their pets? Why not just ask them to abstain? Obviously, animals can't abstain. They're ruled by instinct. But we *can*. If we can't, then we've stooped to the level of Fido and Fidette.

4. Are you saying a couple who needs to avoid pregnancy would have to abstain from sex until menopause in order not to violate their vows?

Let's think it through. Fidelity to the "I do" of the wedding vows means spouses must never do anything of their own will to sterilize any act of intercourse. Menopause actually gives us a good platform for discussion. If a couple past childbearing years chose to have sex, the lack of subsequent pregnancy would not be because of anything *they* did to sterilize the act. The lack of pregnancy would be the result of *God's* choice not to bring a new life into the world, as evidenced by his own design in the way he created a woman's body.

Well, it's also the result of God's design that women *within* their child-bearing years are not always fertile. In fact, the large majority of the time, they're infertile.

Let's return to the couple who is determined never to violate their wedding vows. Out of respect for the meaning of sex, they abstain from intercourse because they have a just reason to avoid a pregnancy. Now let's suppose that on a given day of the wife's cycle they're able to determine that having sex would not result in pregnancy. Would they be doing anything wrong if they chose to have sex then?

If pregnancy did not result, would it be because *they* sterilized the act, or would it be because God chose not to bring a new life into the world as evidenced by the way he designed the wife's body?

This is the very principle of *natural family planning* (NFP). Couples who have been properly trained in modern methods of NFP can determine the fertile time of the wife's cycle with 99 percent accuracy.[4] If they have a just reason to avoid pregnancy, they choose to abstain from intercourse during that time. During the infertile phase of the cycle, if they so desire, they can choose to have intercourse without violating their marriage commitment in any way. The fact that pregnancy doesn't result from these acts of intercourse is *God's* doing, not *theirs*.

5. Isn't that splitting hairs? What's the big difference between sterilizing the act of intercourse yourself and just waiting until it's naturally infertile? The end result is the same thing: Both couples avoid children.

What's the big difference between killing Grandma and just waiting till she dies naturally? The end result is the same thing: dead Grandma. Yes, the end result is the same, but one is a serious sin called murder, while in the other, there's no sin involved whatsoever because Grandma's death is an act of God.

If you can tell the difference between euthanasia and natural death, you can tell the difference between contraception and natural family planning. In natural death and natural family planning, God remains God. In euthanasia and contraception, we take the powers of life into our own hands and make ourselves like God.

As St. John Paul II once said: "Contraception is to be judged so profoundly unlawful as never to be, for any reason, justified. To think or to say the contrary is equal to maintaining that in human life, situations may arise in which it is lawful not to recognize God as God."[5]

This is the question at stake here: Are we free to take into our own hands the powers of life, or does that power belong to God and God alone? We should think long and hard before we answer that question. How we do will determine our stance within the cosmos.

6. Isn't refusing to have sex even more of a contradiction of your wedding vows than having protected sex?

I can't help but comment on this notion of "protected" sex. If your spouse poses some sort of threat to you, against which you must *protect* yourself by erecting a barrier, something's dreadfully wrong.

You can't separate your spouse from his or her fertility. The body expresses the person. To reject your spouse's fertility is to reject an integral aspect of your spouse. True spousal love demands total surrender. There is no place here for "safety nets."

Refusing to have sex could well be a violation of your wedding vows if you were doing it out of spite for your spouse, out of hatred for children, or for some other negative reason. But spouses who mutually agree to abstain from intercourse because they have a *just reason* to avoid pregnancy are acting out of love and utter fidelity to their wedding vows. When spouses choose to "speak" (through intercourse), they must speak the truth. If they have a good reason not to "speak," it's good to remain silent. But nothing justifies speaking a lie by using "protection."

7. The Church's distinction between "natural" and "artificial" birth control makes no sense. Does this mean using polyester is immoral too?

Admittedly, it's difficult to see the important distinction between periodic abstinence and contraception when the emphasis is placed on "natural" versus "artificial" methods. There are lots of things we use that are artificial but not immoral, such as polyester. So why is artificial birth control any different?

Contrary to popular belief, the Church does not oppose artificial birth control *because* it's artificial. She opposes it because it's *contraceptive*. Contraception is the choice by any means *to impede the procreative potential of a given act of intercourse*. In other words, the contracepting couple chooses to engage in intercourse, and foreseeing that their act may result in a new life, they *intentionally* and *willfully* suppress their fertility.

This can be done by employing a large variety of artificial devices and hormones, or by sterilizing surgical procedures. It can also be done without employing anything artificial at all, such as in the practice of withdrawal (*coitus interruptus*). So in order to avoid a great deal of confusion, *contraception* is the best word to use when describing what the Church specifically opposes. "Artificial" really has nothing to do with it and is better left out of the discussion altogether.

Furthermore, the Church approves of NFP (when there is just reason to avoid pregnancy) not because it's "natural" as opposed to "artificial," but because *it's in no way contraceptive*. Never does the couple practicing NFP choose to impede the procreative potential of a given act of intercourse. NFP is not a "natural" method of contraception. *It's not a method of contraception at all*. It's a holistic way of planning a family that fully embraces God's design for sex as a great good.

8. This is just another indication that the Catholic Church is opposed to modern progress and technology. If God gave us the intelligence to control our fertility, we should be able to use it.

As St. Paul VI said in *Humanae Vitae*: "The Church is the first to praise and recommend the intervention of intelligence in a function which so closely associates the rational creature with his Creator; but she affirms that *this must be done with respect for the order established by God.*"[6] Put another way: It is certainly true that God gave us intelligence to understand how our fertility works, and, yes, we should use it. But using our intelligence to act *against* God's design for our fertility is not an intelligent thing to do. Just because we *can* do something doesn't mean we *should*.

Allow me to demonstrate the concept this way. We'd all agree that the proper use of medicine and technology is to serve our health, to make our bodies work the way they're meant to work. For example, if medicine and technology can give sight to a blind man, that's a wonderful, intelligent use of it. But it would be a terrible abuse of medicine and technology *intentionally to blind someone* with perfectly functioning eyes. That would be an act of mutilation.

Well, it's no less a terrible abuse of medicine and technology, and no less a mutilation, *to sterilize someone intentionally*. If someone is fertile, that means his or her body is functioning the way it's meant to function.

As professor Janet Smith points out, we take pills when we're sick. We have surgery to cure maladies and disease. Fertility is not a sickness. Fertility is not a disease. Infertility is the malady that needs to be cured.[7] The only intelligent thing to do when there is honest need to regulate fertility is to come to understand God's design for fertility and work with it. That's what NFP is all about.

9. I still don't see the big difference between NFP and contraception.

Do you *want* to see the difference? Many people don't, because somehow they intuit that it would demand not just a change of behavior in the bedroom but the transformation of their entire view of the world. If that's what you're sensing—you're right.

As we hinted in question 5, the way we understand the order of the universe shifts in one of two irreconcilable directions on this point. Either God is God, and we trust his ordering of the universe, or we're trying to be God and control things ourselves. My advice: Let God be God.

There's nothing to fear. Trusting him is only threatening if he's against us. He's not. He's perfect love. He desires nothing but our good. Let go. Let him in. Trust him.

If you're open to seeing the difference, I think the following analogy will help. Suppose there were a religious person, a nonreligious person, and an antireligious person walking past a church. What might each do?

Let's say the religious person goes inside and prays, the nonreligious person walks by and does nothing, and the antireligious person goes inside the church and desecrates it. (I'm framing an analogy, of course, but these are reasonable behaviors to expect.) Which of these three persons did something that is always, under every circumstance, wrong?

Husbands and wives are called to be *procreative*. If they have a good reason to avoid pregnancy, they are free to be *non-procreative*. But it's a contradiction of the deepest essence of the sacrament of marriage to be *anti-procreative*.

The analogy is even more profound than you may think. According to Ephesians chapter 5, the wife is a sacramental sign of the Church. As exemplified in the Virgin Mary, a woman's womb has truly become the temple of God. If the husband enters this "church," he must pray for God's will to be done. He may have a good reason not to enter the church. But it would be a grievous sacrilege to enter the church and desecrate it by sterilizing her womb.

Here's another analogy.[8] Most engaged couples come to realize in planning their weddings that there are people they know whom, with good reason, they can't invite to the wedding. The proper thing to do is simply not to send them an invitation. Can you imagine sending them a *dis*-invitation"? "We are getting married on June 21, but we do *not* want you to be there. Please do not come." That would be an obvious breach of the relationship.

This is what married couples are doing to God when they contracept. By engaging in intercourse, they are sending God an invitation to join them in bringing about his most creative act, but when God opens the invitation, it says in bold letters: "Do Not Come. We Don't Want You Here." On the other hand, couples who abstain from intercourse to avoid pregnancy are simply not sending an invitation to God. If the couple has a good reason to avoid a pregnancy, God can understand that. There's no breach of relationship.

10. I was always taught that morality is evaluated by intention. Don't couples using NFP and those using contraception have the same intention?

We must be careful to distinguish between *present* and *further* intentions (means and ends). They may have the same *further* intention—to avoid pregnancy for just reasons. But their *present* intentions (the means by which they intend to achieve their common end) are very different. The NFP couple *intends to abstain* from fertile intercourse. The contracepting couple *intends to sterilize* fertile intercourse. These are different intentions altogether.

Take, for example, two students who both have the further intention of getting good grades. With that goal in mind, one intends to study hard, and the other intends to cheat on every test. The end never justifies the means.

11. Where does the Bible say contraception is wrong?

Where does the Bible say that it's wrong to take your neighbor's arm and run it through a meat grinder? It doesn't. But it does say we're called to love our neighbor. Sensible people will draw the conclusion that love of neighbor excludes making hamburger out of his arm.

Nowhere does the Bible say, "Thou shalt not use contraception." But it does say we're created in the image and likeness of God as male and female (see Genesis 1:27). It does say "be fruitful and multiply" (Genesis 1:28). It does say that God slew Onan for "spilling his seed on the ground" (Genesis 38:9–10).[9]

Christ himself taught, in reference to the two becoming "one flesh," that we must not separate what God has joined (see Matthew 19:6), and God's the One who joined sex and babies, isn't he? Ephesians chapter 5 very clearly calls husbands to love their wives as Christ loves the Church. Would Christ ever intentionally sterilize his love?

From beginning to end the Scriptures call us to receive God's love, to love as God loves, and to choose life. Sexual union is perhaps the most pointed opportunity for us to accept this call or to reject it. It's through sexual union that the uncreated love of God penetrates the created world to commune with the love of husband and wife in bringing about the most stunning event in the universe: the creation of a new human person.

Contracepted sex says: "We don't want to receive God's love. We don't want to love as God loves. We don't want to choose life." Is *that* biblical?

12. So what would be just reasons for a married couple to use NFP to avoid pregnancy?

First, we need to look at the general disposition a couple has toward children. A contracepting culture tends to see children as a burden to be resisted, rather than a gift to be welcomed; an obstacle to material wealth, rather than a contribution to family health; a drain on the world's resources, rather than a benefit to society.[10] Within this milieu, couples often enter marriage with an approach to children that assumes they won't have them *unless* or *until* they want them. After the allotted two, it seems a couple would have to find justification for having any more.

Without thinking anything of it, couples who take this approach simply look for the most expedient way to carry out their plan. From this perspective, NFP is just seen as another choice on the long list of methods of avoiding "unwanted" children, and a very undesirable method at that. While it's just as effective at avoiding pregnancy as any contraceptive method, it takes far too much sacrifice to practice.

But suppose such a couple did use NFP. Their negative mentality toward children is already contrary to what they pledged at the altar. Regardless of the fact that they're not intentionally sterilizing their acts of intercourse, they would be guilty of violating their vows "in their hearts."

To return to the wedding invitation analogy, it's not that such a couple is sending a "dis-invitation" to God but that their withholding an invitation is not based on a just reason. It's based on an attitude that God's presence in their union would not be welcome.

This is still an obvious breach of relationship. (How would you feel if a close friend didn't invite you to his wedding without good reason?) So before all else, we need to seek a deep conversion of our hearts to the meaning of sex and the true blessing of children in order to understand the just use of NFP in a marriage.

Every married couple is called to "be fruitful and multiply" (Genesis 1:28). This is the starting point. Children are not something tacked on to married love but are the crowning glory of married love. Thus, instead of avoiding children, the general disposition should be one of receiving children as they come, unless a couple has a good reason not to.

The Church readily recognizes, especially in our day and age, that many couples *do* have good reason not to receive children as they come at certain times of their married life. The Second Vatican Council offers the following guidelines for spouses in planning their family size: Spouses should "thoughtfully take into account both their own welfare and that of their children, those already born, and those that the future may bring. For this accounting they need to reckon with both the material and the spiritual conditions of the times as well as their state in life. Finally, they should consult the interests of the family group, of temporal society, and of the Church herself. The parents themselves and no one else should ultimately make this judgment in the sight of God."[11]

The *Catechism* states that it's the duty of parents to "make certain that their desire [to space births] is not motivated by selfishness but is in conformity with the generosity appropriate to responsible parenthood."[12]

Let's return, once again, to the couple who truly understands the meaning of sex. They have a proper attitude toward children. God is always welcome in their sexual union. Yet they've discerned before God, based on the above principles, that they should avoid another pregnancy, at least for the time being.

Such a couple is not concerned with the amount of sacrifice necessary to be faithful to their vows, so they learn how to use NFP and abstain from sexual activity during the fertile time of the cycle. That is, with good reasons, they refrain from inviting God to create a new life. Such a couple acts justly, responsibly, and in full accord with the commitment they made at the altar.

13. We already have five kids. It is my decision—and should be my decision—to make sure I don't get pregnant again. The pill is what my husband and I have decided is best for our family. It's none of the Church's

business. If the Church really had great love for families, it would allow them to choose the birth control method that works best for them instead of trying to make them feel guilty about the method they choose.

Let me caution you that there are only three ways "to make sure you don't get pregnant again." The first is to abstain from sex altogether until you are post-menopause. If you want to continue having sex, the only other options are complete removal of your ovaries or complete removal of your husband's testicles. No method of birth control, except for these three, is 100-percent effective. Even with vasectomy or tubal ligation, you can't be sure that you won't get pregnant again if you and your husband continue to have sex.

As a mother of five, you can no doubt relate to the following analogy. If you had a fifteen-year-old daughter who wanted to go to an unsupervised party where you knew there would be a lot of drinking, drugs, and promiscuous sex going on, I would imagine that out of love for her you would tell her it's not good to go. Your daughter might not see your love for her in this. In fact, she might scoff at your supposed love and say, "If you really had such great love for me, you would realize that my going to this party is none of your business, and you would allow me to decide for myself what is best instead of making me feel guilty for wanting to go."

As a mother, you're able to see something that your daughter, for whatever reason (maturity level, peer pressure, misinformation, or whatever), is unable to see. Going to this party, no matter what your daughter "believes," is *not* good for her.

In a similar way, we who have been baptized into the Catholic Church are all her sons and daughters. The Church, in a real sense, is our mother. We should have the humility to admit that, even as adults, we don't always know what's best for us. The Church, as a loving mother should, seeks to guide us.

We can resist all we like, just as a child might. But guided by Christ himself, the Church knows the right path for us. It's the narrow path. It's the path on which few are willing to travel (see Matthew 7:13–14). It's the path of following in the footsteps of Christ and living according to his wisdom and not our own "beliefs." It's the path of trusting that God has our best interests in mind even when we don't understand.

In the end, what you choose to do is indeed your decision and can be only your decision. The Church cannot, and never claims to, make decisions for others. As St. John Paul II himself said, the Church "does not impose her teaching, but feels an urgent need to propose it to everyone without fear and indeed with great confidence and hope although she knows that [it] includes the subject of the Cross. But it is only through the cross that the family can attain the fullness of its being and the perfection of its love."[13]

14. When it comes to birth control, the Catholic Church has lost touch with the needs of real people. No other church teaches that birth control is wrong. The Catholic Church loses all credibility right here.

If the Church is wrong about this issue, I would agree. She is "out of touch" and loses all credibility right here. But if the Church is right about contraception, then it's the rest of the world that's "out of touch," and the Catholic Church *gains* all credibility right here.

Contraception is nothing new. In fact, one of the hallmarks of the early Christians that distinguished them from their pagan contemporaries was their refusal to diminish their fertility with the linen condoms, potions, and pessaries (obstructions placed in the vagina) of their day. Until 1930 *every* Christian denomination was unanimous in its condemnation of contraception.

That year, however, the Anglican Church made history as the first Christian body to break with this teaching. At the time, Catholic, Protestant, and even non-Christian voices predicted that acceptance of contraception would logically lead to societal chaos, starting with a dramatic rise in marital breakdown and divorce. You might be surprised to read what several prominent thinkers of the early twentieth century had to say about contraception.[14]

U.S. president Theodore Roosevelt, for example, condemned contraception as "the one sin for which the penalty is national death, race death; a sin for which there is no atonement." Sigmund Freud, the founder of modern psychoanalysis and an atheist, observed: "The abandonment of the reproductive function is the common feature of all perversions. We actually describe a sexual activity as perverse if it has given up the aim of reproduction and pursues the attainment of pleasure as an aim independent of it."

Mohandas Gandhi, the famous Indian nationalist leader and a Hindu, insisted that contraceptive methods are "like putting a premium on vice. They make men and women reckless." He predicted that "nature is relentless and will have full revenge for any such violation of her laws. Moral results can only be produced by moral restraints.... If [contraceptive] methods become the order of the day, nothing but moral degradation can be the result.... As it is, man has sufficiently degraded woman for his lust, and [contraception], no matter how well meaning the advocates may be, will still further degrade her."

T. S. Eliot, the celebrated British poet and literary critic, insisted that by accepting contraception, "the world is trying the experiment of attempting to form a civilized, but non-Christian mentality. The experiment will fail; but we must be very patient in waiting its collapse; meanwhile redeeming the time so that the Faith may be preserved alive through the dark ages before us; to renew and rebuild civilization and save the world from suicide."[15]

When a committee of the Federal Council of Churches in America issued a report that suggested following the lead of the Anglican Church, *The Washington Post* published a stinging editorial with the following prophetic statement: "Carried to its logical conclusions, the committee's report if carried into effect would sound the death knell of marriage as a holy institution by establishing degrading practices which would encourage indiscriminate immorality. The suggestion that the use of legalized contraceptives would be 'careful and restrained' is preposterous."[16]

Wise men and women have always recognized that marriage, sex, and babies belong together … and in that order. God, in his loving design, has united these three realities in a tight knot to reveal in our flesh the truth of his own eternal covenant love and Fatherhood. Contraception not only loosens the knot of this fundamental and society-ordering nexus, it cuts the ties.

Separate sex from babies and you also separate sex from marriage—both in principle and in practice. So long as the natural connection between sex and babies is retained, we realize intuitively that sexual intercourse is the domain of those who have committed themselves to raising children: That commitment is called marriage. Insert contraception into the tight-knot-nexus of marriage-sex-babies and everything will start to unravel as follows.

People throughout history have been tempted to commit adultery. It's nothing new. But one of the main deterrents to succumbing to the temptation has been the fear of an unwanted pregnancy.

Hmm...What would happen if this natural deterrent were taken away through the widespread availability and cultural acceptance of contraception? Not in every marriage, of course, but in a given population, incidents of infidelity would be sure to rise. And what's one of the main causes of divorce? Adultery.

But let's continue with this scenario. Certainly throughout history young people have been tempted to have sex before marriage. Yet one of the main deterrents to succumbing to the temptation has been the fear of unwanted pregnancy. Once again, what would happen if this natural deterrent were taken away through contraception? Not in the case of every hormone-laden young person, but in a given population, incidents of premarital sex would be sure to rise. And premarital sex, as noted in chapter four, is also a key predictor of future divorce.

It gets worse. Since no method of contraception is ever 100-percent effective, an increase in adultery and premarital sex in a given population will inevitably lead to an increase in "unwanted pregnancies." Abortion logically follows (see question 16 for more discussion of this subject).

Not everyone will resort to abortion of course—thanks be to God for that. Some will offer their children up for adoption, a heroic decision. Most mothers, however, will raise these children on their own. This, too, can be heroic, but now the number of children who grow up without a father— which has already been increased by the rise in divorce (brought on by the rise in adultery, brought on by the acceptance of contraception)—will be compounded.

Certainly, God's grace can supply what is lacking and those raised without a father can lead healthy, holy lives. Still, as numerous studies (and common sense) indicate, the chances dramatically increase that "fatherless" children will: grow up in poverty; have emotional, psychological, and behavioral problems; suffer poor health; drop out of school; engage in premarital sex; obtain abortions; do drugs; commit violent crimes; and end up in jail. All of these social ills compound exponentially from generation to generation since "fatherless" children are also much more likely to have out-of-wedlock births and, if they marry at all, divorce.

As history clearly shows, when we begin untying the tight-knot-nexus of marriage, sex, and babies, we end up redefining all three. Babies become mere "clumps of cells." Sex becomes mere uncommitted pleasure-exchange between consenting partners (gender being irrelevant and malleable). And marriage becomes a demanded societal and governmental "stamp of approval" on one's preferred method of sexual pleasure-exchange.

Welcome to the societal/sexual chaos in which we're now immersed, all of which was predicted by wise men and women who understood the power of contraception to alter the course of society by altering people's approach to human life at its source. If marriage is the fundamental cell of society, sexual union is the fountainhead of culture. Oriented toward love and life, it builds a culture of love and life. Oriented *against* love and life, it builds a culture of utility and death.

If nothing governs life at its source, then nothing governs life. A contracepting culture is a culture that is erasing the fundamental purpose and meaning of the gender difference: to generate new life. As such, it's a culture without a future. It's a culture, as T.S. Eliot and Theodore Roosevelt understood, that's committing suicide.

The twentieth century witnessed every major Protestant denomination shift from condemning contraception, not only to accepting it, but oftentimes advocating it. The Catholic Church alone—withstanding unimaginable global pressure—has stood firm. Even staunch Protestant leaders, when they wake up to the evils of contraception (as more and more are), marvel at the courage of the Catholic Church. As one Evangelical Lutheran put it: "That a Roman pontiff would lead the opposition—often painfully alone—to contraception at the end of the twentieth century is no small irony. Perhaps the Catholic hierarchical model, reserving final decisions on matters of faith and morals to a bishop whom Catholics believe is the successor of Peter, has proved more resilient in the face of modernity than the Protestant reliance on individual conscience and democratic church governance."[17]

So, is the Catholic Church out of touch with the needs of real people, or is the prevailing contraceptive culture? Real people need the truth. Real people need to know the good news of our creation in the image of God and our call to love as Christ loves. The Catholic Church proposes this good news to the world. It's our choice whether to embrace it or reject it.

15. You're overlooking a host of benefits. Contraception has helped liberate women, brought more equality between the sexes, and freed married couples to enjoy sex more by relieving the fear of unwanted pregnancies. How can that be wrong?

What does it mean for women to be liberated? What *is* equality between the sexes? What *is* the joy of sex? Let's look briefly at each and see what contraception has done.

Women's liberation. History has demonstrated what the book of Genesis foretold: Men will dominate women (see Genesis 3:16). Women *should* seek liberation from this domination. But if the real problem behind women's oppression is men's failure to treat them properly as persons, contraception is a sure way to keep women in chains. Remove the possibility of pregnancy, and you simply foster men's tendencies to treat women not as persons to love but as things to use for their own pleasure and to discard when they're through.

The first feminist leaders of the nineteenth century recognized this. Women such as Elizabeth Cady Stanton, Victoria Woodhull, and Dr. Elizabeth Blackwell all spoke out against contraception, seeing it as still further degradation of women since it gave men license to indulge their passions without consequence.[18] In a calamitous break with the wisdom of their predecessors, modern feminists would actually come to believe that contraception was the key to women's liberation.[19]

Only after the casualties of the sexual revolution have some modern feminists awakened to the delusion. Germaine Greer, for example, who once encouraged her followers to revel in the "liberties" afforded them by contraception, now laments that "contraceptive technology, instead of liberating women, has turned them into *geishas* [Japanese term for "call girls"] who risk health and fertility in order to be readily available for meaningless sex."[20]

In keeping with the foresight of the first feminists, Paul VI predicted that contraception would result in the further degradation of women in his encyclical *Humanae Vitae*.[21] Gandhi predicted the same. History has proved all of them right.

Equality between the sexes. Our equal dignity as men and women is founded on God's creating us in his image as male and female. But equal in dignity does not mean *sameness*. It's precisely in the beauty of sexual *difference* that we discover our complementary and equally dignified personhood.

Contraception is actually opposed to woman's equally dignified personhood. Its very premise is to turn women into something they're not designed to be: the kind of being that can have sex without getting pregnant. That's called a man. Think about it. If women need to make themselves more and more like men in order to claim "equality" with men, then aren't they already buying into the idea that they are not equal in dignity *as women*? If women's equality is dependent on contraception, it's a sham created by technology, not by God. Men will only treat women as equal in dignity when they come to appreciate woman's unique giftedness as God made her to be. Contraception seeks to eradicate that uniqueness.

The joy of sex. The true joy of sex is loving as God loves in a free, total, faithful surrender of self that's open to life. From this perspective, couples who use contraception don't enjoy sex at all. They may enjoy the pleasure of orgasm exchange, but they don't really enjoy sex.

In fact, a couple that contracepts isn't even really having sex. They don't want to have sex. They're afraid of what sex *is*. They're afraid of what real sex demands of them.

Contraception doesn't relieve people of their fears. It demonstrates how afraid they actually are. Only true love can cast out fear (see 1 John 4:18). Only true love can bring true joy. If all you want is the pleasure of orgasm, it's less hassle just to masturbate.

Could there be some genuinely good things that contraception has afforded? Sure. But trying to justify contraception by pointing them out would be like trying to justify the pornography industry by pointing to the fact that it creates jobs. You can create jobs in morally acceptable ways.

Similarly, any genuine good that has come from contraception can be brought about in other, morally acceptable ways. We may never do evil so that good may result (see Romans 3:8).

16. How can the Church not recognize the contradiction of being against both contraception and abortion? Abortions will continue as long as there are unwanted pregnancies.

St. John Paul II addressed this issue in his encyclical *Evangelium Vitae*: "It is frequently asserted that *contraception*, if made safe and available to all, is the most effective remedy against abortion. The Catholic Church is then accused of actually promoting abortion, because she obstinately continues to teach the moral unlawfulness of contraception. When looked at carefully, this objection is clearly unfounded. It may be that many people use contraception with the view to excluding the subsequent temptation of abortion. But the negative values inherent in the 'contraceptive mentality'...are such that they in fact strengthen this temptation when an unwanted life is conceived."[22]

By using contraception, a couple sets their will *against* the conception of a child. If their contraception fails (as it can and often does), then they're stuck with a child growing in the womb that they didn't bargain for, that they weren't prepared for, *that they didn't want*.

What do they do now? Even a cursory look at the data indicates that in every country that has accepted contraception, abortions have multiplied, not diminished. The United States Supreme Court itself recognizes the inherent connection in a 1992 statement: "In some critical respects abortion is of the same character as the decision to use contraception.... For two decades of economic and social developments, people have organized intimate relationships and made choices that define their views of themselves and their places in society, in reliance on the availability of abortion in the event that contraception should fail."[23]

Thus contraception has afforded the grand illusion that we can sever the inherent connection between sex and babies. People then say the strangest things, such as: "I got pregnant by accident."

Whoa! As Janet Smith is fond of pointing out, if you were having sex and you got pregnant, it doesn't mean something went *wrong*, it means something went *right*. Even doctors, when confronted with their contracepting yet pregnant patients, will ask: "How did this happen?" We really have a problem on our hands when even the medical community has forgotten where babies come from.[24]

"Unwanted babies" are the result of people having sex without being open to children. Pregnancy comes to be seen as a disease—contraception being the preventative medicine, and abortion being the cure. Trying to solve the abortion problem with contraception is like trying to put out a fire by dousing it with gasoline! Only by restoring the full truth about the goodness, the beauty, and the demands of sexual love can we prevent the killing of "unwanted babies."

There's yet a further connection between contraception and abortion that cannot go unmentioned. Many people are unaware that the IUD, the pill, and other hormonal contraceptives such as Depo-Provera and Norplant can at times act not to prevent conception but to abort a newly conceived human being.

Chances are you know someone who got pregnant while on the pill. So obviously the pill doesn't always prevent ovulation. In fact, hormonal contraceptives are believed to have two "backup" mechanisms, should ovulation not be prevented: (1) they prevent sperm from reaching the egg by changing the consistency of the cervical mucus; and (2) they change the lining of the uterus so that a newly conceived child cannot implant in the uterine wall and dies. (It's believed that the IUD works almost exclusively this way.)[25]

Of course, few doctors are telling their patients this. In fact, there has been a push in the medical community to redefine the beginning of pregnancy as the moment of implantation rather than the moment of conception in order to disguise the abortifacient mechanism of these "contraceptives."[26]

17. What if you're on the pill for medical reasons? Is that still wrong?

First let me state the moral principle involved, then I'll address the pill specifically. As St. Paul VI said in *Humanae Vitae*: "The Church…does not at all consider illicit the use of those therapeutic means truly necessary to cure diseases of the organism, even if an impediment to procreation, which may be foreseen, should result therefrom, provided such impediment is not, for whatever motive, directly willed."[27]

Suppose a woman had a hysterectomy to remove a cancerous uterus. Subsequent sexual acts would obviously be sterile, but the intention of the operation was to remove her cancer, not to sterilize her. (Note: A medical reason to avoid pregnancy does *not* justify sterilization.) The fact that she is now sterile is an unfortunate but unintended consequence of a medically necessary procedure.

Taking the pill for medical reasons would be similarly acceptable, but for the fact that the pill is a potential abortifacient. If there were absolutely no medical alternatives for a married woman on the pill for therapeutic reasons, she and her husband would have to abstain from sex *completely* if they were to avoid the risk of aborting their children. The good news is, there are many medical alternatives to the pill. An Internet search for NaPro Technology will lead you to a community of medical professionals who specialize in such alternative treatments.

18. NFP isn't 100-percent effective either. So even if everybody used NFP as the Church says, there would still be the temptation to abort.

This would be the case only if those who were using NFP already had the wrong attitude in their hearts toward children. Let's return, once again, to the wedding invitation analogy (see questions 9 and 12 above). How would you feel if you sent a "dis-invitation" to someone, but that person had the nerve to show up? You'd be upset, wouldn't you? You'd want to tell that person to get out. This is precisely why the contraceptive mentality leads to abortion.

Furthermore, even if a couple wouldn't resort to abortion, we can see how the contraceptive mentality leads to a certain resentment toward children and all that they demand of their parents. Back to the "dis-invited" wedding guest. Suppose you didn't have the nerve to kick him out. Still, you'd resent his presence. And you'd be all the more indignant if he made demands on you at the reception. Quite simply, the lifelong responsibilities of parenthood are not what contracepting couples bargain for.

The mentality of those who make responsible use of NFP is totally different. Suppose you sent a wedding invitation to someone whom you already knew couldn't make it to your wedding. How would you feel if he had a change of plans and unexpectedly showed up? You might be surprised, but you wouldn't want to kick him out. After all, you'd invited him to come. If you did want to kick him out, that would demonstrate that your invitation was insincere in the first place.

This is analogous to the NFP couple having sex during the infertile time. They send an invitation to God saying he's free to create a new life if he so desires, but they are nearly certain he won't. If God has "a change of plans," you might hear the couple speaking of a "surprise pregnancy," but you'll never hear them speaking of an "unwanted pregnancy." If they do, then it will show that their invitation to God was insincere in the first place.

To put it another way, couples who make responsible use of NFP know what the bargain is and embrace it. If God unexpectedly chooses to create a new life, every diaper change, every sleepless night—in short, every parental sacrifice—becomes a continuation of the *yes* they uttered in the ecstasy of that life-giving embrace.

19. NFP couples must have lots of surprises, then. The chart in my doctor's office says natural methods are only 80-percent effective at avoiding pregnancy.

The 80-percent figure often quoted in medical literature is based on studies of people who simply say they use some "natural method of birth control." This could include people who use the older "rhythm method," or those who simply guess when they are or are not fertile, or those who have actually been educated to use a modern method of NFP. It may also include people who knowingly fudge on the time of abstinence.

Grouping this lot together, an 80-percent figure is probably accurate. But if you take the group of people who have been properly educated in modern methods of NFP and who are motivated to follow the rules, the effectiveness rate jumps to 99 percent.[28]

20. I thought NFP *was* the rhythm method. What's the difference?

This is a common misunderstanding. The older rhythm method, popularized by Catholics in the mid-twentieth century, predicted the probable time of fertility in a given month based on the length of past cycles. Thus, it was not very effective for women with irregular cycles. Nor was there any way of determining when fertility would return after childbirth or while breastfeeding.

Progress in understanding the role of cervical mucus throughout the 1950s and 60s led to the development of modern methods of NFP. These are not based on the probability of fertility, but rather on the readily observable signs of fertility and infertility in each cycle (primarily cervical mucus, but also temperature, changes in the cervix, and other signs). Thus, any woman can use modern methods of NFP successfully, even if she has irregular cycles, is breastfeeding, or is premenopausal.

21. So how long do you have to abstain with NFP if you want to avoid pregnancy?

Usually no more than twenty-seven days per cycle. Just kidding. In all honesty, only about seven to twelve days per cycle. Periods of abstinence may be longer during those times of irregular fertility such as after childbirth and premenopause.

22. There's nothing "natural" about abstaining from sex when you're married. Seems to me it could even harm a marriage.

Abstinence could harm a marriage if it were done for the wrong reasons. But when a couple chooses to abstain from sex out of fidelity to their wedding vows, it only serves to strengthen their marriage. We can see this by looking at each of the promises of marriage again through the lens of NFP.

Freedom. Practicing NFP puts a couple's freedom to the test. Even if they find it difficult, periods of abstinence, when chosen in fidelity to the marriage commitment, cannot help but strengthen both husband and wife in the virtue of self-mastery, so essential to the freedom of authentic conjugal love.

Totality. Practicing NFP promotes total self-giving by promoting respect for the total person. The refusal to erect physical or chemical barriers creates an atmosphere that fosters spouses' ability to let go of emotional barriers as well. The willingness to sacrifice and grow in self-mastery of one's sexual desires also fosters mutual trust that enables a couple, when they do have sex, to surrender totally to each other without fear.

Fidelity. Fidelity to the marriage commitment is the *raison d'être* of NFP. Such couples demonstrate their willingness to remain faithful to their vows no matter how difficult, no matter how challenging, no matter how much sacrifice is required. Furthermore, when a couple show themselves ready to embrace the challenges of true self-mastery within marriage, they are all the more prepared to conquer sexual temptations outside their marriage.

Openness to children. Maintaining fidelity to this promise is, of course, the hallmark of NFP. When couples who practice NFP choose to have sex, they always leave the possibility of pregnancy in the hands of God. The Holy Spirit is welcome in their bedroom. The bond of love that unites the Trinity becomes the very same bond that unites them.

There's no question that the periodic abstinence required by NFP can be difficult. But as the Fathers of the Second Vatican Council remind us, "a true contradiction cannot exist between the divine laws pertaining to the transmission of life and those pertaining to authentic conjugal love."[29] Practicing NFP takes self-control, trust in one's spouse, trust in God, honest and open communication, and willingness to sacrifice for each other. But love isn't harmed by these things. Love *is* these things.

Since practicing NFP fosters the very virtues that make for a successful marriage, it shouldn't surprise us that while—across the board—Catholics have about the same divorce rate as everybody else, surveys indicate a virtually nonexistent divorce rate among NFP users.[30] Far from damaging marriage, the faithful practice of NFP is like marriage insurance.

23. NFP is horrible! I'm lying here next to my wife on an extremely rare night when all four of our kids (ages seven to twelve) are spending an overnight at their grandparents'. But I dare not touch her right now because it would almost certainly result in another pregnancy—which our financial situation and her emotional state demand we avoid. Doing things the "Catholic way" is more miserable and frustrating than anything I could have imagined.

First, thank you for your honesty—for just saying it like it is and sharing the naked cry of your heart (when we do that with God, it's called prayer, by the way). I have nothing but reverence for anyone who's in the thick of the battle required of those who embrace the real demands of love. I know that battle well.

In truth, it's not NFP that's horrible. It's the demands of marital love that are horrible: "Husbands, love your wives as Christ loved the Church" (Ephesians 5:25). If the way Christ loved the Church doesn't evoke some level of horror, we have not spent much time pondering the gruesome reality of Roman scourging and crucifixion.

There's no getting around it. We express our wedding vows in a church, under a crucifix, in front of an altar of sacrifice. The vows themselves are a solemn promise to love as Christ loves. That means along with all the real joys of married life, there will be times when the nails are being driven through our palms, the thorns are being pressed into our scalps, and the lance is being thrust through our sides. And we, understandably, will want to exclaim: "This is horrible!"

I'm constantly confronted with how marriage, by its very design, leads me to and through the cross. The temptation in those moments is always to look for a detour. But here's where we need to *press in* rather than *give in*. For on the other side of the horror of the cross lie the ecstasy, joy, and freedom we're really looking for.

I am confident that what you really desire when you're lying there next to your beautiful and fertile (and beautifully fertile) wife is to love her. However, we all have to wrestle in our hearts with desires that want to pass themselves off as love, but when examined more closely, amount to something quite other than love. Marriage does not give us a "free pass" to indulge those desires. Rather, marriage is a call to virtue—to the ordering of our desires toward true self-giving.

As Catholic counselor Dr. Greg Popcak has insightfully observed, we need to recognize that any frustration we feel in practicing the abstinence required of NFP is a sign that NFP is doing the job it's meant to do: It is helping us grow in virtue and authentic freedom. When we feel those frustrations, we must learn to recognize them as the growing pains of personal maturity and the capacity for expressing authentic love. In those times when the growing pains hurt the most, we're not feeling a loving urge that must be satisfied, but a selfish urge that must be crucified if we are to be transformed and reclaim the freedom that our fallenness has taken from us. This is the gift and role of the virtue of chastity.

Remember how I used beautiful piano playing as an analogy for chastity in the last chapter (see question 9)? I hated—and I mean *hated*—piano lessons as a kid. Not only were the weekly lessons themselves miserable, but the need to practice every day made my whole life seem horrible. So I quit. And with my quitting came great relief. Initially.

I can't tell you how many times as an adult I have looked back and wished I'd hung in there and stayed with it. Had I, I'm certain my life would have been greatly enriched by the ability to play the piano.

Here's the thing. We're not all called to become professional pianists, but we are all called to become professional lovers. If we quit when the going gets tough, yeah, we'll feel relieved. Initially. In the long run, however, we'll be missing out on the beauty of the music that would have come if we had stayed with it.

Stay with it, brother! Keep going! There is glory on the other side of the cross. This is God's promise.

24. What's acceptable regarding marital intimacy during the time of abstinence?

Many of the principles that should guide a couple's expressions of affection when they're abstaining during the fertile time have already been discussed. For example, couples shouldn't be seeking the pleasure of climax apart from an act of intercourse. But this doesn't mean they should take a "hands off" (or "lips off") approach, either.

Practicing NFP is a wonderful way for spouses to learn that intimate signs of affection don't always need to lead to intercourse.[31] Being naked together, kissing, embracing, caressing each other tenderly and intimately—such signs of affection are all good in themselves and shouldn't be withheld because a couple doesn't intend to have sex.

We're called to freedom. If a couple can't express genuine affection for one another without being tempted to masturbate, then something's amiss. On the other hand, couples need to know their own limits (these vary greatly from couple to couple) and discuss them openly and honestly to avoid "pushing the envelope" toward climax.

25. I accept what the Church teaches, but my husband insists that we use contraception. What should I do?

Continue patiently to lead him to the truth and meaning of your marriage by your own example of Christlike love. Above all, pray for him. The ultimate goal of your marriage is to lead each other to heaven.[32]

Know that your suffering in this situation is not in vain. Offer it to Christ in intercession for your husband's change of heart. Expect miracles. I've seen them happen. If God can change *my* heart on this issue, he can change anybody's heart.

In the meantime, don't cooperate in the sin of your husband by directly assisting in the contraceptive behavior. For example, don't take the pill or insert a diaphragm for his sake. If he knows where you stand and still withdraws during intercourse, or even forces the use of a condom, then he alone is responsible for the contraceptive behavior.

You also have the option of refraining from intercourse as long as your husband insists on contracepting. Various consequences of this choice need to be weighed, but forcing a spouse to cooperate in objectively sinful behavior is abusive, and you are in no way obligated to submit to it. Out of concern for yourself, and for him, you may want to let him know that, while you yearn for a sexual relationship in keeping with God's plan, you do not want to be treated as a thing for his sexual "relief," all the while loving your husband and helping him to experience a change of heart.

26. I had my tubes tied. Now I regret it. What should I do?

First things first, if you haven't already received the sacrament of reconciliation, find a priest who understands and upholds the Church's teaching, and go. Trust in the Lord's mercy. He heals. He forgives. In addition, you and your husband should seek a fresh start by asking each other's forgiveness for being unfaithful to the commitments you made at the altar.

There are many women (and men who have had vasectomies) in the same boat with you. Some of them don't find peace until they have their sterilizations reversed. If you have the means and you're not a high-risk patient, this is something you should pursue. If you don't have the means and/or you are a high-risk patient, reversal surgery isn't a moral necessity. Nevertheless, genuine contrition and repentance *are* a moral necessity.

One way of showing that repentance is by abstaining from sex for a set time each month as if you were practicing NFP. Many people in your situation find that approach very beneficial as they seek to grow more and more in a true understanding of the meaning of marital love. You could also devote time to spreading the Church's teaching on these issues as a way of preventing others from making the same mistakes.

Above all, trust in God's merciful love. *Nothing* we've done in our lives is beyond the scope of the redemption Christ won for us.[33]

27. We've been contracepting for years. We've never heard any of this stuff. What should we do?

Again, first things first. If you haven't already received the sacrament of reconciliation, find a priest who understands and upholds the Church's teaching, and go. Trust in the Lord's mercy. He heals. He forgives. Seek each other's forgiveness as well.

Then, by all means (even if you're skeptical) *take an NFP class!* Countless couples who have experienced the damaging effects of contraception on their marriage can speak to the healing effects of learning and practicing NFP.[35]

7

"I Do," But Not As God Intends

Reproductive Technologies

Life teaches us, in effect, that love—married love—is the foundation stone of all life.[1]

—St. John Paul II

"Will we still need to have sex?" This was the first question posed by *Time* magazine in a series of articles it published at the turn of the millennium. "Birds do it. Bees do it. But we may no longer have to do it—except for the fun of it," declared the subtitle of this alarming piece. And without a second thought, under an eerie picture of miniature human beings being spawned in test tubes, a caption proclaimed: "The link between sex and procreation, already tenuous, could be severed."[2]

Welcome to Aldous Huxley's *Brave New World*.

This should horrify us. The link between sex and procreation holds the dignity of human life in place. Sever it, and human life is automatically cheapened. Sever it, and human beings come to be treated no longer as persons to love but as things to use.

On the one hand, this utilitarian approach leads to the destruction of human beings when it's supposed that they get in the way of our happiness—both at the beginning of life (abortion) and at the end (euthanasia). On the other hand, it leads to the technological production of human beings when it's supposed that they can bring about our happiness. In either case, human life is not respected for its own sake but is treated as a thing to be acquired or discarded according to personal preference.

Infertility is a real problem, one that has skyrocketed in recent years in developed countries.[3] In response, an entire, ever expanding, and little regulated "reproductive technologies industry" has emerged. While the desire to overcome infertility is certainly legitimate, there are still important moral considerations to take into account.

As good as the desire for children is in itself, it doesn't justify any and every means of "getting" a child. For example, kidnapping another person's baby is wrong no matter how desperately a couple wants children. So also, as the Church teaches, is manufacturing children through technological procedures. In both cases, we're dealing with a *good end* (the desire for children) but a *bad means.*

The pain and even anguish of infertile couples mustn't be dismissed. But much more is at stake in the laboratory generation of human life than is first apparent. The Church's teaching against certain reproductive technologies raises many pressing questions and objections. Before I address them, I'd suggest giving some serious thought both to the following seven questions and to the implications of your answers.

Are we the masters of human life?

Is a child a gift from God?

Can a gift be demanded?

Do couples have a right to children at any cost?

Do couples have a "right" to children at all?

Are we free to determine what is good and evil?

Are God's commandments meant to bring us happiness or keep us from it?

1. The Church is so pro-family and pro-child. I suppose it makes sense that the Church would be against technologies that impede procreation, but what could possibly be wrong with technologies that are intended to bring life into the world?

It does seem contradictory at first. Upon further investigation, however, it becomes evident that the Church would be contradicting herself if she *didn't* teach the immorality of some techniques of generating life. The Church's teaching on reproductive technologies is simply the flip side of her teaching on birth control.[4] While contraceptive methods of birth control divorce sex from babies, many reproductive technologies divorce babies from sex. Consistency in upholding the meaning of love, life, and marriage—the meaning of being created male and female in the image of God—demands that the link between sex and babies, babies and sex, *never* be divorced, regardless of circumstance or motives.

The Church's basic moral principle concerning reproductive technologies is this: If a given medical intervention *assists* the marital embrace at achieving its natural end, it can be morally acceptable, even praiseworthy. But if it *replaces* the marital embrace as the means by which the child is conceived, it's not in keeping with God's intention for human life.[5] Separating conception from the loving embrace of husband and wife not only provokes many further evils, but—even if these are avoided—it remains contrary to the dignity of the child, the dignity of the spouses and their relationship, and our status as creatures. Let's look at each of these issues.

Provocation of further evils. As Christ said, you can judge a tree by its fruit (see Matthew 7:17–20). Separating conception from the marital embrace doesn't *necessarily* entail the following evils, but more often than not, it leads to them in practice: masturbation as a means of obtaining sperm; production of "excess" human lives that are either destroyed through abortion (euphemistically referred to as "selective reduction"), frozen for later "use," or intentionally farmed for medical experimentation; a "eugenic mentality" that discriminates between human beings, not treating all with equal care and dignity; the trafficking of gametes (both sperm and ova) and frozen embryos for use by others; insemination of unmarried women and, therefore, all the evils associated with "fatherless" children outlined in the previous chapter.

The dignity of the child. While there are many acts through which a child *can* be conceived (the marital embrace, an act of rape, fornication, adultery, incest, various technological procedures), only one is in keeping with the dignity of the child. As chapter one explained in some detail, humanity's great dignity is found in our imaging of God. Love is our origin, vocation, and end. Thus human dignity demands that a child be conceived through that act of love that images God. This is marital love, and its defining expression is the embrace of husband and wife in "one flesh."

From the moment of conception, children deserve the respect we owe all persons. They are equal in dignity with their parents. They are created for their own sake, to be received unconditionally as gifts from God. To desire a child not as the fruit of marital love but as the end result of a technological procedure is to treat the child as a *product* to obtain, rather than a *person* to love. For those involved, this creates—consciously or unconsciously, subtly or not so subtly—a depersonalized orientation toward the child.

Products are subject to quality control. When you spend top dollar for a new TV, you want it in mint condition. You don't care about the TV you pulled out of the box for its own sake. You want one that works. If it's defective, you'll take it back for a refund or exchange it for another one.

Similarly, the temptation is all too real for a couple paying thousands (often tens of thousands) of dollars for these procedures to want a "refund" or an "exchange" if their "product" is defective. The mentality of the approach leads people to want not the particular baby conceived for his or her own sake but rather babies in "mint condition," even babies "made to order": this sex, that eye color, this skin tone, that stature. If fact, if the baby is deformed or doesn't otherwise meet the couple's (or the doctor's) specifications, he or she is often "scrapped," and the procedure is started over.

I don't mean to imply that every couple who pays for these procedures automatically begins to think this way. The temptation to apply "quality controls" *can* be resisted. But a depersonalizing mind-set is built into the very nature of the procedure.

The only way to ensure that the dignity of *every* child is respected is to ensure that spouses understand and live the full meaning of sex and never seek to conceive children apart from their union. No child, with whatever "defects" might occur, could ever be unwanted or unloved if he or she were the fruit of the parents' union that imaged God. Unconditional love begets unconditional love.

The dignity of the spouses and their relationship. The Congregation for the Doctrine of the Faith has observed that if the generation of human life is to respect not only the child but also the parents and the dignity of their relationship, it "must be the fruit and the sign of the mutual self-giving of the spouses, of their love and of their fidelity."[6] In other words, in keeping with what we've discussed throughout this book, the generation of human life must be the fruit of the "I do" of wedding vows expressed through sexual intercourse.

The technological generation of human life is simply *not marital.* The child is not the fruit of his parents' wedding vows "made flesh." The child is the product of a technological procedure performed by a third party apart from their union altogether. As the late moral theologian William E. May noted: "Spouses can no more delegate to others the privilege they have of begetting human life than they can delegate to others the right they have to engage in the marital act."[7] The fact that the gametes being used by the technician may be those of a husband and wife is superfluous to the manner of the child's conception.

So yet again, spouses who employ these procedures violate, consciously or unconsciously, the "I do" of their marriage commitment.[8] While spouses may desire to express their "openness to children" through recourse to these procedures, at best they're saying, "I do, *but not as God intends.*" Acting contrary to God's plan for marriage and procreation is simply incompatible with the marriage commitment, even if it's done with the "best of intentions."

Furthermore, numerous couples can attest to the depersonalizing effects of subjecting themselves to numerous tests and repeated procedures that treat their sex cells as "raw material" to be mined for the production of a child. Being artificially inseminated by a doctor with a long syringe isn't on any woman's top ten list of most dignified experiences, either. Some may claim that it was all worth it when their "miracle child" is born. But the underlying realization that their child is a "miracle of science" rather than a miracle of their own marital union cannot help but serve to unravel the basic psychology of family·relationships on which spouses and children alike depend for equilibrium.

The marital embrace is not simply the biological transmission of gametes. If such were the case, it would be much more expedient for couples wanting to conceive to employ *in vitro* techniques rather than leave it up to biological "chance." The marital embrace is a profoundly personal, sacramental, physical, and spiritual reality. To divorce human conception from this sublime union shows a lack of understanding and respect for the "language of the body" and the deepest essence of married love. It depersonalizes all involved.

Our status as creatures. God alone is, as we affirm in the Nicene Creed, the "Lord and Giver of life." Spouses have the distinct privilege of cooperating with God in procreating children, but as creatures themselves, they aren't the masters of life. They're only the servants of God's design.

Technological fertilization, on the contrary, as the Congregation for the Doctrine of the Faith has noted, "entrusts the life and identity of the embryo into the power of doctors and biologists and establishes the domination of technology over the origin and destiny of the human person."[9] Spouses and technicians thereby set themselves up as *operators* instead of *co*operators, *creators* instead of *pro*creators. They deny their status as creatures and make themselves "like God" (see Genesis 3:5).

God created sexual union, as we've been saying throughout, to be a sacramental symbol of his own life and love and of our union with Christ. Seeking human life apart from sexual union is also symbolic. It symbolizes rejection of our union with God: the desire to have life *without* God or, at least, apart from his design for us. As the *Catechism* says, when we prefer our own designs to God's, we thereby scorn him. When we choose ourselves against the requirements of our creaturely status, we act against our own good.[10]

2. Are you saying children conceived from these technologies aren't created by God, or aren't made in his image?

There's not a single person on the planet who would exist if God didn't will for him or her to exist. As soon as sperm meets egg, even if it's in a petri dish, God is there to create an immortal soul. But even though God wills for technologically conceived children to exist, and allows them to come to be in this way, it doesn't mean that God wills for us to use these technologies.

Similarly, God wills the existence of children conceived through acts of rape and incest (if he didn't, they wouldn't exist), but this doesn't mean he wills for us to engage in rape and incest. While all such children themselves bear the image of God and are to be loved and treated like any other human being, none were conceived by an act that images God. This is and always will remain an injustice to them.

Here we find ourselves confronted by the mystery of God's interaction with our freedom. God doesn't intervene in our decisions to act unwisely. To do so would be to deny us our freedom. (What a tremendous gift and what a tremendous responsibility our freedom is!)

It's God's nature, however, to bring good out of our wrong choices, even the greatest good possible—a new human person. Does this mean we should act badly in order for good to result? If we do, according to St. Paul, our condemnation is deserved (see Romans 3:8).

3. We play God every time we have surgery or take medicine. What's the difference with these reproductive technologies?

Fitness, health, and life are written into our very being as part of God's original plan for us. Sickness, disease, and death are all a result of the corruption caused by original sin. God allows them, but he does not *will* them *per se*. So assuming that all the means employed are licit in themselves, we act in complete accord with God's plan when we use medicine and technology to save a life or restore health.

In these cases, we're not acting as the masters of human life but as the stewards that God made us to be. Similarly, when we assist the marital embrace in achieving its natural end, we act as stewards in restoring God's design. But as soon as we *replace* God's design and seek to "force" a conception, we cross the line from steward to master, from being creature to playing God.

4. Didn't you say that infertility is a disease (see chapter six, question 8)? According to your own words, doesn't this imply that it would be a good use of medicine and technology to overcome it?

Yes, infertility is a disease, or perhaps more aptly, a disability. Seeking ways to cure it is a praiseworthy service to the many married couples who suffer greatly because of it. But there are limits to what can be done.

The same statement from *Humanae Vitae* quoted in chapter six is applicable here as well: "The Church is the first to praise and recommend the intervention of intelligence in a function which so closely associates the rational creature with his Creator; but she affirms that *this must be done with respect for the order established by God*."[11] If we use our intelligence to *assist* the marital embrace at achieving its natural end, then we act as stewards of God's design, respecting the order he established. But as soon as we *replace* the marital embrace as the means of conception, we act outside the scope of God's order.

In fact, only by *assisting* the marital embrace can we speak of a true *cure* for infertility. Replacing intercourse in no way cures the couple's malady. It only bypasses it.

God's order isn't arbitrary. It's meant for our good, for our benefit. It's a mystery that God allows some fornicators and adulterers who don't even want children to conceive, while at the same time he allows loving husbands and wives to suffer with infertility. Who can fathom that? But both situations offer an opportunity for those involved to turn to God and abandon themselves to him.

God's ways are not our ways. As high as the heavens are above the earth, so high are God's ways above ours (see Isaiah 55:9). Trust him. This is what Christ teaches us. He himself felt abandoned by God on the cross (see Mark 15:34). But even in this darkest hour, he trusted. And as his resurrection attests, his trust was not in vain.

> Lord, help me to trust you with my life and all the circumstances of it, even—and especially—when I don't understand. Give me the grace to believe in your promise to bring good out of every suffering and disappointment that you allow in my life. Amen.

5. I understand that children are supposed to be the fruit of their parents' love. But children conceived from these technologies can be the fruit of their parents' love on a spiritual level.

It's true that love is spiritual, for God, who is pure Spirit, *is* love (see 1 John 4:8). But human beings are not pure spirits. We are *body-persons* (see chapter three, questions 3 and 11; chapter five, question 6, for a more complete discussion of this issue). It's in and through our *bodies* that we image God and share his love with others. This is nowhere better exemplified than in the expression of love unique to marriage: the union of husband and wife in one *flesh*.

Spouses who seek such technological procedures may do so because they want to have a child to love. And they may certainly love the child once he or she has been produced. Nevertheless, as much as we may like to think it's possible, no amount of mental gymnastics or wishing can transport the couple's "spiritual love" outside of their bodies and onto the procedure of the doctor or scientist. The fact remains that such a child's origin is not the incarnational love of the parents, but rather the end result of depersonalized technological procedures.

6. Why is adoption acceptable? Adopted children aren't the fruit of the couple's sexual union.

Adoption isn't only acceptable. It's laudable. While it's true that an adopted child isn't the fruit of the couple's union, providing a loving home for a child who *already exists* is completely different from manipulating a child into existence.

One is an act of love. The other isn't. Couples who are unable to conceive should prayerfully consider whether God is calling them to open their homes to children in need of adoption.

7. My brother's wife is unable to have children. They've asked me if I'd be willing to be a surrogate mother. I love my brother and want to help. What's wrong with that?

Love *always* chooses the good and helps others to do the same. Genuine love for your brother is incompatible with a willingness to carry his child. Not only is this a grave distortion of the natural order of family relationships, but it would also necessitate *in vitro* fertilization. This is wrong for all the reasons already mentioned.

The best way for you to help your brother would be to encourage him to embrace the truth of God's plan for sex and procreation in his marriage. If that means he'll never have a child that's biologically his own, God will give him the grace to accept that. He need only open his heart to it.

8. Didn't God call us to have dominion over nature?

God called us to subdue the earth and have dominion over the animals (see Genesis 1:28). As long as we're responsible stewards, we're free to manipulate creation for our benefit. There's nothing wrong, for example, with artificially inseminating cattle. They're not called to love in God's image. But this rightful dominion does *not* extend over human beings.

Nor can the body be considered part of the realm of "subhuman" nature over which we do have dominion. As John Paul II warned in his *Letter to*

Families, "When the human body, considered apart from spirit and thought, comes to be used as raw material in the same way that the bodies of animals are used...we will inevitably arrive at a dreadful ethical defeat."[12]

9. Lots of unmarried women have a sincere desire for children. These technologies can fulfill their dreams. What's wrong with that?

These technologies are wrong in and of themselves for all the reasons already mentioned. But there are even further considerations in the case of using them to impregnate unmarried women.

Many women make the heroic effort of raising children when the father is absent due to no fault of their own. They're to be commended for their dedication and sacrifices. But there's an enormous difference between a single mother who *regrets* the absence of her children's father and a single mother who *chooses* to deny her child this irreplaceable relationship. To desire a child in this way can only be self-serving.

Perhaps it's easy to think, "So-and-so's children turned out fine without a father. It's not so terrible." But no child who has grown up without a father is without wounds. It's through the secure and recognized relationship of children to their mother *and father* that they are most naturally and readily enabled to discover their own identity and achieve their own proper human development.[13] What does it do to a child's sense of self when all he or she can possibly know about his or her father is that he masturbated at a sperm bank for money?

10. I can see why single people may not have a right to children. But it's terribly cruel for the Church to deny a loving married couple the right to have a child when they so desperately want one.

A married couple's desire for children couldn't be more natural. The Church is the first to recognize and share in the painful trial of couples who find they are unable to conceive. It's natural to want to alleviate a couple's sufferings by granting them their legitimate aspirations whenever possible. But as we noted previously, we find ourselves on very dangerous ground when we let mere sympathy guide our moral decisions, especially when such decisions concern the very life and destiny of another human being.

The entire body of the Church's teaching is aimed at upholding and defending people's legitimate rights. Spouses, however, cannot claim a legitimate *right* to children.[14]

Children are a gift given by God. No couple is entitled to them, nor can they be demanded. The commitment spouses make at the altar to "receive children lovingly from God" reflects this reality.

Spouses have the right only to engage in the marital embrace and pray for God's will to be done.[15] They are certainly free to make the conditions for conception as optimal as possible, but whether or not a child results from their self-giving must be left in God's hands. The Church's teaching on the intrinsic immorality of technological fertilization actually upholds the only legitimate human right in question: the right of the child "to be the fruit of the specific act of the conjugal love of his parents."[16]

11. So what's a couple supposed to do if they can't have kids but really want them—just suffer?

They can do a number of things. First and foremost, they should take a natural family planning class. NFP is true family planning. Pinpointing the fertile time of the cycle can obviously help a couple achieve a pregnancy as well as help them avoid one.

Believe it or not, most doctors are not even trained to recognize the signs of fertility and what they mean. Many a couple who have had difficulty conceiving have realized after learning NFP that it was simply a problem of timing.[17]

Generally speaking, even if couples are certain they're having intercourse during the fertile time, there's only about a one-in-three chance of achieving pregnancy. Couples aren't considered in need of medical assistance for infertility unless they're certain they've had intercourse during the fertile time for six months without conceiving. For those who are engaging in random intercourse without knowledge of the fertile time, it's twelve months.

At this stage of the process, those intent on conceiving should seek medical advice. For anyone in this situation, I highly recommend doing an Internet search for doctors trained in NaPro Technology, short for natural procreative technology. Such doctors specialize in helping couples in ways that are truly therapeutic—that is, in ways that seek to cure the given malady rather than bypass it, thus allowing couples to conceive naturally through their conjugal union. Their approach is much more successful (and usually much less expensive) than methods that replace sexual intercourse.

Still, there is a certain percentage of couples who, after exhausting all legitimate solutions, find they are still unable to conceive. The Congregation for the Doctrine of the Faith has this to say about their plight: "Couples who find themselves in this sad situation are called to find in it an opportunity for sharing in a particular way in the Lord's cross, the source of spiritual fruitfulness. Sterile couples must not forget [as John Paul II has observed] that 'even when procreation is not possible, conjugal life does not for this reason lose its value. Physical sterility in fact can be for spouses the occasion for other important service to the life of the human person, for example, adoption, various forms of educational work, and assistance to other families and to poor or handicapped children.'"[18]

The sufferings of infertile couples need *not* be in vain. Borrowing words from Archbishop Charles Chaput: "Suffering can bend and break us. But it can also *break us open* to become the persons God intended us to be. It depends on what we do with the pain. If we offer it back to God, he will use it to do great things in us and through us, because suffering is fertile."[19]

Yes, suffering is spiritually *fertile*. These are not empty words of consolation. Through Christ's example, we know these words are "spirit and life" (see John 6:63).

12. My doctor wants to do a sperm count to see if I'm the cause of our infertility. Is it okay for me to masturbate to supply the semen?

No, it's not. Remember that the end does not justify the means. The intention to masturbate is wrong regardless of the further intention for which it's done. It is possible, however, to obtain sperm morally through an act of intercourse in which you use what's known as a "perforated condom." Some sperm are released into your wife's vagina (so as not to be contraceptive), and some sperm are retained for analysis.

13. Sometimes there can be a fine line between assisting and replacing the marital act. How can you tell the difference?

Most of the time it's quite obvious. Either the child is conceived from intercourse, or he or she is not. But you're right: Some procedures may involve an act of intercourse, yet it's difficult to know whether the child actually results from that act.

One such procedure is known as GIFT (Gamete Intra-Fallopian Transfer). Husband and wife engage in intercourse using a perforated condom (as described above). Technicians then place sperm retained in the condom in a small tube separated from the wife's surgically removed ovum by an air bubble. The contents of the tube are then injected into the wife's body with the hope that fertilization will occur.

If a child is conceived, the question remains: Is he or she the fruit of the marital embrace or the end result of a technological procedure? The Church hasn't to date made any definitive pronouncement, and theologians disagree.

It seems to me, however, that assistance or replacement of the marital act can be determined by asking the following question: Is the marital act an essential precursor to the meeting of sperm and egg, or could fertilization have happened just as well without it? It seems that in the GIFT technique, marital intercourse is not essential, since sperm could have just as easily been obtained through masturbation. Furthermore, the sperm that eventually fertilizes the egg was not even ejaculated into the wife's body but was intentionally withheld for the procedure.

That being said, I think it's safer to avoid GIFT and other techniques for fertilization in which intercourse is treated only as a "moral way" to obtain sperm.

14. We have a beautiful daughter conceived by artificial insemination. We prayed and prayed that God would bless us with a child, and we believe he did. We couldn't imagine life without her. I refuse to believe that what we did was wrong.

Admitting that what you did was wrong does not mean you must conclude that your daughter herself is "wrong." Nor does it mean that your daughter's existence is not a gift from God. As we stated earlier, your daughter would not and could not exist if God did not will for her to exist. She *is* a blessing from God.

God is always looking for "excuses" to bless us and show us his love, even (believe it or not) when we act outside his plan. Still, although a great blessing has come from it, the manner of her conception remains an injustice to her. Honesty, and the good of all concerned, calls for that recognition.

I might compare your situation to that of some friends I know. They have a ten-year-old son. They love him very, very much and, like you, couldn't imagine life without him. They know he's a blessing from God in their lives. But they've been married less than ten years themselves. He was conceived out of wedlock.

What they did—having sex outside of marriage—was wrong. To pretend otherwise would be an additional injustice to all involved, especially their son. They know someday he'll do the math, and they'll all talk about it. He'll probably have some issues to work through, but the situation isn't beyond the scope of God's redeeming love. Nothing is, except the pride that refuses to admit when we've been wrong.

15. We knew the Church taught it was wrong but never understood why until now. We wanted a baby so badly, and through *in vitro* we now have twins. Is God angry with us? What should we do?

First of all, continue to love your twins and be grateful to God for them. They are a sign that God loves you and trusted you with these precious lives, even when you turned from his will to your own. What a loving, merciful God we have. We shouldn't presume on his mercy, but when we express true sorrow for our wrongdoing, we should certainly trust in his mercy.

Find a priest who understands these issues, and go to confession. When the priest absolves you of your sins, know that Christ himself is forgiving you.

Is God angry with you? Not in the way we typically understand anger. He's "angry" in the sense that any father would be pained by seeing his children make poor decisions. But he's not vindictive. God's anger and his love, his justice and his mercy, are one and the same reality. Like the father in the story of the prodigal son, he runs to embrace us and welcome us home even when we're still far off in our journey back to him (see Luke 15:11–32). Yes, God is running to you. Run to him.

8

When Saying "I Do" Is Impossible

Same-Sex Marriage and Related Questions

If we don't live the sexual differences correctly that distinguish man and woman and call them to unite, we will not be capable of understanding the difference that distinguishes man and God, and constitutes a primordial call to union. Thus, we may fall into the despair of a life separated from others and from the Other, that is, God.[1]

—Stanislaw Grygiel

The normalization of homosexual relationships and activity to the point of legalizing same-sex marriage is yet another by-product of a culture that has ruptured the natural connection between sex and babies. Indeed, as soon as you sever orgasm from procreation, any (and every) means to genital pleasure becomes fair game. Deliberately sterilizing sexual intercourse effectively nullifies the natural and essential meaning of the sexual difference. When we recognize this, we come to see the hard truth that Christians themselves unwittingly began to homo-sexualize marriage when they began to embrace contraception.

Seventy-two years after the 1930 Anglican decision to allow contraception in marriage, Archbishop of Canterbury Rowan Williams observed that "the absolute condemnation of same-sex relations" has nothing substantial to rely upon in "a church that accepts the legitimacy of contraception."[2] He was correct. But rather than question the legitimacy of contraception, he took that as a given and justified same-sex relations. It's one or the other.

The Catholic Church is admirably and unwaveringly consistent in her teaching. For those who have followed the course we've charted throughout this book, the logic behind her teaching on the intrinsic immorality of homosexual acts is probably already clear. To leave it at that, however, simply doesn't do justice to the issue. The Church's teaching raises pressing questions and objections for those who experience same-sex attractions and for their loved ones.

Real men and women are involved here. Real hearts and lives are affected. Although those who experience same-sex attractions are a relatively small minority in the overall population, when you include their families and friends, those who are not intimately affected by this concern become the minority. As Catholic writer David Morrison, author of the book *Beyond Gay*, put it, that means millions of people "for whom every charge and countercharge, every misunderstanding, every miscommunication, mischaracterization, and slur can strike at the heart of who they consider themselves to be or the kind of life one of their loved ones is trying to build. No wonder questions of same-sex attraction, gay or lesbian rights, and same-sex marriage or adoption have the explosive emotional force they do."[3]

More than one person I love carries this particular cross. I myself went through a painful period in my teenage years of questioning my masculine identity and attractions.

One of my high school religion teachers did a room full of insecure pubescent boys a terrible injustice when she told us we couldn't possibly know whether we were gay until we were at least twenty-five. We all looked around the room and tried to boost our macho facades with a deep-throated, "Yeah, right, not me." But underneath, I was struck with mortal fear that I might wake up one day and discover I was "gay." This fear, coupled with a memory I had desperately tried to repress of "experimenting" with a friend from school when I was about ten, would eventually play a key role in leading me to my knees seeking from God what it means to be a man (see the Introduction to this book).

One of the most healing realities for me was recognizing that there is a God-given *meaning* to my sex. I had been cut off from that meaning, but I discovered that God had a plan to reconnect me with it. When we understand this, no one need be afraid to look deeply and honestly into his or her soul and admit the distortions and confusions found there, *whatever* they might be. We *all* have them. But no confusion, no distortion of our identity as men and women, goes deeper than the cross of Christ. The only tragedy is refusing to label them as distortions and seeking to "normalize" them for fear of the cross.

Lord, you created me to be a man (woman) for a reason. Show me the meaning of my sexual identity, and give me the grace not to fear admitting how far I may be from it. You know me better than I know myself. You know my struggles, my deepest fears, my wounds, my sins. Lead me, one step at a time, closer to your plan for creating me to be a man (woman) in your own

image. I surrender all that I am to you and trust you to bring to completion
the work you've begun in me. Amen.

1. Why does the Church hate gay people? I was born this way. That means *God* made me gay. And God doesn't make mistakes!

The Church does not hate anyone. In fidelity to Christ she loves everyone without exception. Also in fidelity to Christ, the Church knows that to love is to desire a person's true good, and that means inviting everyone to embrace the full truth of his or her humanity as God created it to be "in the beginning."

Of course, this is an invitation that can stir resentment because it challenges us to the core—and we tend not to like such challenges. In that resentment, it's easier to level accusations against the Church than to look honestly at the Church's proposal.

We've been unfolding that proposal throughout this book, but here it is in a nutshell: There was an original, beautiful plan God had for making us male and female; the holy communion of the two in "one flesh" was a sign in the world of his own life-giving Communion, and it was meant to lead us into an eternal participation in that Communion; but an enemy who wanted to keep us from that heavenly joy got in the mix and convinced us that God's design was not to be trusted, so each went his own way.

No, God does not make mistakes; but we do. And the biggest mistake humanity ever made was failing to trust God's plan for our lives. As a result, we now live in a fallen world. And it's not just that there's something wrong "out there" somewhere. If we're honest, we'll recognize that there's something wrong, something seriously "off," in each and every one of us, and this brokenness has registered in our sexuality in a particularly painful way.

The beginning, before sin, is the norm for a proper understanding of how God made us. Hence, Christ's proclamation—"from the beginning it was not so" (Matthew 19:8)—is decisive not just for divorce, but for every other way the human heart has veered from God's original design. The inclination toward an erotic relationship with one's own sex is just one in a very long list of inclinations that, as St. John tells us, come not from the Father, but from the fallen world into which we're all born (see 1 John 2:15–17).

Here's the good news: "Jesus came to restore creation to the purity of its origins."[4] This means it's okay that we're fallen, because God has a remedy. But it's not okay to call our fallenness health. It's not okay to call our fallenness "the way God made us." So long as we do, we close ourselves off to the beautiful plan God has to remake us in Christ. As St. John Paul II observes, if we are to live as the men and women God made us to be, we *"must rediscover the lost fullness of [our] humanity and want to regain it."*[5]

2. My priest said the Church teaches it's okay to be gay, just not to act on it. Is that true? Seems like a contradiction to me.

It seems this priest is referring to the wise distinction the Church makes between the homosexual *tendency* and homosexual *acts*. The tendency is typically something people discover within themselves, not something they choose to have. Hence, having the tendency is not a sin in itself. But acting on the tendency would, indeed, "miss the mark" of God's plan for human life, and that's what the word "sin" means.

There's no contradiction here. Because of original sin, we all have tendencies in us that are not good to follow.

Still, this priest's statement needs to be clarified. When someone labels himself as "gay" (or herself as "lesbian"), it can often imply, "This is the way I *am*. I will always be this way, and I plan to pursue romantic same-sex relationships." However, if we understand that our true humanity lies "in the beginning" (see the answer to the previous question), then we have to recognize that no one is *ontologically* (in his or her deepest being) oriented toward the same sex. Because of the fallen world in which we live, same-sex attractions are an aspect of some people's lives, but these attractions can never define *who* a person *is* in the essence of his or her identity.

It's true that a person's identity can't be separated from his or her sexuality. But *sexual identity* refers to the fact that "from the beginning God made them male and female" (Matthew 19:4). The meaning of our sexual identity is inseparable from our complementary call to life-giving communion in the image of God. Original sin has obscured this call in each of us to some degree or other. But it hasn't changed the fact that this is who God created us to be.

As we've discussed throughout this book, the body is the revelation of the person, and, as is plainly obvious, a man's body is oriented toward a woman's body and woman's body is oriented toward a man's. In other words, a man and a woman's genitals are biologically designed for each other. This alone makes our gendered humanity intelligible. If someone experiences a strong sexual or romantic attraction toward the same sex, this is more properly described as a *disorientation*, since it departs from the natural, God-given complementarity of the sexes. Again, since people generally discover they are attracted to the same sex rather than choosing to be so, there's no moral fault connected with this. Even so, it's very important to realize that sexual or romantic attractions toward one's own sex is itself, as the Church describes it, an "objective disorder," in that it departs from the original order established by God.[6]

Returning to the original question, we can see that the statement "it's okay to be gay" needs some qualification. If your priest meant this in the sense that I mentioned in the previous answer—it's okay that we're fallen, because God has a remedy—then that is certainly true. But we shouldn't give the impression that erotic or romantic same-sex attractions are something morally neutral or good. If they were "okay" in this sense, it *would* be contradictory to claim that acting on such desires is always immoral. But such attractions cannot be neutral, much less good, because they're aimed at something intrinsically opposed to God's plan for human life and human love.[7]

But let's remember that fallen human beings are attracted to many things that are immoral; homosexual romance and activity is only one such thing on a very long list. As noted earlier, disordered desire is called *concupiscence*. It comes from sin and entices to sin but isn't sinful in itself. It's merely a given of the fallen human condition.

But precisely because concupiscence comes from sin and entices us to it, it's something we're called to resist—whether it manifests itself in a disordered attraction to one's own sex or the opposite sex, or in a disordered desire for food or drink.

Like everyone else, those who experience homosexual attractions are called to live chastely; that is, they're called to experience the redemption of their sexuality through an ever-deepening appropriation of Christ's work in their lives (see chapter four, question 12). To be sure, same-sex attractions can be a difficult cross to bear. But God's liberating grace is ever-present to help us live according to his original plan of love. Indeed, through the grace of baptism, we've become "a new creation: the old things have passed away; behold, new things have come" (2 Corinthians 5:17). This is why the Church's teaching about sex, including her teaching on homosexuality, is good news.

3. That is *so* offensive to call a gay person disordered!

What's disordered is not the person, *per se*. The person—every person, without exception—is a wonderfully made child of God. What's disordered, in this case, is his or her experience of sexual desire. But guess what: *Every* human being has disordered sexual desires (not to mention all kinds of other disordered desires).

No one is off the hook here. We all fail to live according to God's original order in making us male and female. It's part of the universal inheritance of original sin.

This is why it is a terrible injustice to define ourselves based on how we experience sexual desires. To do so is to fail to go deep enough into the real roots of our humanity. To do so is to fail to recognize that "the beginning"—before original sin distorted our desires—is where we find the full truth of what it means to be human. This is why the Catholic Church insists that the

> human person, made in the image and likeness of God, can hardly be adequately described by a reductionist reference to his or her sexual orientation. Every one living on the face of the earth has personal problems and difficulties, but…strengths, talents and gifts as well. Today, the Church provides a badly needed context for the care of the human person when she refuses to consider the person as a "heterosexual" or a "homosexual" and insists that every person has a fundamental Identity: the creature of God, and by grace, his child and heir to eternal life. [8]

As St. John Paul II proclaimed so powerfully: "We are not the sum of our weaknesses and failures; we are the sum of the Father's love for us and our real capacity to become the image of his Son." [9]

4. What could possibly be wrong with two people of the same sex loving each other? If love is of God, it can't be wrong.

You're right. It's never wrong to love. But what *is* love? The truth of love comes from God because *"God is love"* (1 John 4:16). If we are truly to love others, whatever their sex, our love must conform to the image of God in us. Otherwise, it's simply not love.

Unfortunately, the English language doesn't distinguish between different kinds of love. A man's relationship with his wife, his mother, his best friend, even with his favorite dessert, are all described by the word *love*. All of these loves can participate in God's mystery of love, but each does so in different ways.

Sexual or erotic love is a very particular way of imaging God. The purpose of this book has been to demonstrate that erotic love images God only when a man and woman are expressing the "I do" of wedding vows: the free commitment to indissolubility, fidelity, and openness to children in and through the gift of themselves to each other whereby they become "one flesh."

It's simply *impossible* for two people of the same sex to make this commitment to each other. Another way of saying this is that, despite common parlance, it's simply impossible for two people of the same sex to have sex (in the true sense of the term). Whatever same-sex genital acts may consist of, they are not and cannot be acts of true sexual union. Sexual union is brought about by the inseminating union of sexual organs, of the genitals. A man's genitals cannot unite with another man's genitals, nor a woman's with another woman's. It's simply impossible. Hence, as the Church observes,

> To choose someone of the same sex for one's sexual activity is to annul the rich symbolism and meaning, not to mention the goals, of the Creator's sexual design. Homosexual activity is not a complementary union, able to transmit life; and so it thwarts the call to a life of that form of self-giving which the Gospel says is the essence of Christian living. This does not mean that homosexual persons are not often generous and giving of themselves; but when they engage in homosexual activity they confirm within themselves a disordered sexual inclination which is essentially self-indulgent. [10]

Yet again we're confronted by the "problem" of our bodies. Any attempt to divorce our souls from the fundamental orientation of our bodies (yes, our genitals) is to embrace a ruptured view of the human person who was created by God as a profound unity of body and soul.

Those who seek to justify homosexual acts are *ipso facto* guilty of Gnosticism, that ancient heresy that splits body and soul (see chapter three, question 11). The dissenting Catholic group called Dignity, for example, shows the root of its error when it seeks to undermine the procreative meaning of sexual expression with insinuating questions such as this: "Is the biological or the personal the key aspect of sex among human beings?"[11] The biological *is* personal. It's *the body* that shows us who we are and defines our call to sexual love. There's no way around it. Divorce love from the truth of the body and, at best, you're left with a shadow of love; at worst, its antithesis.

There is absolutely nothing wrong with two persons of the same sex loving each other. But romantic/sexual love (and all the emotions and activities associated with it, from the first spark to the full flame of consummation in the marital embrace) is a love the Creator designed to be experienced and expressed in and through the sexual difference. To impose or project this kind of love onto a same-sex relationship is to miss the mark of what romantic/sexual love *is* in the divine plan. As such, it is inherently contrary to the virtue of chastity.

True love is chaste love. It always chooses the good of the person loved. It never does wrong or entices another to do so. People who are truly loving one another will resist all temptations to engage in unchaste behavior with each other specifically *because* of their love.

5. Everything you're saying is a denial of true equality. Love is love and neither Church nor State should ever deny people the right to marry whomever they want.

"Love is love" is a slogan that's cleverly designed to appeal to our sense of equality and justice while obfuscating what's really at stake. It intentionally dodges the fact that there is a fundamental *difference* between the (sexual/romantic) love of a man and a woman and the love of two men or two women—a difference that is no small matter since it pertains directly to the very origin and survival of the human race.

The best definition of philosophy I've ever heard (philosophy literally means "the love of wisdom") is the art of making meaningful distinctions. The slogan "love is love" is evidence that we have lost this art in the modern world. We've become blind to the critical distinction between what is properly called *marital* love and other human loves. As we've already said, there are many genuine ways in which men are called to love other men and women are called to love other women. But not all love is worthy of the name *marriage* (nor is all "love" worthy of the name *love*; see chapter four, questions 1–3).

Since we're so familiar with "brand identities" in our culture, perhaps we could look at it this way. Nike has every right to safeguard its brand to maintain its distinctive line of shoes in the marketplace, and it would be seriously wrong for the courts to allow a *different* shoe company to call itself Nike. It's the same with marriage. Marital love is a specific kind of love—a specific "brand" of love—manifested in husband and wife becoming "one flesh" for the sake of their own good and for the procreation and education of children. People of the same sex can express genuine love for each other in a great many ways, but not in *this* way, not in a *marital* way. It's physically, biologically, and ontologically impossible.

As noted in the answer to the previous question, there's no getting around our bodies. More specifically, there's no getting around our genitals and all that they reveal about human identity, human dignity, and the divine design for sexual love. Underneath other concerns, this is the fundamental issue at stake in debates about the nature and meaning of marriage: What is the nature and meaning of the sexual difference? More specifically, what is the nature and meaning of our genitals?

It used to be obvious to everyone: Genitals are meant to generate. As we learned in grade school, "First comes love, then comes marriage, then comes the baby in the baby carriage." These were the undisputed "facts of life." Today, thanks to the reality-warping impact of effective contraceptive technology, the facts of life are entirely up for grabs. It takes some time due to what sociologist William Ogburn called "cultural lag,"[12] but introduce effective contraception on a wide scale and eventually the fundamental link among gender, genitals, and generating will all but vanish from the way we understand our personal relationships and our personal identities.

In an attempt to snap out of our collective fog, imagine, if you will, that an alien being from a sexless galaxy landed on earth to study the human race. This alien would readily observe that each member of the human species is amazingly self-sufficient in his or her functions as an organism. The heart, the lungs, the kidney, the pancreas, the stomach, the bladder, the rectum, etc. all carry out their own functions. And both sexes have all the same organs... *except*... except what we fittingly call *the sexual organs.*

There is one function, this alien has discovered—and a critical function indeed—that simply cannot be carried out without cooperation from another member of the species. And that other member of the species *must* be of the opposite sex (i.e., must have *different* sexual organs) or said function doesn't function. This is the light that illuminates for the alien the most basic purpose of the genitalia. Men and women are quite literally organ-ized for each other. The sexual organs of male and female *work together* in a stunning, harmonious interdependency to *generate* (hence the term "genitalia") new members of the species.

Furthermore, since the baby born to them cannot survive on its own, the alien rightly realizes that the man and the woman who cooperated to bring this life into existence, if they are to be responsible, must commit themselves to rearing their child. Precisely *this* commitment (the commitment to responsible genital intercourse as the foundation of future generations) is called *marriage.*

Although many modern States have abandoned it, the State has the right to safeguard and reward responsible genital intercourse as the foundation of future generations (marriage) precisely because it has a vested interest in its own survival. The State has no such interest in the genital activity of two men or two women. And the Church has a vested interest in protecting this relationship because, among other things, it's the foundation of the entire sacramental order—the order in which God makes his invisible mystery visible to us and prepares us for eternal union with himself. The genital activity of two men or two women is actually a countersign of this divine mystery, a contradiction of our call to love in the image of God.

The argument in support of same-sex marriage reveals its spuriousness right here: It is based on the idea that the sexual difference is essentially meaningless. As we've been learning throughout this book: Not only is the sexual difference not meaningless; it is *pregnant with ultimate meaning*.

Behind phrases like "marriage equality" and "love is love" lies the assertion (often masked, but nonetheless present) that whether it's a man and a woman or two people of the same sex, their genital acts are "the same." No ideology and no ruling of the courts can change the fact that the genital acts of a husband and wife are stupendously, wondrously *different* than the genital acts of two men or two women. And they are *not* "the same" precisely because of the sexual *difference*.

So, may I point out that what you are calling "true equality" is actually *false equality* because you are *falsely equating* the genital activity of a husband and wife with the genital activity of two men or two women.

But this I will readily grant you: While it's impossible to *raise* what same-sex couples do with their genitals to the level of what husbands and wives can do with theirs, it *is* possible to *reduce* what husbands and wives do with their genitals to the level of what same-sex couples do with theirs: engage in the pursuit of sterile pleasure. That's what contraception has done to marriage: It has *reduced* it to the same thing pursued in same-sex relationships.

When we look for real answers as to how the modern world came to embrace the unprecedented social experiment of same-sex marriage, it becomes increasingly clear that contraceptive practice and mentality is the foundation on which the entire premise of justifying homosexual activity and, thereafter, demanding "marriage equality" stands.

The alternative—a frightening one for many to concede—is to consider that maybe, just maybe the Catholic Church has been correct in her insistence that contraception is a contradiction of authentic marital love. Something worth pondering.

5. You can't reduce marriage to genital activity! Marriage is so much more than that! Denying marriage to people of the same sex is nothing but blatant discrimination.

It's true that marriage can't be reduced to genital activity. But, as we learned earlier, it's also true that without the possibility of engaging in genital intercourse, there's no possibility of the relationship properly called marriage. The possibility of genital intercourse, as we discussed earlier (see chapter three, questions 10–12), is the *defining* element of marriage.

Establishing proper definitions for things is critical in order to makes sense of the world. Definitions make things just that: definite. An orange is not an apple and vice versa. Both are fruits, but they're not the same kind of fruits. To confuse the two is, well, confusing. Words mean something, and must mean something. When words can mean anything, they mean nothing.

Discrimination itself is a word that has become confused in its meaning. It has become a buzzword *in*discriminately linked with injustice. It seems we have forgotten that there is such a thing as *just* discrimination. We discriminate—that is, we differentiate and discern by recognizing mean-ingful distinctions—all the time, and *must* do so. It's called love of wisdom (*philo-sophia*).

Discrimination is unjust when the distinction recognized has no bearing on the matter at hand. Discrimination is just—and required—when the dis-tinction matters.

For example, it is unjust discrimination for the State to deny blind people the right to vote. It is just discrimination for the State to deny blind people driver's licenses. It is unjust discrimination for the State to prevent a twelve-year-old from buying a bottle of water at the local convenience store. It is just discrimination for the State to prevent a twelve-year-old from buying a bottle of whiskey at the local liquor store.

So, is denying marriage to those of the same sex just or unjust discrimi-nation? The question at hand is this: Does the sexual difference have any real bearing on marriage? If it does not, any institution denying marriage to those of the same sex would be drawing meaningless distinctions. But if the sexual difference is intrinsic to what marriage *is*, then the real problem is not think-ing discriminately about marriage, but thinking *in*discriminately about it.

7. What's the difference between the sexual acts of a husband and wife known to be sterile and same-sex acts? Neither one is "open to children."

As we discussed earlier, remaining open to children means never inten-tionally rendering a sexual act sterile or seeking climax in a way not designed for the generation of life. Even if a married couple is known to be infertile through no fault of their own, they can still engage in a genital union (an intercourse of their genitals). Their union is still the kind of union that God has intended for the procreation of children, even if children do not result.

On the other hand, it's physically impossible for two members of the same sex to engage in a genital union (an intercourse of their genitals). It's physically impossible for two members of the same sex to engage in the kind of act that God designed for the generation of life.

So, in the case of a husband and wife known to be infertile, they are experiencing a *defect* in the natural order of things. But in the case of homosexual activity, people are choosing to engage in acts that are *contrary* to the natural order of things.

8. What kind of cruel God do we have that would give people these feelings and then tell them they can't act on them?

Recall from my answer to the first question in this chapter that God doesn't give people homosexual attractions and desires. Nor does he give people lust in their hearts for the opposite sex. *Both* are the result of the fallen world in which we live. In this sense, we're *all* in need of "reorienting" our sexual desires toward the truth of God's original plan. And the healing is the same for everyone: to find our true identity as men and women in Christ.

I don't mean to suggest that if we just had enough faith all our problems, confusions, and wounds would disappear in a flash. It's a lifelong journey to become the men and women we're created to be (in fact, for most of us, that journey extends to the next life, too—thanks be to God for purgatory!). We need healthy community to do it, and we should make use of all that's good in counseling, spiritual direction, spiritual reading, and whatever else is truly helpful.

God's call on our lives is not impossible to live. It's difficult, sometimes extremely difficult. But God never asks the impossible. That *would* be cruel. If we think our weakness is stronger than God's strength, we've emptied the cross of its power.

9. Are you saying it's possible for homosexuals to change and become heterosexual?

Before I answer the question, I need to clarify the terms being used. We use the words *homosexual* and *heterosexual* to distinguish between those who are sexually attracted to the same sex and those who are attracted to the opposite sex. They are useful words in some contexts, but there's an inherent tendency in *naming* such things that leads to treating them as concrete realities when they're not.

Evil is a useful word, for example. But evil doesn't exist in its own right. Evil is the absence of good, just as cold is the absence of heat, and darkness is the absence of light.

My point is that *"homo*-sexuality" doesn't exist in its own right. Nor is there really any such thing as *"hetero*-sexuality." These words, in fact, are a relatively recent invention.[13] All that really exists is *sexuality*: the call of men and women to love in the image of God either through marriage or in a celibate gift of self. Any other desire or attraction (whether geared toward the same or opposite sex) is a privation, a lack, of this good. Any other desire or attraction is like cold in the absence of heat, or darkness in the absence of light. Cold cannot "change" into heat. The presence of heat vanquishes cold. Darkness doesn't "change" into light. The presence of light vanquishes darkness.

Similarly, homosexuals don't "change" into heterosexuals. Men and women simply become further aligned with who God truly created them to be. That is, as the sun rises in the cold and darkness, people can and do experience warmth and light. The truth of sexuality can and does vanquish distortions of sexuality.

To continue with the sunrise analogy, few will ever be at "high noon" in this life with *all* the cold and darkness banished. It's probably more accurate to say we live at dawn: a mixture of light and dark, cold and warmth. But whatever our particular struggles, everyone can, through an ongoing appropriation of Christ's redemption, experience more and more the truth of sexuality as God intended it to be in the beginning. And even if not in this life, in the next life Christ will bring to completion the work he has begun in each of us (see Philippians 1:6).

We must remember, however, that it's precisely *the cross* from which we receive the power to become who we were created by God to be. This means suffering will be part of our journey. This suffering may mean dying to a lifetime of diseased ways of thinking and behaving. This suffering may mean letting go of the very thing, perhaps, in which a person has wrongly posited his or her identity, and *re-positing* that identity in the eternal plan of God the Father which is offered to us through the death and resurrection of his Son.

This means the journey of becoming who we're made to be *ain't easy*. I wouldn't want to imply that a person who experiences same-sex attractions (or any other disorders of the sexual appetite) could simply rid himself or herself of them by praying hard enough or having enough faith. But, as numerous men and women testify, it is possible for those who experience disordered attractions to come to a more ordered experience of their attractions. Our struggles may persist, but Christ has opened for us a world of wonders through his death and resurrection. And this means there is always hope for us to become more and more the men and women we are created to be. Yes, there is *always* hope!

10. You know that a host of homosexuals would vehemently disagree with everything you're saying and accuse you of being a homophobe.

Yes, I do. But a host of others, whose voices are often silenced in the popular media, would agree wholeheartedly.

In saying this, however, I'm not trying to shore up the sides of two warring camps. Even those who would vehemently disagree have something to say. There's always some element of truth to be found in our desires, regardless of how distorted they may have become. (A distortion, after all, is simply a twisting of truth.) There's always some genuine human need that people are seeking to meet in the way they live their lives. There's always a person behind it all who is longing, as everyone is longing, to be loved and affirmed as a human being—to be wanted, chosen, appreciated, desired.

While compassion shouldn't lead us to compromise what's true, it *should* lead us to affirm the beautiful humanity of everyone, regardless of his or her sexual attractions. It *should* lead us to reach out and listen. It *should* lead us to want to understand everyone's heart.

When we do reach out in love, lo and behold, those of us who think we have everything "straight" actually find that we have a lot to learn about life from the dreams and experiences, hopes and fears, of those who experience same-sex attractions. Charity, from both "sides," is the only human response. Dismissing those active in a "gay lifestyle" as "sinners" and "sodomites" is just as uncharitable as when they dismiss those who disapprove of their behavior as "homophobes."

I don't mean to ignore the fact that fear and mistreatment of those who experience same-sex attractions exist. More often than not, it seems this fear results in those people with a tenuous grasp on their own sexual identities. Such people often feel threatened by the mere existence of those who pursue romantic/erotic relationships with their own sex. They may even act violently against such persons in a perverse attempt to bolster their own fragile sense of sexual identity, rejecting in others the emotions and desires that they cannot face in themselves. Tragically, Christians themselves have sometimes been party to malice and violence in this regard. It shouldn't even need mentioning that such violence is unconditionally condemned by the Catholic Church.

11. I know a lesbian couple who live right across the street. They're so kind and loving toward us and toward each other. I refuse to believe that they're "living in sin."

Are you kind and loving toward your family and neighbors? Does that mean that you never sin in other ways? Of course not.

Even people who base a large part of their lives on something objectively sinful are able to show genuine love and human kindness, oftentimes even more so than people who may not have anything "large and looming" on their own laundry list of sins. I'm sure you're right to say they're genuinely kind. I'm sure there are elements of genuine love that they share for one another.

Still, whatever is romantic or "erotically charged" in their relationship is not in keeping with what God authored into our humanity "in the beginning." This doesn't mean they're inherently "bad people." It just means they're in need of Christ's redemption like the rest of us.

12. I'm married with three kids. I've never admitted this to anybody, but sometimes I'm attracted to other men. Does this mean I'm gay? I'm afraid this will ruin my marriage. What should I do?

No! It does *not* mean you're gay. Remember, no one *is* gay, ontologically speaking.

First of all, if we don't find people of our own sex "attractive," either we're not looking hard enough, or we've shut down a healthy aspect of our own humanity. Our culture has become so toxically "eroticized" that even normal and natural attractions to the goodness in others gets labeled as something romantically or sexually charged. And when we take on those false labels as an "identity," it can become a self-fulfilling prophecy—the desires may well become romanticized or eroticized.

Regardless of the origin, sentiment, or character of your attractions to other men, once again, it does not mean "you're gay." It means you live in a fallen world and you may be cut off at times from your own masculine identity. Welcome to the human race.

Your struggle is *not* an insurmountable hurdle to a healthy, holy marriage. If you're committed to facing your struggles and seeking Christ's help to be the husband and father you're called to be, there should be no reason for this to ruin your relationship with your wife and kids. We all have certain "thorns" of weakness throughout our earthly journey (see 2 Corinthians 12:7). Even so, God's grace is sufficient for you to be a strong and faithful husband and father.

Perhaps it would be helpful for me to tell you more about my own struggles and how the Lord has worked in my life to affirm me in my identity as a man. As I already mentioned, as a teenager (and even into my early twenties), I went through a painful period of questioning my masculine identity. I was very troubled by the fact that I found myself somewhat attracted or drawn to men who I thought were more masculine than I. Whenever I'd be in such a person's presence (the college campus "stud," for instance), I'd feel terribly insecure about myself.

Listening to lectures of a conference on gender issues and personal healing finally helped me to make sense out of this troubling inner dynamic. Several of the talks were given by a man who had lived an active homosexual life for many years. Although the attractions I experienced were never fully eroticized as his were, as he very candidly shared his struggles and his healings, his story resonated with me.[14]

Boys, by virtue of the fact that they're boys, have an inherent need to identify with what is masculine. They have an inherent need to *become men*. In the natural course of things a boy meets this need through healthy relationships with male role models whom he very naturally aspires to be like (such as his father, uncles, grandfathers, teachers, coaches).

In the absence of healthy relationships, that is, in the absence of male role models worth aspiring to be like, boys and young men will naturally seek to fill the void. They will admire, want to be with, and be attracted to those men whom they perceive to have "become men." This desire doesn't always become eroticized, but it can and sometimes does.[15]

The fact that most every boy hangs posters of his "heroes" on the wall points to this dynamic. Boys are looking for what it means to be a man. Unfortunately, what the world holds out is gravely distorted.

Consequently, boys and young men end up positing the meaning of manhood in all sorts of false images: the "ladies' man," the "muscle man," the "macho man," the "successful man,"—you name it. And consciously or unconsciously, they long to become the image that has lodged in their souls as the "ultimate masculine."[16] If they don't measure up to that image, they become terribly insecure, particularly in the presence of those men whom they think embody the image more than they themselves do.

This inner dynamic became a very pointed reality for me one day as I was working at one of my first jobs out of college. The woman who sat behind me was the kind of girl who hung Chippendale posters in her cubicle. These images of muscle-bound studs in tight spandex pants and bow ties tapped into all my insecurities, so I avoided her cubicle like the plague. One day I reluctantly overheard a conversation she was having with a friend. She described a dream she'd had of a similar stud who rode up the beach on his white stallion and had wild sex with her in the waves.

I'm not one who regularly receives visions, but I had one right then and there as I was trying my darnedest not to listen to her conversation. I saw the man she described walking down the beach. He was everything that years of living in this society had convinced me it meant to be a man: muscle-bound, attractive, sleek. He wasn't just *a* man. He was *the* man. At some place in my soul, he was what *I* wanted to be, but wasn't.

Then I saw another man walking beside him. He was everything that society had convinced me was not manly. Nothing drew me to him at all. He was weak, disfigured, beaten, bloody. He wore a crown of thorns on his head and had scourge marks all over his body.

Then a voice posed a question to me. I can only assume it was the voice the Holy Spirit, which said: "Who is the *real* man, and with whom do you wish to identify?"

I was stunned. I realized at that moment that I had been believing, even *worshipping*, a lie.[17] I realized at that moment that all my insecurity as a man stemmed from positing my identity in a false image of masculinity.

My heart cried out: "Jesus, you're the real man. I choose to identify with you!"

Then my heart sank. *Wait a minute*, I thought. *If I choose to identify with Christ, if I choose to seek the very meaning of my manhood in him, I'll be treated just like he was. The world won't affirm me as a man. The world will mock me, laugh at me, spit in my face, crucify me.*

I shuddered. But Truth drew me to himself and gave me the grace to renounce my idol.

I've had many turning points in my life. This was one of the big ones. The cause of years of insecurity and fear was encapsulated for me in that vision.

Within days I purposely went into that woman's cubicle to stare those Chippendales in the face. The lie no longer had a grip on me. I was able to see those distorted images for what they were and stand secure in claiming my masculine identity in Christ. In fact, I realized that those men in the spandex and bow ties should want to be like me. Not because I'm so great, but because I'm seeking Christ.

It's not like I was instantly healed of all my insecurities, but there was a dramatic shift in my soul that day that continues to anchor me whenever I've been tempted to believe lies about the meaning of manhood.

There's no magic formula for healing confused emotions and desires, but St. John Paul II spoke of three infallible and indispensable means for living out the true theology of our bodies: a deepening life of prayer; regular confession of our sins; and frequent reception of the Eucharist.[18] These means are infallible because, when they are properly understood and lived, they can't possibly steer us wrong. And they're indispensable because we simply can't live the Christian life to the full without them.

At first, recommending prayer and the sacraments just sounds like "standard Catholic stuff" you've heard before. John Paul II's "spousal theology," however, gives us a fresh, *mystical* perspective that (sadly) you probably didn't hear growing up in the Church. Let's take a look.

1) *Prayer.* The Fathers of the Church tell us that prayer is nothing but a longing for God. If we have the courage to follow it the whole way through, this longing, says John Paul II, will take us through "painful purifications (the 'dark night'). But it leads, in various possible ways, to the ineffable joy experienced by the mystics as 'nuptial union.'"[19] To clarify, he's talking about "nuptial union" with the eternal, with the divine. This is how the greatest saints describe it.

Behind all our disordered desires for love and union in this life, this is what we really yearn for: eternal love and union with the God who has revealed himself as eternal Love and Union. The healing of desire comes as we learn, as Fr. Jacques Philippe observes, that "one passion can only be cured by another—a misplaced love by a greater love, wrong behavior by right behavior that makes provisions for the desire underlying the wrongdoing, recognizes the conscious or unconscious needs that seek fulfillment and...offers them legitimate satisfaction."[20] This is what happens in a genuine life of prayer.

2) *Regular Confession.* If sin is a misguided attempt to satisfy a genuine human need, the grace of Confession is essential to help redirect that need toward its true object. Whenever we commit serious sin, we should be going to confession. That may mean quite frequently for lots of us. But this does not mean we should not also be going regularly if we haven't done anything "big, bad, and horrible."

As the *Catechism* says, "Without being strictly necessary, confession of everyday faults (venial sins) is nevertheless strongly recommended by the Church. Indeed, the regular confession of our venial sins helps us form our consciences, fight against evil tendencies, let ourselves be healed by Christ and progress in the life of the Spirit."[21]

Prayerful reception of this sacrament is where we "let our masks fall and turn our hearts back to the Lord who loves us, so as to hand ourselves over to him as an offering to be purified and transformed."[22] In other words, confession is where we "get naked" before God, allowing him to love us as we are and transform us into what we're made to be.

3) *Frequent Reception of the Eucharist.* The Eucharist, wrote St. John Paul II, is "*the sacrament of the Bridegroom and of the Bride.*" Christ instituted the Eucharist, he continued, "to express the relationship between man and woman, between what is 'feminine' and what is 'masculine.'"[23] What wealth of truth is contained in these astounding statements! Please read them again. The Eucharist expresses the ultimate truth about our creation as male and female: it's all a "great mystery" that reveals the Holy Communion of Christ and the Church (see Ephesians 5:31–32). This means the truth of your masculine identity is found in the Eucharist.

Our confused (and confusing) attractions often stem from what we admire in others but fear we lack in ourselves. When we see that particular quality in others, sometimes we want to *take it in* to ourselves so badly that it can become an obsession. Untwist these distorted desires, and you'll find that what you desire to *take in* to yourself is Christ. And praise be to God, Christ gives us his very flesh to *eat* in the Eucharist. If you allow the Eucharist to be the wellspring of your identity as a man, you'll find yourself on the path to discovering the man you truly are.

One more important word of advice for your journey: *don't go it alone.* Share your struggles with a trusted friend, spiritual director, or counselor whom you know will give you sound Christian advice. Sharing our lives— our real needs, questions, and struggles—with others who have been on the journey is not a luxury, but a necessity of human nature.

One program that offers an encouraging community setting in which to exchange misbegotten ideas about ourselves for the truth of our most authentic selves is *Living Waters* offered through Desert Stream Ministries. I couldn't recommend them more highly. *That Man Is You* is also doing great work helping men form real bonds of communion among themselves as they seek to grow in masculine virtue and holiness. *Eden Invitation* is also an excellent resource for those with questions about sexual orientation and gender identity (a simple Internet search will lead you to these ministries).

13. My son insists on a same-sex wedding. He knows that I do not support this decision, but not attending will cause irrevocable damage to our relationship. What should I do? Is it against Church teaching for me to attend?

Your son's decisions have put you in a very difficult position. While there is no definitive teaching on this matter from the Church, there are, indeed, moral principles that should shape a person's conscience in making such a decision.

On the one hand, Christ attended gatherings of public sinners. Of course, he attended as a light in the darkness, and not as one endorsing or celebrating people's sin. And that is the matter at stake. Even if your son knows you do not support his decision, would your attendance be perceived by others as an endorsement of same-sex marriage? Perhaps there is good reason to believe your attendance would be well understood in the same spirit in which Jesus associated with those who were in open rebellion against God's plan for our lives—with a love for the sinners but not for the sin. But only you can know the answer to that.

The *Catechism* observes that we share in the responsibility for the sins committed by others when we cooperate in them by: participating in them directly and voluntarily; praising or approving them; not disclosing or not hindering them when we have an obligation to do so; or protecting evildoers in their evil doing.[24]

Fidelity to the truth can, indeed, cause divisions within families. Christ himself warned of this: "Do not think that I have come to bring peace upon the earth. I have come to bring not peace but the sword. For I have come to set a man against his father…and one's enemies will be those of his own household" (Matthew 10:34–36). This is sometimes the difficult and painful price of fidelity to Christ.

While I can't give a definitive answer to your question, I can provide the two extremes to avoid. On the one hand, a rigid, legalistic, cold conformity to the Church's moral teaching that takes no account of people's weaknesses, questions, circumstances, and struggles does not serve anyone. But, on the other hand, nor does compromise of the truth. Somewhere between these two extremes lies an appropriate path forward in this difficult situation.

14. Our daughter recently told us she's a lesbian and the woman we have known for years as her best friend is actually her "lover." It's put a terrible strain on our relationship with her. My husband and I don't know what to do or where to turn.

Certainly you already have and will continue to go through a range of emotions over your daughter's announcement. Be patient with yourself as you work through your feelings, but be careful not to *act* on emotional impulse, especially in a way that would make your daughter feel isolated or ostracized. Perhaps now more than ever, your daughter needs to know that you love her. Whatever the tensions caused, don't break off contact. Don't reject her.

None of this means, however, that you must approve of the choices she's making with her life. In fact, it would be unloving to say nothing of your concerns, but this must be done carefully and tactfully. It may mean waiting until your daughter initiates conversation with you or seeks your counsel or perspective. In that moment, trust the Holy Spirit for the right words such that she will be certain of your love and will know that you desire her growth in holiness, just as you desire that for anyone else. Let Christ's example guide you. While he was uncompromising with sin, he was ever patient and loving toward sinners.

Perhaps the most important thing you can do for your daughter is to pray for her, not out of a sense of self-righteous indignation but out of a loving desire to see her become the woman she's created to be. Some parents in your situation fear for their child's salvation. While no one can know the state of another person's soul before God, this you can rely upon: The Lord desires her salvation more than you do yourself. Trust in his mercy. Never lose hope for your daughter's conversion of heart.

Furthermore, seek support for yourselves as parents and, if she's willing, for your daughter. Desert Stream Ministries' *Living Waters* program and *Eden Invitation*, as previously mentioned, are resources I highly recommend. *Courage* is also a support group devoted to helping Catholics who experience same-sex attraction to live holy, chaste lives in keeping with the Church's teachings. A sister group, called *EnCourage*, offers support to parents of children who experience same-sex attraction (a simple Internet search will lead you to them).

Finally, if you're willing to receive it as such, your daughter's announcement is actually an opportunity for growth for your whole family. In our fallen world, the term "dysfunctional family" is redundant. Every family has its share of dysfunction because every family is made up of fallen human beings. While countless factors in today's world influence the lives and decisions of our children, it must be acknowledged that family dynamics often do play a role in the development of a child's problems later in life, including sexual and gender identity problems. Just as love is diffusive of itself, so are sin and dysfunctional relating.

Don't be afraid to bring the light of Christ into all the family "closets." Open wide the doors to Christ. Don't be afraid to admit and seek forgiveness from your adult children for mistakes that were made, patterns of relating that were unhealthy, and even sexual sin that may have been (or still is) part of your own marriage.

While you may think your sex life is none of your kids' business, and in some respects, that's true, look at it this way: because your sex life is the very origin of your children's lives, their identity is intimately intertwined with what goes on in your bedroom. I've worked with enough wounded people to know that parental sins such as adultery, pornography, contraception, and divorce have a deep and lasting effect on children. Prudence may dictate otherwise in some situations, but open discussion with your adult children about your own failings is often a crucial step in healing family wounds. If you have reason to believe such discussions would be explosive, the presence of a wise family counselor is a good idea.

Christ entered the world through a family in order to restore the family. He can bring healing and forgiveness to our families. But we must open our wounds to his healing touch. There is always hope. Always!

9

Trapped in the Wrong Body?

Gender Identity Questions

Various forms of an ideology of gender...promote a personal identity and emotional intimacy radically separated from the biological difference between male and female. Consequently, human identity becomes the choice of the individual, one that can also change over time.... It is one thing to be understanding of human weakness and the complexities of life, and another to accept ideologies that attempt to sunder what are insepa-rable aspects of reality. Let us not fall into the sin of trying to replace the Creator. We...are called to protect our humanity, and this means, in the first place, accepting it and respecting it as it was created. [1]

—Pope Francis

The moment you were born (or sooner with modern technologies), someone examined your body in order to *identify* you. Where did that person look? Your eyes? Your elbows? Your kneecaps? All lovely, I'm sure. But that's not where the person looked. Someone looked directly at your genitals and announced, "It's a girl!" or "It's a boy!" From that first reve-lation (and even from before it) until now, a wide array of factors both of nature and of nurture have shaped your level of comfort or discomfort with your being either a male or female human being.

I once heard a therapist propose that, like a train, we need two solid tracks on which to travel if we are to grow up with a healthy sense of our own gender: the track of gender identification and the track of gender com-plementarity. To the degree that a girl grows up with healthy women in her life and learns to identify with them, and to the degree that she grows up with healthy men in her life who know how to honor and welcome her complementary differences while sincerely offering their own, her train will carry her into adulthood with an accordingly healthy sense of herself as a woman. Obviously, the tracks of identification and complementarity are reversed for boys, but the same holds true.

No one grows up with a perfect set of tracks for his or her train, however. And in today's world, many of us grow up with large sections of both tracks missing altogether. Hence, it shouldn't surprise us in the least that people's trains are getting derailed with regard to their identity as male or female. When over half of America's children grow up without the stable witness of their mother and father's married love;[2] when 28 percent of youth report being sexually victimized by the age of seventeen;[3] and when the gross distortions of hard-core pornography have become the frame in which our culture understands masculinity and femininity, a gender identity crisis is inevitable.

Hence, as Pope Francis admonishes in the quote that started this chapter, we must indeed be understanding of human weakness and the complexities of life in this regard. At the same time, we serve no one by accepting ideologies that divorce human identity from the human body. An eye-opening video that went viral on YouTube demonstrates where such ideologies lead.[4] Therein a 5'9" white adult male asks some college students the following questions:

Interviewer: So if I told you I was a woman, what would your response be?

Student 1: Good for you, okay, yeah.

Interviewer: If I told you that I was Chinese, what would your response be?

Student 1: I might be a little surprised, but I would say, good for you, like, yeah, be who you are.

Interviewer: If I told you that I was seven years old, what would your response be?

Student 1 (after some hemming and hawing): If you feel seven at heart, then, so be it, yeah, good for you.

Interviewer: So, if I wanted to enroll in a first grade class, do you think I should be allowed to?

Student 1: If that's where you feel, like, mentally you should be, then I feel like there are communities that would accept you for that.

Interviewer: If I told you I am 6'5", what would your response be?

Student 2: If you truly believed you're 6'5", I don't think it's harmful. I think it's fine if you believe that. It doesn't matter to me if you think you're taller than you are.

"It shouldn't be hard to tell a 5'9" white guy that he's not a 6'5" Chinese woman," the video concludes, "but clearly it is. Why? What does that say about our culture?"

It says, among other things, that our culture has swallowed the ancient Gnostic heresy hook, line, and sinker (see chapter three, question 11). Indeed, governments around the world are now demanding in law that we identify every-body without identifying any-body. But when we identify some-body without reference to his or her body, we identify, quite literally, no-body. Our material bodies become immaterial.

In turn, a fork in the relationship between the human body and human identity creates a fork in the tongue.[5] Words like *male* and *female*, *boy* and *girl*, *man* and *woman*, *he* and *she*, *sex* and *gender* become meaningless. Separate the human body from human relationships and the meaning of words like *husband* and *wife*, *father* and *mother*, *brother* and *sister*, *uncle* and *aunt* also get totally eclipsed. New words are then invented to reinforce the rupture and impose it on the rest of the world.

Tune into the secular conversation on these matters and one begins to wonder if something of the world George Orwell warned about in his famous dystopian novel *1984* isn't upon us. Therein he described a totalitarian state that manipulates the masses by continually distorting language. Orwell observed that "if thought corrupts language, language can also corrupt thought."[6] This is why we must defend the integral relationship between words and the determinate realities to which they refer. If we don't, freedom becomes slavery and speaking the truth in love becomes hate speech.

This is a window into the all-out human crisis we are now facing as the logic of the sexual revolution marches on. This chapter will seek to navigate these treacherous waters with sensitivity and understanding for those who experience gender dysphoria (a condition of persistent and deep discomfort with one's God-given sex), while at the same time lovingly holding out the full truth of our humanity as an integral union of body and soul.

1. I notice that you seem to use the terms sex and gender interchangeably. Don't you know that sex refers to your biology while gender refers to how you identify on the inside?

I do know that this is how the dominant culture and media want us to use these words. But I also know that to accept this distinction is to embrace that death-dealing rupture between body and soul that we've discussed repeatedly throughout this book. Because of the profound unity of body and soul in God's design, sex cannot be sequestered to the (supposedly) impersonal realm of "biology." The human being is a sexed being through and through, physically and spiritually.

"*Sexuality* affects all aspects of the human person in the unity of his body and soul," observes the *Catechism*.[7] It "is by no means something purely biological," St. John Paul II affirmed. Rather, sexuality "concerns the innermost being of the human person."[8] And this means that *the body* reveals the deepest truth of the person. "It is, thus, in all its materiality... penetrable and transparent," wrote John Paul II, "in such a way as to make it clear who man is (and who he ought to be)."[9]

If a certain distinction between sex and gender is warranted, we might say that gender refers to the social expression of one's sex. But even if sex and gender can in this sense be distinguished, they are nonetheless inseparable. Any attempt to rend one's gender from the reality of one's body is the fruit of having embraced that tragically faulty Cartesian view of the person as a "thinking thing" housed in meaningless, crude matter (see chapter three, question 3).

When we embrace Descartes' dictum, it's only a matter of time until "I think, therefore I am" plays itself out logically as "I think, therefore I am whatever I think I am." In this view, subjective thoughts are no longer answerable to objective reality. "Reality" gets reduced to what I *think* and *feel* about it. If a man *thinks* he is a woman, then, contrary to all the evidence, the modern world demands that we all recognize him *as* a woman. Then we invent false distinctions between sex and gender to justify what we think and feel.

None of this is said to make light of the real persons involved and the pain they experience. It would certainly be agonizing to feel interiorly cut off from one's own body and sex. But rather than seeking to address that underlying pain and heal it, the modern "solution" is to mask it with a cosmetic alteration of one's outward appearance. In all charity, it must be said: This approach has exchanged the truth for a lie. If genuine healing is to come to those who suffer with gender dysphoria, we must begin by standing firmly on the truth that our identity as male or female is rooted not in our *feelings* but in our *bodies*.

Much wisdom can be regained here simply by looking at the root of the word *gender*. It shares the same root as words like *generous, generate, genesis, genetics, genealogy*, and *progeny*. *Gen* means "to beget or give birth to." A person's *gen*-der, therefore, is based on the manner in which that person is designed to *gen*-erate new life, and that is determined by the kind of *gen*-itals he or she has (we will address those rare cases of ambiguous genitalia in questions 6 to 8 of this chapter).

When a culture understands and reverences the meaning of our genitals, that culture will understand and reverence the meaning of gender. Attack the meaning of our genitals and an attack on the meaning of gender is inevitable. Stated another way: Once a culture starts draining *sexual activity* of its meaning, it is only a matter of time before it starts draining *sexual identity* of its meaning too. The two stand or fall together.

Hence, it shouldn't surprise us that yesterday's sexual ideology (which was all about rupturing gender from life with contraception and abortion politics) has led us to today's gender ideology (which is all about rupturing life from gender with identity politics).

This is not to say that prior to the sexual revolution we had a wonderfully balanced understanding of gender. Without a doubt, a correction of socially constructed gender roles that exaggerated the sexual difference (and almost always favored men) was sorely needed. But in the process, it seems we have forgotten that there are two roles—one belonging only to men and the other only to women—that are in no way fabricated by society; they're ordained by God, given in nature, and they just so happen to be absolutely indispensable for the survival of the human race: fathering and mothering a child through the generative act which is made possible precisely by the fact that we are gendered creatures.

This is the only coherent way in which to classify and understand *the natural purpose* of the sexual difference. As we put it in the previous chapter, the sexual difference literally *organizes* men and women for each other, which is to say a man and a woman have been given *organs* that allow them to work together as one *organism*, as it were, for the generation of new human beings.

Until the *dis-organizing* impact of modern contraceptive technology intervened, society as a whole naturally *organized* itself around this truth. While people have always bucked this organizing principle, the regulating effect of fertility naturally kept such movements on the fringes of society. Today, of course, new gender ideologies (more aptly: "genderless" ideologies) have gone mainstream. As we observed in the last chapter (see question 5), introduce effective contraception on a wide scale and eventually the fundamental link among gender, genitals, and generating will all but vanish from the way we understand our genital relationships and our "gender identities."

St. Paul VI himself warned us in *Humanae Vitae* that a contracepting world not only becomes a world of rampant infidelity, a world where women and childbearing are degraded, and a world in which governments trample on the rights and needs of the family. He also warned that it becomes a world in which human beings believe they can manipulate their bodies at will. [10]

In a 1984 interview, the future Pope Benedict XVI explained the progression from contraception to gender confusion this way: We will atone in our day, he said, for "the consequences of a sexuality which is no longer linked to...procreation. It logically follows from this that every form of [genital activity] is equivalent.... No longer having an objective reason to justify it, sex seeks the subjective reason in the gratification of the desire, in the most 'satisfying' answer for the individual." In turn, he observed that everyone becomes "free to give to his personal *libido* the content considered suitable for himself. Hence, it naturally follows that all forms of sexual gratification are transformed into the 'rights' of the individual." From there, he concluded that people end up demanding the right of "escaping from the 'slavery of nature,' demanding the right to be male or female at one's will or pleasure." [11]

But why limit it to male and female? Not long ago Facebook listed over fifty gender options to choose from when filling out a personal profile. After complaints that terms such as "intersex," "cisgender," "gender fluid," "gender noncomforming," "gender variant," "neutrois," "non-binary," "pangender," "two-spirit," and multiple other variations on these themes were still too limiting, the site added a "free-form field" in which people could "customize" their gender identity. "We recognize that some people face challenges sharing their true gender identity with others," said Facebook's diversity team in a statement, "and this setting gives people the ability to express themselves in an authentic way." [12]

What does it mean—really—to speak of "true gender identity" and to express it "in an authentic way"? Whatever number of "gender identities" the modern world may claim exists, Christ's teaching is very clear: "Have you not read that he who made them from the beginning made them male and female?" (Matthew 19:4). And with a mercy and compassion that literally *bleeds* to reach us where we ourselves are bleeding most, Christ wants not only to show us who we really are, but empower us to become who we really are.

This means the woman who was sexually abused as a girl, who was subjected to other forms of misogyny, internalized that and hated herself, and began to identify with the masculine as a way of protecting herself—she can begin the grand adventure of rediscovering the true gift of her femininity through the tender mercy of the God who loves the unrepeatable woman he made her to be. This means the creative boy who was cruelly bullied, found no bridge into masculine identification, and who early on lost himself in dazzling icons of empowered women—he can begin the grand adventure of rediscovering the true gift of his masculinity through the tender mercy of the God who loves the unrepeatable man he made him to be.

Yes, we must proclaim it loudly and clearly: Whatever our inner struggles, whatever our battles, wounds, and confusion, there is always hope of becoming who we truly are through the *real power* of Christ's death and resurrection.

2. If people who are labeled one sex at birth feel like they are the other sex, what's the problem with them acting on these feelings, especially if they were born this way? Surgical intervention could help them live as they really are on the inside.

Once again, we must show our sincere compassion for those who endure the gut-wrenching struggle of feeling like they were born in the wrong body. But what does true charity call us to in these painful situations?

"Truth is the light that gives meaning and value to charity," affirmed Pope Benedict XVI. "Without truth, charity degenerates into sentimentality. Love becomes an empty shell, to be filled in an arbitrary way."[13]

Offering love without truth is unloving. Offering truth without love is untruthful. Our desire must be to offer love truthfully and speak truth lovingly. That's been the spirit with which I've written this book and with which I'll try to respond to the above question.

Allow me first to address the notion, in vogue in today's world, that we are "labeled" one sex or the other at birth. This is another example of an Orwellian manipulation of language intended to rend us from the truth of things. To describe one's sex as a "label" applied at birth is to frame an objective, fixed reality as something arbitrary, restrictive, and inaccurate. This immediately appeals to our sense of justice (we all intuit that no one should be bound by arbitrary, restrictive, and inaccurate labels) while skirting the fact that there is absolutely *nothing* arbitrary, restrictive, or inaccurate about someone looking at a newborn's penis and saying, "It's a boy," or looking at a newborn's vulva and saying, "It's a girl."

In the beginning, God didn't "label" us male and female. He *created* us male and female. This is who and what we are and always will be. As St. John Paul II observes, our creation as male and female is "the fundamental fact" of human existence in every stage of history.[14]

Now, to get to your question: What's the problem with people acting on the feeling that they are the opposite sex? If we hold that feeling up to the light of truth, we will recognize that it does not coincide with reality. To act on that feeling would be a betrayal of truthfulness. Think about it from this perspective: Is there any man on the planet who would not feel deceived if the woman he had been dating for some time suddenly revealed that she (actually he) had undergone gender reassignment surgery? That man would feel deceived because what his date did in presenting himself as a woman *is*, in fact, a deception.

What's the problem with people acting on the feeling that they are the opposite sex? By replacing objective reality with their subjective feelings, they are setting themselves up as the arbiters of what is real. They are making themselves "like God" and that is the original human problem, the problem behind all our problems (see Genesis 3:1–5).

What's the problem with people acting on the feeling that they are the opposite sex? They are embracing a false view of their humanity that radically separates body and soul, placing the physical and spiritual dimensions of their humanity in opposition. Rather than seeking to heal that opposition, those who act on the feeling that they are the opposite sex are reinforcing the opposition of body and soul, almost cementing it, as it were.

When you assert that such people were "born this way," it would appear that you mean to say their dissociation from their bodies is somehow to be understood as a "given" of nature and that their desire for a different body should therefore be embraced. However, ever since the dawn of original sin, what we are given at birth is a *fallen nature*. Part of fallen nature is, indeed, the experience of a certain rupture or incongruity of body and soul. The entrance of shame after original sin indicates that the body has ceased drawing on the power of the spirit, and in conjunction with the disorder of our sexual appetite this causes, as St. John Paul II expressed it, "an almost constitutive *difficulty in identifying oneself with one's own body*."[15]

This means *all* of us struggle to one degree or another to harmonize the inner and outer realities of our humanity, to live the integral unity of body and soul. This struggle is particularly sharp and agonizing for those who experience gender dysphoria. The desire for some relief, for some resolution to the struggle is not only understandable, but it points to the good (very good) desire we all have to harmonize that which is physical and that which is spiritual in our humanity.

But is the lack of harmony a physical problem or a spiritual and psychological one? In the case of physical birth defects, such as those born with ambiguous genitalia (we address this in more detail in questions 6 to 8 below), surgical intervention may well be warranted. But very few people who consider themselves transgender had ambiguous genitalia at birth. For the large majority, their God-given gender was plain for all to see.[16] In these cases, surgical alteration of their bodies isn't helping them "live as they really are." It's actually cooperating in their ailment and reinforcing their malady. It's calling sickness (their psychological condition) health and health (their properly functioning sexually organized bodies) sickness.

What these men and women need is the real hope of an *inner* healing. But it would seem most mental health professionals have given up on that prospect. Instead of seeking the needed inner transformation, they hand their patients over to surgeons for outward transformation.

Some individuals believe they are disabled people trapped in fully functional bodies. It is an actual condition called body integrity identity disorder (BIID). Medical professionals would be making a horrible mistake if they suggested the proper treatment program for those with BIID was to drug their bodies into a state of dysfunction or to amputate healthy limbs to coincide with how these people feel on the inside. Is it any different when doctors prescribe hormones and perform surgeries to make people appear like the opposite sex? Excising perfectly healthy body parts (such as a woman's breasts or a man's genitals) is called mutilation.

These are just a few initial reasons why acting on feelings that one is the opposite sex is not the right path to follow.

3. What trans people do is no one else's business. These people aren't hurting anyone. The Church should just respect their feelings, mind its own business, and stop trying to rob people of their rights and their freedom.

The Church is the first institution on the planet to speak up and defend people's true rights and true freedom. But, as we learned in chapter one, freedom does not give us the right to do whatever we want. Freedom is given to us by God as the capacity to choose whatever is good, whatever is in keeping with the truth of our humanity. Truth and freedom are so intertwined they stand or fall together.

We can all recognize that truth without respect for freedom leads to tyranny (this is why the Church doesn't impose her teaching, but proposes it; see chapter two, question 11). But it seems the modern world has forgotten that freedom without respect for truth also leads to tyranny.

If there is no *objective truth* to which we are all equally answerable, then all that exists is a power struggle between opposing *subjective opinions*. Those with the most money, media influence, or military muscle will inevitably impose their views on the rest of the world: Might makes right. "In this way democracy, contradicting its own principles, effectively moves towards a form of totalitarianism," as St. John Paul II observed. "The state... is transformed into a *tyrant state*." [17]

The fact is, when people embrace falsehoods that attack the deepest roots of what it means to be human and then lobby medical, educational, media, and governmental institutions to embrace and promote these falsehoods, they are, to be sure, causing tremendous harm to others. When the state enshrines these falsehoods in law and punishes those who don't comply, a tyrant state is, indeed, upon us.

The Catholic Church, by standing up oftentimes as the lone voice in defense of the truth of the human person, is defending everyone on the planet from those tyrannical forces that seek to rob us of our true rights and our true freedom.

4. We've decided to raise our children gender neutral so they can choose what gender to be when they're ready. We think it's a matter of respecting their freedom.

It is good, indeed, to respect others' freedom. However, part of respecting your children's freedom means providing a proper education in the true nature of it. Human freedom is not absolute self-determination. There are countless truths about ourselves that we do not and cannot determine for ourselves. Your children can no more choose their gender than they can choose their parents or their race and nationality.

The exaltation of "choice" as pure autonomy ends in meaninglessness. Choice presupposes a willingness to engage and to wrestle with ultimate questions about the nature, meaning, and purpose of the universe, of our own lives, and of the difference between good and evil. Not every choice is a good choice. If that were the case, authentic choice would not exist; we would only be prey to our own (or others') whims, seductions, and prejudices.

The Supreme Court of the United States, in its attempt to justify abortion as a "good choice," flipped reality right on its head when it asserted: "At the heart of liberty is the right to define one's own concept of existence, of meaning, of the universe, and of the mystery of human life." [18] It almost sounds like a religious statement, but it's the religion of the father of lies who since the beginning has set out to convince us that we can be "'like God,' but 'without God, before God, and not in accordance with God.'" [19]

Human beings possess an extremely far-reaching freedom. This is symbolized in Genesis by the fact that we are free to eat from "every tree in the garden" (Genesis 2:16). However, our freedom is not unlimited. We must halt before the "tree of the knowledge of good and evil," for we are called to accept reality as it is given by God. [20]

Helping our children to recognize and embrace reality, rather than invent reality, is how we teach them proper lessons about freedom *and its limits*. To set your children up as the arbiters of their own gender places them squarely in a false vision of themselves and the universe and will inevitably create a world of uncertainty and confusion in their lives.

5. God blessed me by making me transsexual for the same reason he made wheat but not bread and grapes but not wine: because he wants us to share in the act of creation. By conforming my body to my gender identity, I am only doing the good works here on earth as God intended.

We've discussed throughout this book that "the beginning" (before original sin harmed and distorted our humanity) is the norm for understanding how God made us. I won't reiterate those points here.

Rather, I want to comment on the very important aspect of the human being's role in creation that you're calling to mind. As the *Catechism* puts it:

> To human beings God…gives the power of freely sharing in his providence by entrusting them with the responsibility of "subduing" the earth and having dominion over it. God thus enables men to be intelligent and free causes in order to complete the work of creation, to perfect its harmony for their own good and that of their neighbors.[21]

So you are indeed right that God left plenty of room for us to take the raw material of creation and transform it according to our needs and creativity. As technology has advanced throughout human history, so has our ability to transform the world around us. This is all very fine and beneficial when placed at the service of humanity's true good. It makes for better bread and better wine, to use your example. Who doesn't benefit from that?

This is why the *Catechism* describes science and technology as "precious resources." However, they "must be at the service of the human person" and used "in conformity with the plan and the will of God." By themselves science and technology "cannot disclose the meaning of existence and of human progress" and this means "guiding principles cannot be inferred from simple technical efficiency." [22] In other words, just because we *can* do something doesn't mean we *should* do it.

As we learned previously (see chapter seven, question 8), the human body must never be considered "raw material" over which we have dominion. What we do to the human body we do to the human person, and the person is not a "thing" we can manipulate at will. The human person is in a moral category altogether different than subhuman creation over which we have dominion.

We do not violate the dignity of wheat when we turn it into bread. We do not violate the dignity of grapes when we turn them into wine. But we *do* violate the dignity of the human person when we flood the body with hormones and perform mutilating surgeries in an attempt to make someone look like the opposite sex.

Medical intervention upon the human body is only justified when it serves its health, which is to say, its objectively proper functioning. We must never employ science and technology to harm our healthy functioning bodies nor use it in a way that contradicts God's plans and purposes as revealed through our bodies and their proper functioning (see chapter six, question 8 and chapter seven, questions 3–4). This is why bodily mutilation is always against the moral law. [23]

6. There's a spectrum to gender. The very existence of people born with different chromosomal configurations and/or ambiguous genitalia proves it. And that proves that the Catholic position on binary gender is wrong!

As we've observed several times, Catholic teaching on gender has its foundation in God's plan for creating us male and female "in the beginning." This is where we find the blueprint for human nature, not just in regard to gender, but regarding everything else that makes human beings what they are.

Tragically, because of the mystery of humanity's fall into sin, painful anomalies have been introduced into creation that were never part of God's perfect design. He allows them, obviously, but he does not *will* them (see chapter seven, question 3).

We know, for example, that human beings are meant to have arms and legs. Sometimes, however, people are born missing one or more of them. We know, also, that human beings are meant to see, hear, and speak, but sometimes people are born blind, deaf, and mute. It's tragic when birth defects occur precisely because something has gone wrong. Here it's important to recognize that that person's physical development *departed* from the natural order of things; it did not *change* the natural order of things. We still know people are meant to have arms and legs even if some, sadly, are born without them.

It's the same in the rare cases of those with chromosomal disorders or ambiguous genitalia. Disorders of sexual development do not alter the reality of human nature. It remains true that we are meant to be, and are designed by God to be, one sex or the other, even if anomalies are sometimes introduced in our fallen world that can make it unclear to which sex a person belongs.

7. Why does God allow such things? Are those whose sex is unclear at birth just condemned to a life of suffering, of not knowing who they really are?

Your question confronts us with the horror of evil and suffering. No human being can ignore these vexing questions. And no believer can bypass the conundrum of how an all-loving God could possibly allow innocent people to suffer. Why does God turn a blind eye to our misery?

Does he?

By contemplating the mystery of a God who suffers *with* and *for* us in his passion and death, we discover a God who is "rich in mercy" (Ephesians 2:4). *Misericordia*, Latin for mercy, means "a heart which gives itself to those in misery." God never promises to take away our sufferings in this life. But he promises to be *with us* in our misery. He promises us that we can *find him there* and that, in the end, he will bring great good out of our suffering. Indeed, he has already born our misery in his passion and death—all human misery from the beginning to the end of human history, including mine and yours—and transformed it into glory in his Resurrection.

Only from "within" this mystery of Christ's death and Resurrection can we look at all the suffering in the world and in our own lives and still conclude "God is love" (1 John 4:8). As St. John Paul II once wrote, "If the agony on the cross had not happened the truth that God is love would have been unfounded." [24]

The *Catechism* observes that God permits sin and evil in the world "because he respects the freedom of his creatures and, mysteriously, knows how to derive good from it." [25] While birth defects are attributable to the mystery of sin in a general sense (original sin, and what it unleashed on the world), this does *not* mean they are immediately attributable to that person's sinfulness.

Recall that when the disciples saw a man blind from birth and asked Jesus who sinned to cause it, he insisted: "Neither he nor his parents sinned." Rather, he was born blind "so that the works of God might be made visible through him" (John 9:3).

We can certainly say the same about other birth defects, including those rare cases of ambiguous genitalia or chromosomal disorders. God has a plan, yet to be fully revealed in us, for bringing great good out of all the suffering he allows in our lives. And with our faith firmly placed there, we can "consider that the sufferings of this present time are as nothing compared with the glory to be revealed in us" (Romans 8:18)

Medical science can almost always determine the true sex of a child when it is unclear, and surgical intervention is legitimate in the case of correcting actual birth defects. But even in those rare cases when science cannot be certain about the sex of a child, God knows that person's true identity and it will be fully revealed in that person's resurrection. For, as St. John Paul II clarified, the sexual difference will not only be preserved in our resurrected humanity, our creation as male or female will be "newly constituted" in our glorified bodies. [26]

There are many things we can do to help this world become a better place, and, with respect for the plan God wrote into creation, we must work toward that. However, we must be humble enough to recognize that certain problems can only be resolved by God, and we must be patient enough to wait for such resolutions in the next life, lest we seek false remedies and illusory solutions to our problems in this life. The next world is where our true happiness lies. If we hope only for happiness in this world, "we are the most pitiable people of all" (1 Corinthians 15:19).

The Lord has promised to those who trust in his mercy that in the next world every last ounce of evil, sorrow, and suffering will be fully redeemed. "Then the eyes of the blind shall see, and the ears of the deaf be opened; then the lame shall leap like a stag, and the mute tongue sing for joy" (Isaiah 35:5–6). And, we can add, then those whose sex was unclear in this life will be revealed as the man or woman God had always intended them to be. For the Lord "will change our lowly body to conform with his glorified body" (Philippians 3:21).

In this fully redeemed, resurrected state, we will know for certain that God permitted suffering and evil in the world and in our own lives, says the *Catechism*, "only as occasions and means for displaying all the power of his arm and the whole measure of the love he wanted to give the world." [27]

8. When someone is born with ambiguous genitalia, I've heard that doctors will randomly decide one or the other gender based on what's easier in the operating room. Who can decide which gender these children should be?

Only God can decide a person's gender. In the case of a child born with ambiguous genitalia, doctors have a responsibility to determine, as far as is possible, the underlying sex of the child (this can almost always be determined at the chromosomal level). Arbitrary decisions based on expediency have a chance of being wrong about a reality that "is by no means something purely biological, but concerns the innermost being of the human person."[28]

9. Janet meets transgendered Jane (born male). Janet sees Jane as the man he truly is and falls in love with him. Jane, however, continues to live as a transgendered female. Can they still get married in the Church since the Church sees Jane as a man?

Recall from chapter three (see question 6) that a person must be psychologically capable of committing to marriage. As the sacramental alliance of masculinity and femininity, marriage demands and presupposes the acceptance of one's God-given sexual identity. Therefore, an unaddressed deep-seated gender dysphoria would be considered one of those psychological maladies that invalidates marital consent. There is always hope for a person with gender dysphoria to come to a healthy acceptance of his or her God-given sex, but a person who embraces a false sexual identity cannot marry validly.

10. Haven't things changed so dramatically in the modern world that we should just allow for these new perspectives in gender identity out of compassion? Wouldn't God also allow for these new perspectives out of compassion?

Compassion means to "suffer with," or to "suffer together." What is it to which true compassion for those who experience gender dysphoria calls us?

A world of pain and personal trauma lies beneath the failure to identify with one's own body. Divorcing one's identity from one's body does not heal that pain; it only masks it.

As we discussed earlier (see question 2 above), all of us struggle to one degree or another to harmonize the inner and outer realities of our humanity. This means we are all in need of a redemption that heals the rift in us between body and soul. This is the hope that the death and Resurrection of Christ offers the world. There is *real power* flowing through the sacraments to enable us to become the men and women God created us to be "in the beginning." That's where the roots of our humanity lie. The rift in us caused by sin does not define us! Let us never consign ourselves to identify with that rift!

God shows his compassion for us not by "allowing" us to dissociate from our bodies, but by *allowing himself to associate with our bodies*, and, in taking on a body, absorbing all the sorrow and suffering we endure because of that painful rift of body and soul. This is what Christ's death *is*. And his Resurrection is the open door to the hope of the healing of our rift, too.

This is the true hope not just of those who experience gender dysphoria. This is the true hope of every human being who longs for life and life to the full.

11. How should we respond to those who insist on being addressed with pronouns that don't reflect who they really are or that are constructed for the sole purpose of being "non-binary" (like ze, zer instead of he or her)? Many governments are now enforcing laws that label refusals to use preferred pronouns as "hate-speech."

Allow me to call to mind a key line from the statement of Pope Francis with which we began this chapter. He observed that it is "one thing to be understanding of human weakness and the complexities of life." Those who prefer pronouns that do not correspond to their God-given bodily identity are, indeed, caught in a painful web of complex difficulties that call for our patience and understanding. However, it's another thing, Francis continued, "to accept ideologies that attempt to sunder what are inseparable aspects of reality."

Those who insist on being addressed with pronouns that do not correspond to their God-given bodily identity have not only accepted such ideologies themselves, they are demanding that others do so as well. As you note, they have even successfully lobbied certain governments to make it a criminal offense if others do not accept such ideologies. Here we can see very clearly how freedom loosed from truth becomes tyranny. If there is no objective reality to which we are all answerable, then those with the most power will impose their own subjective ideology on everyone else (see question 3 above).

Those who wish to remain faithful to the truth mustn't succumb to these ideologies. In our dealings with others, we should always be of the mind of wanting to help them come to an acceptance of the truth about themselves, and that has direct bearing on the language we use to refer to people. Of course, the appropriate means for helping others come to the acceptance of truth may differ from case to case.

As a general rule, I think maintaining the use of pronouns that refer to a person's God-given bodily identity is appropriate. That said, we are called to bear with one another (see Ephesians 4:2 and Colossians 3:13) and I have encountered situations in which the patient endurance of another's error (which is not the same as assenting to another's error) seemed warranted.

I have in mind a faithful Christian minister I know who cared for the destitute and the homeless. It was obvious when a certain person came to his center for help that he was a male presenting himself as a female. When he signed in with a female name, the minister did not press him for his real name. That would not have been appropriate to their relationship at that stage. Over time, however, as he got to know the person's story and earn his trust, he learned his male name and eventually began to use it, along with corresponding pronouns. Both the minister's willingness to bear with him in his confusion and the minister's decision, at the right time, to use his given name were instrumental in helping this man come to terms with his God-given identity.

In short, receiving people in a given pastoral moment may mean accepting the use of names and pronouns that do not correspond to their God-given identity. However, we cannot pretend that the journey into deepening self-honesty ends there.

12. How should faithful Catholics treat friends or family members who experience gender dysphoria?[29]

Faithful Catholics should love them with all of their hearts and, above all, let them know that God loves them with all of his heart. They should let them know that they're willing to journey with them through their suffering (remember compassion means to "suffer with") without encouraging illusory remedies for that suffering. They should bear with them in the midst of their struggles and do all they can to be an inspirational, joyful light pointing to the truth (even when it is difficult to do so).

Those who adopt a transgender identity are attracted to the narrative that that ideology proposes. They see it as a way out of their sufferings and a way into a community of other people like them who will embrace them unconditionally. Who *wouldn't* find that attractive, especially when people (wrongly) perceive the Church's vision as oppressive and (often rightly) perceive Christian communities as judgmental and rejecting of those who don't "measure up"?

We must be convinced deep in our bones that the Church's true vision of human life is *far more attractive* than any other vision the world has to offer, and we must learn how to share that vision with others in all its liberating splendor. Furthermore, we must build genuine Christian communities where everyone is welcomed on equal footing—not based on a worldly "I'm OK/you're OK" mentality, but on the truthful recognition that "I'm broken and you're broken," and we are all equally in need of a savior. We must all allow Jesus to take us on the journey of becoming totally reliant on his mercy, like the poor sinner who cried out from his depths and was heard while the self-righteous Pharisee pretended to pray, but only boasted of his own accomplishments before God (see Luke 18:9–14).

In view of the above, faithful Catholics can lead those who have adopted a transgender identity to resources that seek faithfully and joyfully to unfold Catholic teaching on what it means to be human (see also the resources listed in chapter ten, question 10). They can lead them to resources like *Eden Invitation* and ministries like Desert Stream and its *Living Waters* program that help people open the roots of their personal and relational brokenness to Christ's healing light within a welcoming, nonjudgmental community of fellow journeyers.

Of course, people cannot be forced to pursue integration with their God-given gender, but all can be encouraged. And we should take heart in the many persons who through Christ and his Church have experienced the grace to detach from a long cultivated "self" of the opposite sex. Today they walk on the splendid journey toward authentic self-acceptance.

13. My nine-year-old son has always had a sensitive temperament and has always seemed threatened around other boys, especially more physical and aggressive ones. I've found him wearing his sister's clothes and when his teacher recently asked him what he wanted to be when he grew up he said he wanted to be a woman. Now the teachers and staff at his school are encouraging him to embrace his "true identity as a girl" and my priest seems unequipped to help. I don't know what to do or where to turn.

The first thing I would encourage you to do as a person of faith is prayerfully entrust your son's precious and unrepeatable heart to the hearts of Jesus and Mary. They know and share the cry of your heart for your son's well-being and they have full knowledge of God's perfect plan to bring a greater good out of this trial than would have been possible without it.

Recall the train analogy I used at the start of this chapter (i.e., we all need healthy models of gender identification and gender complementarity for our train to stay on track). When we purify ourselves of the hyper-pious and almost inhuman images many people have of Jesus and Mary and rediscover their authentic, incarnate humanity, we discover that they provide the perfect tracks of gender identification and complementarity. As his mother, you have spiritual authority that you can exercise in prayer to place your son's train, so to speak, on those tracks. Pray a prayer something like this every day for your son:

Jesus, you are the perfect track of gender identification for my son, and, Mary, you are the perfect track of gender complementarity for him. I entrust his fragile sense of himself as a boy to your merciful love and care. You know all the contours of his precious, unrepeatable heart—his wounds, his fears, his hopes, and dreams—and you know how to reach him there. Please reveal yourselves to him. Please show him the goodness of his being a boy in a way that he can know it and embrace it as the divine gift that it is, and help him grow into the man he's created to be. Amen.

In addition to the importance of prayer, your son's situation could benefit greatly from proper professional attention. Both Pastoral Solutions Institute and CatholicPsych Institute are trustworthy organizations that will steer you in the right direction (an Internet search will lead you to them).

I'd also encourage you to educate yourself on the issues. For starters, I have found Ryan T. Anderson's book *When Harry Became Sally: Responding to the Transgender Moment* a very helpful resource. It has an entire chapter devoted to the issue of childhood gender dysphoria. I'm sure you'll be encouraged by Anderson's well-documented finding that "the vast majority of children with gender dysphoria—80 to 95 percent—naturally grow out of it, if they aren't encouraged to transition." [30]

Since the teachers and staff at his school *are* encouraging him to transition, I think it is important to remove him from that environment as soon as possible. At an age when he is especially susceptible to the influence of adults, it is very important that he be surrounded by those who know how to guide him sensitively into a proper understanding of his God-given identity as a boy and paint an appropriate picture of growing into a man that attracts his unique heart and affirms his individuality.

As Anderson reports, gender dysphoria in children can be a sign of anxiety about the roles, attitudes, or characteristics they mistakenly assume are a fixed part of their sex, but are actually rooted in rigid and misleading stereotypes. Hence, as he observes, "Part of an effective treatment plan for gender dysphoria in children is to cultivate a mature and nuanced view of gender, so the child understands that there are various ways to be real boys and real girls." For example, we shouldn't promote "rigid stereotypes that might lead a boy to think he should be a girl because he is sensitive and artistic, or a girl to think she might be a boy because she prefers sports over dolls. Acknowledging the richly diverse ways of being male and female," Anderson counsels, "can help children more readily identify with and accept their own embodiment." [31]

Pope Francis made the same point when he observed that a rigid approach to certain gender roles

> turns into an overaccentuation of the masculine or feminine, and does not help children…to appreciate the genuine reciprocity [of men and women]. Such rigidity, in turn, can hinder the development of an individual's abilities, to the point of leading him or her to think, for example, that it is not really masculine to cultivate art or dance, or not very feminine to exercise leadership.[32]

None of this implies falling into androgyny, of course. That's just the other extreme of rigid stereotypes. For a balanced view of gender, as Anderson advises, we need to allow boys and girls to express both their individuality *and* their sex-based differences.[33] And, in terms of educating yourself in this balanced view, I know of no resource that is richer, more insightful, or more liberating than St. John Paul II's Theology of the Body, the importance of which I highlight in my answer to the next (related) question. There I also place your trial in a wider spiritual context and outline the divine plan for victory, our only true hope.

14. How are faithful Catholics to make sense out of what's going on in the world today? I'm fearful for my kids who are getting indoctrinated with "gender theory" at school. What can we do to protect our children from all this confusion and how can we turn the tide in the wider culture?

Jesus invites us to read "the signs of the times" (Matthew 16:3). As St. John Paul II unfolds so compellingly in his Theology of the Body, the greatest sign we've been given in all of creation is the human body in its masculinity and femininity—and in our times this great sign is under violent attack. How are we to "read" this?

The following statement might be one of the most important and profound things I say in this entire book, so you'll want to pay attention. It's no coincidence that Ephesians 6 comes *after* Ephesians 5. Stupid joke aside, the connection between these two chapters is indeed quite important if we are to understand the signs of the times. I'll unfold that connection and then use it as a launching point to address your question.

What do we learn in Ephesians 5? We learn that the union of husband and wife in "one flesh" is a "great mystery" that refers to Christ and the Church (see Ephesians 5:31–32). And this "great mystery," St. John Paul II tells us, is "the central theme of the whole of revelation, its central reality. It is what God…wishes above all to transmit to mankind in his Word."[34]

What does God wish above all to tell us in his Word? He loves us. He loves us as a Father and brother and friend, to be sure. But he loves us in a particular way as a Bridegroom. In fact, we could summarize the entire Bible with these five words: "God wants to marry us." When we proclaim Christ's saving love to others, we are proclaiming the love of the eternal Bridegroom for his Bride and we are inviting them to say "yes" to heaven's marriage proposal.

As we've been learning throughout this book, God wanted this eternal "marital plan" to be so plain to us, he stamped an image of it right in our bodies by making us male and female and calling the two to become "one flesh." For those with eyes to see, *this* is the good news about sex, gender, and marriage: they reveal the eternal plan of God for the universe.

The divine Word is inscribed in our flesh. Not only that: the divine Word *became flesh*—male flesh, born of female flesh (it's always male and female together that reveal the "great mystery")—in order to make known to us the plan of God's mystery that all things would be made one, consummated in Christ (see Ephesians 1:9–10).

Here's the problem: There is an enemy of this Word, an anti-Word, who is hell-bent on turning the *great mystery* of human sexuality into a *great misery*. "The devil (*dia-bolos*) is the one who 'throws himself across' God's plan" as the *Catechism* puts it.[35] Lucifer, created by God as the brightest and most glorious of all the angels (*Lucifer* means "angel of light"), fell out of envy, as we learned in chapter one. In his pride he could not accept that God would take on flesh, thereby divinizing the human body and raising it higher than the angels (see Hebrews 1:1–14).

And so, from the beginning, his diabolic fury has been aimed at our bodies—more specifically at our gender (our ability to generate offspring). Most specifically, his enmity has been aimed at woman, since her fertility would give flesh to the One who would "crush his head" (see Genesis 3:15).

Which brings us to Ephesians 6. There St. Paul follows up his presentation of the good news about sex and marriage by basically saying, "If you want to live what I was just telling you about, get ready for a war." Then he outlines the plan for victory.

1. *Know your enemy.* To win a battle, we have to know whom we are fighting and what kind of battle it is. Righteous anger at your children's school board, the teachers, or those who lobbied to infuse the curriculum with "gender theory" is understandable, even justifiable, but they are not the enemy. This is a spiritual battle for the life of the world and the enemy is *the* Enemy: "For our struggle is not with flesh and blood but...with evil spirits"

(Ephesians 6:12). Those responsible for this curriculum are caught up in a web of deception that ultimately comes from the father of lies. If we fight the wrong battles, against the wrong forces, with the wrong weapons, we'll lose.

2. *"Draw your strength from the Lord and from his mighty power"* (Ephesians 6:10). In other words, don't rely on your own powers to win this battle (you'll be taken out). The spiritual forces we are fighting are much stronger than we are, but they are *nothing* compared to God's "mighty power" which has already defeated the enemy. We need to heed Christ's instruction to Peter: "Put your sword back into its sheath..." (Matthew 26:52) and learn the mysterious "way" of Christ's victory—a victory that comes by way of an apparent defeat. Only by allowing Christ's way of victory to reign in us can we, too, "crush his head."

3. *"Put on the armor of God so that you may be able to stand firm against the tactics of the devil"* (Ephesians 6:11). And do you know what the *first* piece of armor is that the apostle invites us to don? Before the helmet of salvation, before the shield of faith and the breastplate of righteousness, St. Paul exhorts us to *gird our loins with the truth* (see Ephesians 6:14–17).

The Enemy has been after our loins since the beginning, to divert us from speaking the truth of divine love in order to speak his own language—lies! Here we find ourselves "at the center of the great struggle between good and evil, between life and death, between love and all that is opposed to love."[36] In fact, John Paul II believed that the modern world may now be "experiencing the highest level of tension between the Word and the anti-Word in the whole of human history."[37]

How do we recognize the Word? He's the One manifested in the flesh (see John 1:14). How do we recognize the anti-Word? He's the one who attacks God's Word manifested in the flesh (see 1 John 4:2–3; 2 John 1:7). Yes, it's a spiritual battle we're fighting, but the battleground is the human body and the divine secret it reveals.

If we are to protect our children from the confusion descending on the world and make any difference in the wider culture, we must understand how the Enemy gained access to the divine message inscribed in our bodies. In the twentieth century, a Trojan horse, shall we say, entered the City of God. Christians the world over opted to gird their loins with the lies of latex rather than the truth of the Trinity. And now in the twenty-first century—as was foretold by wise men and women who understood the power of contraception to disorient civilization at its roots (see chapter six, question 14)—we reap the whirlwind.

But let us never forget that where sin abounds, grace abounds even more (see Romans 5:20). Another sign of the times is a great outpouring of divine mercy. *Misericordia*: a heart that gives itself to those in misery (see question 7 above). This is the Lord's heart toward *all of us* in these terribly confused and confusing times. In fact, the Lord takes our misery upon himself—unto the most gruesome death—to save us from it. Unfathomable as it is to human wisdom, this is God's path to victory over evil: the apparent defeat of the Bridegroom.

We must ponder this anew if we are to understand what is happening in our world today. The good news about sex and marriage, it would seem, is going the way of its prime exemplar. It's being put on trial, condemned, mocked, rejected, spat upon, scourged, and crucified. But when things are as dark as dark can be, victory is right around the corner. Give it "three days" and watch what happens.

We don't know how and we don't know when, but this we do know: After this great trial, God's plan for man and woman will somehow be resurrected "and all flesh will see the salvation of God" (Luke 3:6). Then the sun of justice will arise with its healing rays (see Malachi 3:20) and, we can hope, our confused world will be reoriented toward the light.

That's what the sun does: It *orients* us. And that's why the Bride (the Church) traditionally prays toward the east (the Orient), because the rising of the sun, as Scripture says, symbolizes the coming of the Bridegroom (see Psalm 19:5).

In a world that believes in an infinite number of sexual identities and orientations, the Catholic Church continues faithfully to hold out a vision of sexual identity that's *oriented toward the Infinite*. The body in its sexuality is an icon, a sign that's meant to point us to the Infinite satisfaction for which we yearn. When we aim our yearning for the Infinite at the finite, however, the icon degenerates into an idol.

That's how the sexual revolution began, with the promise that unfettered sexual indulgence would provide ultimate fulfillment. But idols can never deliver on the promises we invest in them. This is why we eventually come to despise whatever we idolize. That's where we are today—on the final lap, it seems, of the sexual revolution. What began by worshipping the body and sexuality is now ending with a violent hatred of the same. (When it's in vogue to mutilate the body and amputate its sexual organs, how else can we describe it?)

If we are to protect our children from the confusion descending on the world and turn the tide in the wider culture, we must recover a sense of *primordial wonder* at the divinely inspired beauty of the human body. We must come to recognize in the human body the revelation of the human *person* whose dignity demands he never be used or manipulated (let alone mutilated). We must rediscover *the treasure* of human sexuality as a stupendous sign of God's image in our humanity, and as an invitation to human freedom to live this image through the sincere gift of one's life in marriage or in celibacy for the Kingdom (see next chapter for a discussion on Christian celibacy). And we do all of the above by prayerfully pondering the good news about sex, gender, and marriage found in divine revelation. [38]

For such a time as this have we been given St. John Paul II's Theology of the Body. Yes, the Holy Spirit has provided the theological antidote for the sexual chaos and gender confusion that's sweeping our world like a virus. But theological antidotes are useless if we do not inject them into our bloodstream. This book is a good start, but I cannot encourage you enough: If you really want to protect your children and make a difference in the wider world, continue immersing yourself in St. John Paul II's Theology of the Body and educate your children in that vision.[39] This book has only scratched the surface. (See chapter ten, question 10 for a list of suggested resources that will help you continue the adventure.)

"We are certainly not seduced," John Paul II wrote, "by the naive expectation that, faced with the great challenges of our time, we shall find some magic formula." [40] No, the Theology of the Body is not some magic formula. Its power lies in the fact that, if we let it, it will lead us into ever deeper intimacy with Christ the Bridegroom where we learn to rest in "the assurance which he gives us: *I am with you!*"[41] It is this assurance that is our hope and salvation.

10

Saying "I Do" to God Alone

Sex and the Celibate Vocation

Then I saw a new heaven and a new earth; for the first heaven and the first earth had passed away, and the sea was no more. And I saw the holy city, new Jerusalem, coming down out of heaven from God, prepared as a bride adorned for her husband; and I heard a great voice from the throne saying, "Behold, the dwelling of God is with men." [1]

—St. John the Apostle

Sex and the celibate vocation? Isn't that a contradiction of terms? More aptly, it's a *paradox*.

We can't understand the Christian mystery without facing the tension of paradox. We must affirm the truth of one God in three Persons; of the Man who is also God; of the Virgin who is also Mother. In marriage, two become one flesh. In our walk with God, we must die to live, surrender to be free, lose our lives to find them.

These are not the teachings of a schizophrenic God or a Church gone mad. If they strike us as "double-speak," it's because we are not accustomed to making peace within the realm of mystery.

Marriage, sex, and the celibate vocation reveal a "great mystery" and are much more interrelated than we might first think. They're also interdependent. When each is given proper esteem and respect, the delicate balance among them is maintained.

On the other hand, if any of the three (marriage, sex, or celibacy) is devalued, overvalued, or otherwise disrespected, the others inevitably suffer. It's no mere coincidence, for example, that the sexual revolution brought both a dramatic rise in divorce *and* a dramatic decline in vocations to the priesthood and religious life. Nor is it mere coincidence that historical misinterpretations of the celibate vocation have led to a disparagement of sex and marriage.

All such error stems from failure to deal with the tension of paradox. There's something mentally torturous about reconciling the (seemingly) irreconcilable poles of paradox. So to avoid the discomfort we focus on one aspect of truth and end up denying others.

But it's precisely by *pressing into* the tension of paradox that we discover the fullness of truth. We must find our home in that tension. Only then can we properly understand the profound interrelationship among marriage, sex, and the celibate vocation.

1. If the call to "spousal love" reveals the fundamental truth of our existence and the way we fulfill ourselves as human beings, why does the Church promote celibacy?

At first glance, it seems as if the Church's promotion of celibacy is a contradiction of everything we've said about the dignity and importance of sex and marriage. Upon further investigation, however, we discover that the celibate vocation is actually the ultimate *fulfillment* of everything we've discussed.

As a sacrament, the "one flesh" union of marriage is only a sign and foreshadowing of things to come. According to the analogy, we're created for spousal union with God. That's what sexual desire ultimately points us to—our desire for heaven.

There, Christ will make a gift of himself to humanity in a beatifying experience completely beyond anything proper to earthly life. Our reciprocal gift of self will be our response to the gift of the Bridegroom.[2] The marriage of divinity and humanity will be eternally consummated (see chapter three, question 19).

Only by looking toward this heavenly reality can we properly understand the celibate vocation. As we read in the Gospel, Christ calls some of his followers to embrace celibacy, not for celibacy's sake but "for the sake of the kingdom" (Matthew 19:12). "The kingdom" is precisely *the heavenly marriage*. In short, those who choose celibacy are "skipping" the sacrament in anticipation of the real thing. By expressing the "I do" of a marriage commitment directly to God, celibates step beyond the dimension of history—while living within the dimension of history—and dramatically declare to the world that the kingdom of God is here (see Matthew 12:28).

Both vocations, then, in their own particular way, are a fulfillment of the call to "spousal love" revealed through our bodies. As St. John Paul II wrote: "On the basis of the same spousal meaning of being, as a body, male or female, there can be formed the love that commits man to marriage for the whole duration of his life (see Matthew 19:3–9), but there can be formed also the love that commits man for his whole life to continence 'for the kingdom of heaven' (see Matthew 19:11–12)."[3]

We can't escape the call of our sexuality. Every man, by virtue of the fact that he's a man, is called in one way or another to be both a husband and a father; and every woman, by virtue of the fact that she's a woman, is called in one way or another to be both a wife and a mother. Celibate men become an icon of Christ; their bride is the Church. Celibate women become an icon of the Church; their bridegroom is Christ. And both bear many spiritual children.

Thus the terms husband, father, brother, son and the terms wife, mother, sister, daughter are just as applicable to the celibate vocation as they are to marriage and family life. Both vocations are indispensable in building the family of God. Each vocation complements the other and demonstrates the other's meaning. Marriage reveals the spousal character of celibacy, and celibacy reveals that the ultimate purpose of marriage is to prepare us for heaven.

2. Does the Church still teach that celibacy is a "higher" calling than marriage?

Yes, but this must be carefully qualified. History has seen some grave distortions of St. Paul's teaching that he who marries does "well," but he who refrains does "better" (see 1 Corinthians 7:38). It's led some to view marriage as a second-class vocation for those who can't handle celibacy. It's also solidified people's erroneous suspicions that sex is inherently tainted, and that only those who abstain can be truly "holy." Such errors led St. John Paul II to assert firmly that the "superiority" of celibacy *"never means in the authentic tradition of the Church a disparagement of marriage* or a belittling of its essential value."[4]

Celibacy is "better" than marriage only in the sense that heaven is better than earth. Remember that celibacy is not a *sacrament* of heaven on earth. It's more of an immediate participation even now in the heavenly marriage. But this shouldn't lead those who are called to marriage to devalue their vocation.

Celibacy is "better" only in the objective sense. Subjectively speaking, the better vocation is the one to which a person is called by God. As St. Paul puts it, "Each has his own special gift from God, one of one kind and one of another" (1 Corinthians 7:7).

Each of us should respond to the gift we've been given. If we're called to celibacy, then we shouldn't choose marriage. If we're called to marriage, then we shouldn't choose celibacy. Hence the important need to discern our vocation prayerfully.

3. Why can't married men become priests?

Actually, they *can*. We often forget in the West that there are many Eastern Rite Churches that have married priests. They are no less priests than priests of the Roman rite, which maintains a celibate priesthood. Furthermore, in some cases, married priests from other denominations (Anglican, for example) who convert to the Catholic faith are able to be ordained as married priests in the Roman rite.

Thus celibacy isn't essential to a valid priesthood. It's simply a discipline upheld in the Western Church in order to conform more closely to the example of Christ.

Christ was not married to one particular woman because he came to marry *the whole human race*. The Church is his eternal Bride. Ordained priests become a sacrament of Christ. They make the love of the heavenly Bridegroom efficaciously present to the Church, particularly in the Eucharistic sacrifice. Acting in the person of Christ, priests also marry the Church.

This important symbolism is better retained when a priest is not also married to a particular woman. As St. Paul said, the celibate is not "divided" in his service, but is able to devote himself entirely to the service of the Church (see 1 Corinthians 7:32–34).

I think it's unfortunate in some ways that we define celibacy with a word that points to what the person has given up rather than defining it in terms of what the celibate person has *embraced*. Much confusion could be avoided if we described the celibate vocation as the "heavenly marriage," for instance. This is the marriage in which priests and all consecrated celibate persons participate.

4. Celibacy is simply unnatural. It's no wonder that so many priests have sexual problems. This type of scandal would end if priests were allowed to marry.

In some sense, you're right to say celibacy is *un*-natural. As Christ reveals, celibacy is *super*-natural. It's celibacy for the sake of the kingdom. By calling some to renounce the natural call to marriage, Christ established an entirely new way of life, and in doing so, he demonstrated the power of the cross to transform lives.

For those who are stuck in a fallen view of sex with no concept of the freedom to which we're called in Christ, the idea of lifelong celibacy is complete nonsense. But for those who understand and embrace Christ's call to experience the transformation of their sexual desires, the idea of making a complete gift of our sexuality to God not only becomes a possibility; it becomes very attractive. The celibate vocation is *not* a rejection of sexuality. If some approach it this way, according to St. John Paul II, they're not living in accord with Christ's words.[5]

Celibacy is a grace, a gift. Only a small minority of Christ's followers are given this gift. But those who *are* given this gift are also given the grace to be faithful to their vows, just as married couples are given the grace to be faithful to their vows.

In both vocations people can and do reject this grace and violate their vows. Certainly there's a need in the typical Catholic diocese for greater openness about sexual woundedness and for development and promotion of ministries that bring Christ's healing to those in need, including priests. But the solution to marital and celibate infidelity is not to concede to human weakness and redefine the nature of the commitments. The solution is to point to the cross as the font of grace that it is, a font from which we can drink freely and receive *real power* to live and love as we're called.

Furthermore, the statistical rates of sexual misconduct among celibate priests are no higher than that of clergy in Christian denominations who are allowed to marry. There is absolutely no evidence that allowing priests to marry would solve or even alleviate this problem.

There's also a dangerously misguided approach to marriage inherent in the idea that marriage is the solution to the sexual scandal of priests. As has been stressed throughout this book, marriage does not provide a "legitimate outlet" for disordered sexual desire. Celibacy does not *cause* sexual disorder. Sin does. Simply getting married does not *cure* sexual disorder. Christ does. If a priest, or any other man, were to enter marriage with deep-seated sexual disorders, he would be condemning his wife to a life of sexual objectification. The only way the scandal of sexual sin (whether committed by priests or others) will end is if people learn how to open their sexual brokenness to the power of redemption flowing from the death and resurrection of Christ.

5. Why can't women be priests?

For many women, the fact that the Catholic Church reserves priestly ordination to men stirs a cauldron of intense emotion fired by the "historical consciousness" of women's oppression. Only in recent years, it seems, has the Church been willing to acknowledge and ask forgiveness for the fact that, as St. John Paul II expressed in his *Letter to Women*, "objective blame [for this oppression], especially in particular historical contexts, has belonged to not just a few members of the Church. May this regret," he continues, "be transformed, on the part of the whole Church, into a renewed commitment of fidelity to the Gospel vision."[6]

This Gospel vision is precisely what we've been discussing throughout this book: the great "spousal mystery" of Christ's union with the Church symbolized from the beginning by our creation as male and female. Fidelity to this vision calls us to uphold woman's dignity at every turn and to resist the ways in which gender roles have been exaggerated to favor men. But it also calls us to resist the other extreme that views men and women as interchangeable.

As mentioned previously, equality between the sexes doesn't mean *sameness*. It's the fundamental *difference* of the sexes that reveals the great "spousal mystery." It's the fundamental *difference* of the sexes that quite literally brings life to the world.

A culture that levels this difference is a culture committing suicide, a culture of death. Professor Stanislaw Grygiel, former vice-president of the John Paul II Institute for Studies on Marriage and Family, aptly described the danger of a "unisex" world in the quote that begins the previous chapter. As a preface to that statement, he said that to understand "the miracle of sexual difference...is the beginning of a path in which we discover the ultimate and fundamental difference for human beings: the difference between God and Man."[7] To blur sexual difference is to blur the great spousal mystery: the call to life-giving communion between man and woman, and between God and us.

Men and women have different callings in this life-giving communion. It's the bridegroom who gives the seed or inseminates; it's the bride who receives the seed within and conceives new life. The physical truth reveals the spiritual truth. A man trains to be a priest in the *seminary* and, once ordained, is called *father*. A woman cannot be ordained a priest because she is not ordained by God to be a father; she is ordained by God to be a mother. This is where the sexual difference matters—in the call to holy communion and generation. If a woman were to attempt to confer the Eucharist, the relationship would be bride to bride. There would be no possibility of Holy Communion and no possibility of generating new life.

Of course, a world that insists two women can marry will also insist that a woman can be a priest, but both ideas come from the same failure to recognize the essential meaning of the sexual difference. Since grace builds on nature, when we're confused about the natural reality, we're also confused about the supernatural reality: "If I have told you earthly things and you do not believe," asks Jesus, "how can you believe if I tell you heavenly things?" (John 3:12).

The more deeply we enter into the "great mystery" of Christ's spousal love for the Church (see Ephesians 5), the more we will see how and why the sexual difference is just as important to the Holy Communion of the Eucharist as it is to the holy communion of marriage. As St. John Paul II reminded us: "It is *the Eucharist* that above all expresses *the redemptive act of Christ the Bridegroom towards the Church, the Bride.* This is clear and unambiguous when the sacramental ministry of the Eucharist, in which the priest acts 'in the person of Christ,' is performed by a man."[8] Here, through the masculinity of the priest and the feminine mystery of the Church, we recognize that the "*Eucharist is...the sacrament of the Bridegroom and of the Bride.*"[9]

Men and women must receive the calling they've been given as a gift from God if they are ever to be at peace with themselves. Should men complain that God hasn't given them the amazing privilege of carrying a child in the womb? For a woman to complain that she can't be an ordained priest is just as misguided.

6. If even men become the "bride of Christ" as members of the Church, why can't women become the bridegroom as a priest?

First let me offer a brief discussion of the masculine and feminine principles in each of us. If it's male and female *together* that encompasses what's fully human, and if every man and woman is not merely half human but *fully* human, then it's proper to conclude that every man and woman is in some way an interior "marriage" of that which is masculine and that which is feminine. Thus in some sense we can speak of feminine principles in men and masculine principles in women. Still, this interior marriage manifests itself as essentially *male* in men and *female* in women.

The Church, in turn, as a "corporate person," is a marriage of men and women that manifests itself essentially as *feminine,* as *Bride.* There are masculine and feminine principles in this Bride in which both men and women partake. So, as much as men become "bride" as members of the Church, women also become "priest" as members of the priesthood of all believers (see 1 Peter 2:9). Every baptized man *and woman* participates in Christ's priesthood by living a sacrificial life in union with him.

But we enter a different realm altogether as soon as we talk about an individual person becoming an efficacious sign of a spiritual reality. For sacraments to be efficacious, the physical reality must properly symbolize the spiritual reality. For instance, if someone said the baptismal formula while pouring motor oil over a person's head, there would be no sacrament because the cleansing symbolism of water is necessary to bring about the spiritual cleansing from sin. Without an accurate symbol (motor oil symbolizes making dirty), nothing happens in the spiritual realm.[10]

Women certainly do participate in the priesthood of all believers (just as men participate in the "bridehood" of all believers). However, women individually are the proper sign of the Church, the Bride; they are not the proper sign of the Bridegroom. Hence, if a bishop proclaimed the words of priestly ordination over a woman, nothing would happen in the spiritual realm to make her a priest in the *sacramental* sense. This is why it's not a matter of the Church's stubborn unwillingness to ordain women to the priesthood. It's a matter of *impossibility*.

7. Didn't St. Paul say there is no longer male or female, but all are one in Christ Jesus?

Yes (see Galatians 3:28). But how do we become *one* in Christ Jesus? Specifically through the *difference* of the sexes. Sexual union symbolizes union in Christ. Husband and wife are no longer two (male and female) but one. Yet the only way they can become one is by being *male* and *female* in the first place. Thus St. Paul is not leveling sexual difference but showing where it leads (or, at least, where it is meant to lead)—to unity in Christ.

8. I'm single. If "spousal love" is so important, what about me?

There's a difference, I'd say, between a person who chooses to remain single in the world in order to devote himself or herself to worthy causes and a person who is single not by choice but by circumstance. The former has made a vocational choice in some ways parallel to the celibate vocation and, by living a life in service to others, is fulfilling the call to make a sincere gift of self in imitation of Christ. The latter is, in some sense, still waiting to make that definitive gift of self.

This doesn't mean that the latter person's life need remain on hold. He or she can live a very fruitful life as a gift to others while maintaining the hope of one day finding a spouse and making a definitive vocational choice.

In any case, no one should think his or her life is meaningless without a spouse. The ultimate meaning of life is *heavenly marriage*. This is the gift

Christ offers *everyone*—the gift of his very self.

Accepting this gift and giving ourselves back to Christ is how we *all* fulfill our call to spousal love, whether we're married or not. In fact, if we're seeking our ultimate fulfillment in earthly marriage, we're setting ourselves up for serious disillusionment. As the saying goes, never hang your hat on a hook that cannot bear the weight. Peace comes in our lives only in as much as we learn how to direct that "ache" we all feel for love and union toward the Love and Union that alone can satisfy: the Marriage of the Lamb.

> *Lord, help me, especially in my times of deepest loneliness, to trust in your promise of everlasting love and fulfillment. Direct my desires according to your design so I can reach my destiny: the communion of the saints in communion with the Communion of the Trinity for all eternity. Amen.*

9. Why does the Church say Joseph and Mary never had sex? The Bible itself says Jesus had brothers.

While Scripture speaks of Jesus's brothers in various passages (see Matthew 12:47; Mark 3:31), "brothers" for the Jewish people often referred not only to people who shared the same parents, but to other close relatives. Hence, as the *Catechism* observes,

> The Church has always understood these passages as not referring to other children of the Virgin Mary. In fact James and Joseph, "brothers of Jesus," are the sons of another Mary, a disciple of Christ, whom St. Matthew significantly calls "the other Mary." They are close relations of Jesus, according to an Old Testament expression.[11]

Many tend to think of the Church's teaching on Mary's perpetual virginity as proof of the Church's negativity toward sex. Some very confused Christians may give that impression, but nothing could be further from the truth! As the French philosopher Fabrice Hadjadj rightly insists, "Mary's virginity is not a rejection of sexuality as is frequently thought, but, on the contrary, its most perfect fulfillment. Mary is not asexual, but a woman made of blood and bone."

Sexuality, Hadjadj continues, "is above all an opening onto transcendence. It is, which is especially important here, a fertile opening. It enters into a drama and this drama is connected with being fruitful. In Mary this opening is radical. She reveals that the essence of sexuality is not a passing pleasure, but being open to...God himself." Hence, Hadjadj concludes that "in the case of Mary we are dealing with the revelation of the very essence of sexuality."[12]

This is what Joseph and Mary's celibate marriage is all about: the full revelation of the very essence of sexuality understood as a call to union with the divine. Mary, having virginally conceived God's Son, was given the unique privilege of already living on earth a certain consummation of the eternal nuptials. To have engaged in sexual relations with Joseph would have been a step backward from the heavenly reality toward the earthly sign. Instead of stepping backward, it's as if Mary reached out to Joseph and said, "Let me take you *forward* with me into these eternal nuptials!"

St. John Paul II spoke about the difficulty for many of accepting "the sublime mystery" of Joseph and Mary's spousal love. How could anyone with a young man's libido, the sentiment goes, have lived in the same house with the most beautiful woman God ever created and honor her vow of perpetual virginity?

One way of dealing with this "difficulty," wrote John Paul II, was "to think of Joseph as advanced in age and to consider him Mary's guardian more than her husband." But this approach fails to recognize the real possibility of sexual virtue, the real possibility of inner transformation of desire. We overcome the "difficulty" of Joseph and Mary's virginal marriage by "supposing that he was not an elderly man at the time," but by recognizing that "his interior perfection, the fruit of grace, led him to live his spousal relationship with Mary with virginal affection."[13]

Virginal affection means *pure* affection. When the Church gives Joseph the title "Most Chaste Spouse," this does *not* mean he was fearful or prudish with regard to his masculinity and Mary's femininity. It means he was pure. It means he saw the mystery of God revealed through himself and his wife and the Son she bore.

Reread question 1 of chapter four where we defined chastity. Joseph had *that* virtue in its highest degree, making his celibacy not only possible, but joyful, because he understood it as "a promise of immortality."[14]

Yet, in order to get to that place of freedom and joy, Joseph himself had to work through various questions and fears. St. John Paul II reflects:

I think that every man, whatever his station in life or his life's vocation, must at some point hear those words which Joseph of Nazareth once heard: "Do not be afraid to take Mary to yourself" (Matthew 1:20). "Do not be afraid to take" means *do everything to recognize that gift which she is for you*. Fear only one thing: that you try to appropriate that gift. That is what you should fear. As long as she remains a gift from God himself to you, you can safely rejoice in all that she is as that gift. What is more, you ought even to do everything you can to recognize that gift, to show her how unique a treasure she is.... Perhaps God wills that it be you who is the one who tells her of her inestimable worth and special beauty. If that is the case, do not be afraid. [15]

God gave Joseph and Mary an exceptional calling: to live the marital vocation *and* the celibate vocation *at the same time*. Remember what the celibate vocation is? It's the heavenly marriage. Joseph and Mary's celibate marriage is the marriage of the earthly marriage and the heavenly marriage. *It's the marriage of heaven and earth.*

And what's the fruit of their marriage? The marriage of heaven and earth: *the Word made flesh*—Jesus Christ, the center of the universe and of history.[16]

This is why the Church's teaching on sex is good news. From the beginning, the "one flesh" union of Adam and Eve was a foreshadowing of the union of God and Man in the flesh of Jesus Christ; it was a foreshadowing of the Incarnation. God created sex as the fundamental revelation in creation of his plan of life and love—his plan to marry us by becoming one in the flesh with us.

This is the great "spousal mystery" of the universe in which we're all called to participate. This is why we crave sexual union: beneath it all we're craving union with God. And this is why the devil so often tempts us to distort sexual union: malign the sign and the window to heaven closes.

There really is an enemy who is hell bent on keeping us from the eternal nuptials. The good news is that Christ came to save us from his lies so we could live the full truth of our humanity as men and women made in the image of God. May we have the courage to embrace that truth and fight the good fight to uphold it! If we do, we'll find ourselves on the path that leads to the fulfillment of the very meaning of our being and existence. We'll find ourselves on the path that leads to the bliss of the eternal marriage of Christ and the Church.

I pray this book has been of service to you on your journey toward that everlasting embrace.

Come, Lord. Let it be done to us, your Bride, as you will. Amen.

(One final question…)

10. Where do I go from here to continue learning about the Theology of the Body?

Consider joining a worldwide online community of men and women who are receiving ongoing formation. Learn more by visiting the website theologyofthebody.com.

If you have the aptitude, I encourage you to read St. John Paul II's actual text *Man and Woman He Created Them: A Theology of the Body*. If you need help with his scholarly approach, read it in conjunction with my extended commentary, *Theology of the Body Explained*, or my *Theology of the Body for Beginners*. Visit theologyofthebody.com and click on "shop" for a listing of various books and additional resources.

I'd also encourage you to explore what other authors and teachers have written. There are many good resources out there today offered by different teachers with their own emphases and insights. Do an Internet search for "theology of the body resources" and start exploring.

Consider taking a five-day Immersion Course through the Theology of the Body Institute. Learn more at tobinstitute.org.

And for more in-depth study, consider the Theology of the Body Institute's Certification Program or the graduate degree programs offered by the Pontifical John Paul II Institute for Studies on Marriage and Family. An Internet search will lead you to them.

Acknowledgments

My thanks to all those who submitted their honest questions, for both the 2000 and the 2018 editions of this work. I'm grateful to Bill Howard, Jason Clark, Wendy West, and Bill Donaghy for reading drafts and offering comments and suggestions. Special thanks to Andrew Comiskey, Hudson Byblow, and Anna Carter for their help with chapters eight and nine.

Notes

Author's Note on the Updated, Revised & Expanded Edition

1. John Paul II, *Man and Woman He Created Them: A Theology of the Body* (Boston: Pauline, 2006). Translation by Michael Waldstein, 23:2. Hereinafter TOB.

2. TOB 23:2.

3. *Catechism of the Catholic Church* (Washington, DC: USCCB, 1994), 2336. Hereinafter *Catechism*.

Introduction

1. *Redemptor Hominis*, 10.

2. The Theology of the Body is the collective title given to the 129 short talks St. John Paul II delivered in his Wednesday General Audiences between September 5, 1979, and November 28, 1984. In them, through a searching analysis of three key teachings of Christ that takes us on a tour from Genesis to Revelation, John Paul presented a depth of understanding of the human person and the meaning of our call to "spousal love" never before articulated. Many of these insights are set forth in chapter one of this book. Subsequent chapters also draw heavily from this work. Hereafter, we will refer to it as TOB, followed by the number and paragraph of the General Audience cited. The entire catechesis was originally published by the Daughters of St. Paul in four volumes now out of print (*Original Unity of Man and Woman, Blessed Are the Pure of Heart, The Theology of Marriage and Celibacy*, and *Reflections on Humanae Vitae*). A copyedited version of the Theology of the Body was published in 1997. In 2006 the Daughters of St. Paul published a new and much improved English translation of the TOB, which included some undelivered content, bringing the total number of talks to 135. Quotes used in this book are taken from this 2006 translation.

3. This work was written in 1981 following the 1980 Synod of Bishops on the Family. It is an excellent and comprehensive presentation of Catholic teaching on sex, marriage, and family life. Hereafter, in the notes we will refer to it as *Familiaris*.

4. Karol Wojtyla (John Paul II), *Love and Responsibility* (San Francisco: Ignatius, 1993), p. 43 (hereafter referred to as *Love*). This work was first published in Poland in 1960, eighteen years before Karol Wojtyla became Pope

John Paul II. Based on years of the author's dialogue and pastoral work with young men and women, as well as engaged and married couples, the book examines ordinary human experience to demonstrate that Catholic moral teaching on sex and marriage corresponds perfectly with the dignity of the human person. A "personalist" philosophy, as John Paul's position has been called, recognizes that persons are subjects toward whom the only proper attitude is love. A person must never be made merely an object of use. John Paul II argued that failure to accept the demands of the Catholic sexual ethic inevitably turns people into objects to be used.

Chapter 1: The Great Mystery

1. John Paul II, *Letter to Families*, 19 (hereafter referred to as *Families*).
2. See TOB 15.
3. TOB 15:5.
4. See *Families*, 19.
5. See the *Catechism of the Catholic Church*, n. 370 (hereafter referred to as *Catechism*).
6. See *Catechism*, 370.
7. See TOB 103. John Paul II brought a development to the Church's understanding of the sacramental sign of marriage. Historically, most theologians posited the sign of marriage in the exchange of wedding vows, as opposed to another view that posited the sacramental sign in the act of consummation. John Paul II brought the two views together by recognizing that the words of the wedding vows "can be fulfilled only by conjugal intercourse." In conjugal intercourse, he said, "we pass to the reality which corresponds to these words. Both the one and the other element are important in regard to the structure of the sacramental sign."
8. Supposed you asked a scientist and a poet both to describe a tree. They would give very different reports. Could one say that the scientist disproves the poet? Still, the creation stories in Genesis are not merely someone's poetry. While they're mythical, they're not just a myth. They are the inspired Word of God. They speak truth—deep truth—about the meaning of life, who God is, and who we are as men and women. The Church interprets the symbolism of biblical language in an authentic way, teaching that our first parents were constituted in a state of holiness and justice but fell through a deed that took place at the beginning of human history (see *Catechism*, 375 and 390).
9. At this point in the story, "Adam" (which literally means "man") is a generic human person and represents all humanity, not just the male. In fact,

the biblical account does not make the distinction between male and female until the woman is created from Adam's side.

10. *Gaudium et Spes*, 24 (hereafter referred to as *Gaudium*). Being created for "our own sake" means, among other things, that we can never rightly be *used* as a means to another person's end. In contrast, the rest of creation is created not for "its own sake" but for *our* sake. So long as we are good stewards, we can *use* the created world for our benefit. But we must never *use* another person.

11. See TOB 8, note 15.

12. TOB 15:1.

13. *Catechism*, 391.

14. See TOB 7:2.

15. What follows is a generalization, of course, but it does seem to be true for the most part that men experience their fallen sexual desires as geared toward physical gratification at the expense of a woman, while women experience their fallen sexual desires as geared toward more of an emotional kind of gratification at the expense of a man. That's not to say that women don't have physical desires or that men don't have emotional ones. It's only to acknowledge that we tend to experience their interplay differently as men and women. As the common observation goes, men will often use love in order to get sex, while women will often use sex in order to feel loved. It should also be mentioned here that some men and women experience sexual desires toward members of the same sex. While same-sex attractions, since they are most often not freely chosen, are not in themselves sinful, they are, to be sure, part of the disorder of the sexual appetite caused by original sin. See chapter eight for more discussion of this matter.

16. TOB 44:7.

17. See TOB 20:1.

18. See *Catechism*, 411.

19. It's important to realize that the marriage of the New Adam and Eve is a "mystical" marriage. It takes place beyond the realm of blood and family relationships as we understand them. "Adam-Christ" and "Eve-Mary" are to be understood as archetypes of "man" and "woman." There is no reason, then, to be troubled by the fact that it is Christ's mother according to flesh and blood who, in some sense, represents all of us as Christ's mystical Bride (see *Catechism*,773). Furthermore, when Jesus wants us to understand Mary as the New Eve, both at Cana and at Calvary, he doesn't refer to her as his mother but as "the woman"—a reference to Genesis 3:15.

20. As St. John Paul II said, "All human beings—both women and men—are called through the Church, to be the 'Bride' of Christ.... In this way 'being the bride,' and thus the 'feminine' element, becomes a symbol of all that is 'human'" (*Mulieris Dignitatem*, 25). Elsewhere in the same text he said, "From this point of view, woman is the representative and the archetype of the whole human race: she represents the humanity which belongs to all human beings, both men and women" (4).

21. *Catechism*, 1617.

Chapter 2: Who Says?

1. See *Catechism*, 889.

2. *Lumen Gentium*, 12.

3. See *Catechism*, 889.

4. St. Augustine, Homily on First Letter of John.

5. *Catechism*, 27.

6. G.K. Chesterton, *Orthodoxy* (New York: Ignatius, 1995), p. 102.

7. Lorenzo Albacete, *God at the Ritz: Attraction to Infinity* (New York: Crossroads, 2002), p. 154.

8. This has only happened twice in the history of the Church. In 1854 Pope Pius IX infallibly defined the dogma of the Immaculate Conception (the teaching that, in light of Christ's redemptive work, Mary was conceived without original sin). And in 1950 Pope Pius XII infallibly defined the dogma of Mary's Assumption, body and soul, into heaven.

9. See *Lumen Gentium*, 25.

10. *Catechism*, 2051, emphasis added.

11. *Catechism*, 892.

12. For an excellent study of the essential role of hierarchy in the ordering of not only the Church but society at large, see Joyce Little, *The Church and the Culture War* (San Francisco: Ignatius, 1995). Some of the thoughts expressed here were gleaned from her insightful work.

13. *Familiaris*, 9.

14. Whatever your questions, you'll always do best by going to the source for answers, such as the *Catechism*. This is the sure norm for knowing what the Church teaches and believes. Books like the one you're now reading, that attempt to explain what the Church really teaches and why, are also a great resource. Furthermore, there are various apostolates within the Church whose purpose is to clarify and explain the official teachings of the Catholic faith. Two such organizations are *Catholic Answers* and *Catholics United for the Faith*. Both organizations will turn up with a simple Internet search.

15. To demonstrate this ambivalence, consider how many slang terms you know for your elbow. In contrast, how many slang terms do you know for those parts of the body that distinguish men and women from each other? Makes you wonder, doesn't it?

16. Credit is due to Christopher Derrick and his book *Sex and Sacredness* (San Francisco: Ignatius, 1982) for many of the insights expressed here.

17. See TOB 97:5.

18. *Familiaris*, 11.

19. See TOB 46:6.

20. See TOB 43:7.

Chapter 3: What Are You Saying "I Do" To?

1. John Paul II, "The Love Within Families," *Origins* 16 (April 23, 1987): 799.

2. See *Gaudium*, 48, and *Code of Canon Law*, Canon 1055.

3. See *Gaudium*, 49.

4. Even if a marriage is not consummated, no human power can claim to dissolve it. However, the Church, in very rare cases, does have the more than human power, given by God, to dissolve nonconsummated marriages.

5. *Gaudium*, 48.

6. See Canon 1055.

7. *Familiaris*, 13.

8. *Baltimore Catechism*, 304.

9. See Tertullian, *On the Resurrection of the Flesh*, chapter 8.

10. TOB 19:4.

11. See TOB 97:4.

12. TOB 98:2.

13. *Catechism*, 1617.

14. Peter Kreeft, *Everything You Ever Wanted to Know about Heaven* (San Francisco: Ignatius, 1990), pp. 86–87.

15. In Catholic Churches of the Eastern rite, however, the priest is understood as the minister of the sacrament of marriage (see *Catechism*, 1623).

16. I'd recommend *Annulment: The Wedding That Was* by Rev. Michael Smith Foster (New York: Paulist, 1999). Written in question-and-answer format, it makes complex issues of canon law easy to understand.

17. Canons 1083–1090.

18. Men who are already married may be ordained as permanent deacons. If a deacon's wife dies, however, he is not free to remarry.

19. Canon 1108.

20. Canons 1095, 1102, 1103.

21. *Familiaris*, 32.
22. TOB 92:6.
23. See John Paul II, *Novo Millennio Inuente*, 33.
24. *Catechism*, 1821.

Chapter 4: What to Do Before "I Do"
1. John Paul II, "The Love within Families," 799.
2. This interview is from Benjamin Nolot's (brutally painful to watch) documentary *Liberated: The New Sexual Revolution* (2017) which explores the disturbing trends of hookup culture.
3. Nolot, *Liberated*.
4. See *Love and Responsibility*, Karol Wojtyla's philosophical work on human sexuality (San Francisco: Ignatius, 1993), p. 167.
5. *Love*, 139.
6. See TOB 106:4.
7. Nolot, *Liberated*.
8. George Weigel, *Witness to Hope* (New York: HarperCollins, 1999), 343.
9. See Jason Evert, "Why are the divorce rates so high for couples who lived together before marriage?" https://chastityproject.com/qa/why-are-the-divorce-rates-so-high-for-couples-who-lived-together-before-marriage/.
10. Premarital sex almost always involves the consistent use of contraception. Yet even if a couple engaging in premarital sex were desirous of conceiving a child, they could not be considered "open to life" in the full sense of that expression. A proper openness to life is inherently marital—that is, it recognizes the right of the child to be conceived by parents who are already committed by marriage to the child's upbringing in a stable, loving environment.
11. Even if a person is willing to or *wants* to be used, we are *never* to use. Our dignity is not contingent upon our awareness of it. In fact, if a person is unaware of his or her dignity, we are all the more obliged to show that person his or her dignity through our love.
12. See *Love*, 43.
13. See *Catechism*, 2342.
14. *Catechism*, 2350.
15. Paul Quay, *The Christian Meaning of Human Sexuality* (San Francisco: Ignatius, 1985), pp. 74–75.
16. See *Catechism*, 2352.
17. The disordering of the passions caused by original sin is called *concupiscence*. Concupiscence, in its broader sense, encompasses more than the disordering of the sexual appetite. Concupiscence inclines us toward sin but

isn't sinful in itself, because it's not freely chosen. It's simply a "given" of fallen human nature.

18. *Love*, 46.

19. TOB 48:4.

20. See TOB 46:6.

21. TOB 49:3.

22. See TOB 57:3.

23. Here are a few suggestions:

Integrityrestored.com

LovePeopleUseThings.fm

CovenantEyes.com (accountability/filtering)

ProtectYoungMinds.com (for parents)

FortifyProgram.org (an online recovery program)

BloomForWomen.com (for wives struggling with betrayal/trauma)

FightTheNewDrug.com (excellent site for youth and young adults)

YourBrainOnPorn.com (provides helpful research on the subject)

Chapter 5: "I Do"-ing It

1. *Families*, 12.

2. St. John Paul II, Homily at Kinshasa, May 3, 1980.

3. *Love*, 225.

4. *Love*, 272, 275.

5. See *Love*, 233.

6. *Love*, 234.

7. See John Harvey, "Expressing Marital Love During the Fertile Phase," *International Review of Natural Family Planning* (Winter 1981): 207.

8. TOB 35:5.

9. In one such manual from the early twentieth century, Dominican Fr. Benoit Merkelbach wrote: "To begin union in the undue vessel, e.g., the backward vessel...with the intention of consummating it in the vagina, and again to touch the backward vessel with the genitals...is not a mortal sin, as long as the pouring out of semen is prevented and the sodomitic emotion is excluded.... Indeed, when they are sought as the only means and preparation for the due act and a sufficient reason is present, e.g., because someone cannot be aroused in another way, then they are not a sin" (*Questiones de Castitate et Luxuria*, fourth edition [La Pensee Catholique, 1936] p. 110). Another example comes from Fr. Heribert Jone who wrote in his authoritative 1956 book *Moral Theology*: "Excluding the sodomitic intention [that is, the intention to ejaculate] it is neither sodomy nor a grave sin if intercourse

is begun in a rectal manner with the intention of consummating it naturally" ([TAN, 1993] section 757). I think the conclusions drawn here betray a certain "objectivism" common in moral manuals of the past and are, thus, in need of revisions that take into consideration not only objective criteria, but the dignity and inviolability of the person as a subject and the symbolic meaning of our sexual acts. This is the gift of St. John Paul II's "personalistic" and "sacramental" approach to sexual ethics.

10. See Canon 1061.

11. Quay, 83.

12. In *Love and Responsibility* (see pp. 270–278), John Paul II made a distinction between "technique" in marital relations and the "culture of marital relations." The very term *technique* implies an artificial or depersonalizing analysis of sexual intimacy. A proper "culture of marital relations," on the other hand, leads to true fulfillment because it allows both husband and wife to penetrate and experience each other's "worlds." Disinterested (altruistic) tenderness in marital relations, he said, affords "the ability to enter readily into the other's emotions and experiences [which] can play a big part in the harmonization of marital intercourse." For example, on the husband's part, this disinterested tenderness leads him to understand his wife's more gradual rise in sexual arousal and to control his own response so as to bring his wife to climax with him. Without such tenderness, there is the danger that the husband may seek just to subject his wife to the demands of his own body. So, with motives always of love, spouses deliberately work at their timing in order to bring each other to the fullness of joy in their union. This is quite a different thing from the hedonistic attempt to maximize physical pleasure.

13. *Love and Responsibility*, p. 135.

14. See *Love and Responsibility*, pp. 87–88.

15. TOB 115:2.

16. *Catechism*, 1642.

17. Talking through your experiences with a spiritual director or counselor is very helpful. There are also various programs (some better than others) designed specifically to help adults deal with sexual and relational wounds from the past in order to build healthy relationships in the present and future. One such program is called *Living Waters* hosted by Desert Stream Ministries (a simple Internet search will bring up their information). If you've been abused sexually, I would strongly urge you to seek professional counseling. Here are three good resources I can recommend, each of which can provide help via phone or online:

Pastoral Solutions Institute

http://www.catholiccounselors.com

Doctor Peter Damgaard-Hansen

http://www.docpeter.com/counseling.html

CatholicPsych Institute

http://catholicpsych.com

18. TOB 33:2.

19. The Second Vatican Council marked a shift in Church's language regarding the ends of marriage. The *Catechism* now speaks of the "twofold end" of marriage as the "good of the spouses themselves and the transmission of life" (2363). This change in language stems in part from a development in understanding of the role of conjugal love in the relationship of the spouses. Those who sought to find the place of conjugal love within the traditional hierarchy of ends too often equated it with the *mutual help of the spouses*. This secondary end of marriage actually refers to the help and support that sharing a common life as husband and wife affords on a very practical level. Equating *mutual help* with "mutual love" led to the mistake that the Church taught that procreation takes precedence over love. The Second Vatican Council clarified the matter beautifully by demonstrating that conjugal love is not an *end* of marriage at all. It's the very *essence* of the marital relationship from which the ends of marriage flow. The ends of marriage are one and the same as the ends of conjugal love. As Vatican II stated, "By their very nature, the institution of matrimony itself *and conjugal love* are ordained for the procreation and education of children" (*Gaudium*, 48, emphasis added). "In this renewed orientation," wrote St. John Paul II, "the traditional teaching on the ends of marriage (and on their hierarchy) is confirmed and at the same time deepened from the viewpoint of the interior life of the spouses" (TOB 127:3).

20. John Paul II, homily, April 8, 1994.

21. See TOB 32.

22. See TOB 84 and 101.

Chapter 6: "I Do...Not"

1. Deuteronomy 30:19.

2. Ronald Lawler, Joseph Boyle, and William May, *Catholic Sexual Ethics* (Huntington, IN: Our Sunday Visitor, 1985 and 1998).

3. See *Familiaris*, 32.

4. Ninety-nine percent effectiveness means that out of one hundred couples following the rules of NFP for one year, only one couple would conceive a child. See P. Frank-Herrmann, J. Heil, C. Gnoth, et al., "The effectiveness of a

fertility awareness based method to avoid pregnancy in relation to a couple's sexual behaviour during the fertile time: a prospective longitudinal study," *Human Reproduction* 22(5) (2007):1310–1319.

5. *L'Osservatore Romano*, October 10, 1983, p. 7.

6. *Humanae Vitae*, 16; emphasis added.

7. Listen to the audio presentation "Contraception, Why Not?" by Janet Smith. A simple Internet search will lead you to it.

8. I'm indebted to Dr. Donald DeMarco for this analogy. See his book *New Perspectives on Contraception* (Dayton, Ohio: One More Soul, 1999), p. 114.

9. Traditional interpretations of this passage have always seen in it God's condemnation of any and every method of deliberately sterile orgasm (masturbation, contraception, sodomy, etc.). The term *Onanism* was coined specifically in reference to such behaviors. Only modern proponents of contraception, it seems, have sought to avoid the conclusion that God slew Onan for spilling his seed.

10. This anti-child mentality is epitomized in a catalog I once saw selling a doormat that read: "Pets welcome. Children must be on a leash." The caption below the picture proclaimed, "This unwelcome mat is guaranteed to keep Fertile Myrtle and her rambunctious brood at bay."

11. *Gaudium*, 50.

12. *Catechism*, 2368.

13. *Familiaris*, 86.

14. Unless otherwise noted, the following statements were cited in Patrick Fagan, "A Culture of Inverted Sexuality," *Catholic World Report*, November 1998, p. 57. (Credit is also due Patrick Fagan for some of the thoughts presented in response to question 14.)

15. T.S. Eliot, *Thoughts after Lambeth* (London: Faber and Faber, 1931), p. 32.

16. "Forgetting Religion," *The Washington Post*, March 22, 1931.

17. Allan C. Carlson, "The Ironic Protestant Reversal: How the Original Family Movement Swallowed the Pill," *Family Policy* 12 (1999): 20.

18. For a wealth of interesting information on what early feminists thought of contraception see Linda Gordon, "Voluntary Motherhood: The Beginning of Feminist Birth Control Ideas in the United States," *Feminist Studies* 1 (Winter-Spring 1973): 5–22.

19. This shift in the feminist approach to contraception is due largely to the influence of Margaret Sanger and Planned Parenthood, the institution she founded. For a shocking look into the influence of Planned Parenthood on the modern world's view of human life and sexual morality, see Robert G.

Marshall and Charles A. Donovan, *Blessed Are the Barren: The Social Policy of Planned Parenthood* (San Francisco: Ignatius, 1991).

20. Quoted from Donald DeMarco's article "Contraception and the Trivialization of Sex," retrieved from www.cuf.org/july99a.htm, 6.

21. *Humanae Vitae*, 17.

22. John Paul II, *Evangelium Vitae*, 13.

23. Planned Parenthood v. Casey, 1992.

24. Listen to the audio presentation "Contraception, Why Not?" by Janet Smith. A simple Internet search will lead you to it.

25. See "Birth Control Pill: Abortifacient and Contraceptive" for helpful information on this topic from the American Association of Prolife OBGYNs, https://aaplog.org/birth-control-pill-abortifacient-and-contraceptive/.

26. Using figures of probability of conception and patterns of sexual activity, John Kippley has estimated that use of the IUD accounts for 247,800,000 "unknown" early abortions worldwide each year. The pill he estimates at 34,400,000 "unknown" early abortions worldwide each year (See *Birth Control & Christian Discipleship*, second ed. [Cincinnati: Couple to Couple League, 1998], p. 14.)

27. *Humanae Vitae*, 15.

28. See note 4 above.

29. *Gaudium*, 5.

30. In a survey by Dr. Josef Rotzer, out of fourteen hundred married couples using NFP, there was not a single divorce among them (see DeMarco, 115).

31. Countless wives who use NFP in their marriages speak of the joy of being kissed without the suspicion that their husbands "want" something. This is the freedom and joy that NFP affords. It enables spouses to love each other for their own sake.

32. A source of encouragement for any wife hoping and praying for the conversion of her husband is the diary of Elisabeth Leseur entitled, *My Spirit Rejoices* (Manchester, NH: Sophia Institute, 1996).

33. The organization One More Soul has a national network of doctors who provide sterilization reversals. Call 800-307-7685 for more information.

34. Call your local diocesan offices to find where classes are offered in your area. An Internet search for NFP classes in your area may also prove helpful. Taking a live class is always recommended, but a home study course is also available through the Couple to Couple League, which you can find through a simple Internet search.

Chapter 7: "I Do," But Not As God Intends

1. "The Love Within Families," 799.

2. *Time* magazine, November 8, 1999, 66–69.

3. More than a few doctors have recognized the irony in the fact that they spend the first fifteen years of a woman's reproductive life helping her impede pregnancy and the second fifteen helping her conceive. Is it any wonder that a promiscuous culture bent on impeding pregnancy with high doses of fertility suppressant drugs and intrusive mechanical devices would experience a dramatic rise in rates of infertility when conception is desired?

4. History's first test tube baby, Louise Brown, was born on July 25, 1978. This just so happened to be the tenth anniversary of the release of Pope Paul VI's encyclical *Humanae Vitae*, which upheld the intrinsic link between sex and procreation. Coincidence? Or is God making a subtle point? (Approximately one hundred thousand technologically produced children have been born in the United States alone since then.)

5. See Congregation for the Doctrine of the Faith, Instruction on Respect for Human Life in Its Origin and on the Dignity of Procreation (*Donum Vitae*), 7. Hereafter referred to as *Donum*.

6. *Donum*, A1.

7. William E. May, *Marriage: The Rock on Which the Family Is Built* (San Francisco: Ignatius, 1995), p. 98.

8. Spouses further violate their vows when they make recourse to the gametes of third parties (technically termed *heterologous fertilization*) or "use" the womb of a surrogate mother for gestation, since the spouse's commitment to fidelity "*involves reciprocal respect of their right to become a father and a mother only through each other*" (*Donum*, A1).

9. *Donum*, B5.

10. See *Catechism*, 98.

11. *Humanae Vitae*, 16, emphasis added.

12. *Families*, 19.

13. See *Donum*, A1.

14. See *Donum*, B8.

15. Here again we see how the interior logic of contraception and technological reproduction is related. Couples who engage in contracepted intercourse don't want God's will to be done in their sexual relationship but their own. Similarly, those who have recourse to technological fertilization aren't satisfied with God's will but seek their own. You might say we're dealing here with a "faucet approach" to fertility. Instead of trusting and respecting God's design, people demand the power to turn their fertility off when *they* want it off, and on when *they* want it on.

16. *Donum*, B8.

17. The following tragic story, told to me by a friend who teaches NFP, demonstrates how little some medical professionals know. After giving a presentation on how to interpret the signs of fertility, she noticed that a woman in the audience was beside herself with grief. It turned out she had been unable to conceive and for years had been following the advice of her doctor, who told her she could increase her chances if she waited to have intercourse until *after* her temperature shifted in her cycle. In actuality, the temperature shift indicates the *infertile* period of the cycle. Just prior to the temperature shift is the *most* fertile time.

18. *Donum*, B8; quoting *Familiaris*, 14.

19. *Denver Catholic Register*, July 21, 1999, p. 2.

Chapter 8: When Saying "I Do" Is Impossible

1. Stanislaw Grygiel as quoted in "The Church Must Guide the Sexual Revolution" (Zenit International News Agency, August 31, 1999), retrieved from www.ewtn.com/library/Theology/ZSEXREV. HTM.

2. "The Body's Grace," Rowan Williams, in *Theology and Sexuality: Classic and Contemporary Readings* (New York: Blackwell, 2002), p. 320.

3. David Morrison, *Beyond Gay* (Huntington, Ind.: Our Sunday Visitor, 1999), p. 14.

4. *Catechism*, 2336.

5. TOB 43:7.

6. See Congregation for the Doctrine of the Faith, *The Pastoral Care of Homosexuals*, 3. Hereafter referred to as *Pastoral*.

7. See *Pastoral*, 3.

8. Congregation for the Doctrine of the Faith, *Letter to the Bishops of the Catholic Church on the Pastoral Care of Homosexual Persons* (October 1, 1986), 16.

9. Address at World Youth Day, July 28, 2002.

10. Congregation for the Doctrine of the Faith, *Letter to the Bishops of the Catholic Church on the Pastoral Care of Homosexual Persons*, 7.

11. "Catholicism, Homosexuality, and Dignity," brochure published by Dignity, cited in *Beyond Gay*, p. 56.

12. See Mark Regnerus, *Cheap Sex: The Transformation of Men, Marriage, and Monogamy* (New York, Oxford, 2017), pp. 146–148.

13. Credit is usually given to Austrian-born Hungarian journalist Karl-Maria Kertbeny for coining the terms in 1868. See https://en.wikipedia.org/wiki/Karl-Maria_Kertbeny.

14. Mario Bergner, the man who gave these talks, has written a book that tells his story, called *Setting Love in Order* (Grand Rapids: Baker, 1995).

15. It's beyond the scope of this book to debate different theories about the origins of homosexuality. There are several. My only point here is to explain briefly what made sense for me out of my own "identity crisis" and to note that these same insights have helped men with any and every degree of same-sex attractions better understand themselves.

16. Ask a man with same-sex attractions about his sexual fantasy life, and almost inevitably he'll describe himself uniting with idealized images of the masculine. This is simply the dynamic that I'm describing, as it happened in my own life, taken to its eroticized extreme. Leanne Payne, a counselor with years of experience helping homosexual men, describes this phenomenon as a "cannibal compulsion." Cannibals, apparently, typically eat only people they admire with the hopes of acquiring their traits. Men who act on their same-sex attractions, she believes, seek to acquire that masculine part of themselves that they see in their sexual partner (or fantasized partner) but fear they lack in themselves. Her books *The Broken Image* (Grand Rapids: Baker, 1981 and 1996) and *Healing Homosexuality* (Grand Rapids: Baker, 1996) are well worth reading whether or not you experience same-sex attraction.

17. St. Paul was tapping into a fundamental truth when he described the root of same-sex attraction as idolatry (see Romans 1:23–27).

18. See TOB 126:5.

19. *Novo Millennio Inuente*, 33.

20. Jacques Philippe, *Interior Freedom* (Strongsville, Ohio: Scepter, 2007), p. 113.

21. *Catechism*, 1458.

22. *Catechism*, 2711.

23. *Mulieris Dignitatem*, 26.

24. *Catechism*, 1868.

Chapter 9: Trapped in the Wrong Body?

1. *Amoris Latitiae*, 56.

2. Pew Research Center, "Fewer than half of U.S. kids today live in a 'traditional' family," http://www.pewresearch.org/fact-tank/2014/12/22/less-than-half-of-u-s-kids-today-live-in-a-traditional-family/.

3. As reported by the National Center for the Victims of Crime, http://victimsofcrime.org/media/reporting-on-child-sexual-abuse/child-sexual-abuse-statistics.

4. "Gender Identity: Can a 5'9", White Guy Be a 6'5", Chinese Woman?" https://www.youtube.com/watch?v=xfO1veFs6Ho.

5. My thanks to Daniel Moody for this turn of phrase. See *The Flesh Made Word: A New Reason to be Against Abortion* (n.p.: Amazon, 2016).

6. George Orwell, "Politics and the English Language," http://www.orwell.ru/library/essays/politics/english/e_polit.

7. *Catechism*, 2332.

8. *Familiaris Consortio*, 11.

9. TOB 7:2.

10. *Humanae Vitae*, 17.

11. Vittorio Messori and Cardinal Joseph Ratzinger, *The Ratzinger Report* (San Francisco: Ignatius, 1985), pp. 85, 95.

12.Facebook Diversity policy, https://m.facebook.com/facebookdiversity/photos/a.196865713743272.42938.105225179573993/567587973337709/?-type=3.

13. *Caritas in Veritate*, 3.

14. TOB 18:4.

15. TOB 29:4.

16. See Ryan T. Anderson, *When Harry Became Sally: Responding to the Transgender Moment* (New York: Encounter, 2018), p. 92.

17. *Evangelium Vitae*, 20.

18. Planned Parenthood vs. Casey, 1992.

19. *Catechism*, 398.

20. See *Veritatis Splendor*, 35.

21. *Catechism*, 307.

22. *Catechism*, 2293, 2294.

23. See *Catechism*, 2297.

24. John Paul II, *Crossing the Threshold of Hope* (New York: Knopf, 1994), p. 66.

25. *Catechism*, 311.

26. See TOB 66:4.

27. *Catechism*, 760.

28. *Familiaris Consortio* 11

29. For a more thorough answer to this question, I recommend a prayer guide called *Becoming Good News* written by my friend Andrew Comiskey, executive director and founder of Desert Stream Ministries (an Internet search will bring you to it). Andrew has worked in this field for nearly four decades, first as a Protestant, and more recently as a convert to Catholicism.

30. Anderson, p. 119.

31. Anderson, p. 119.

32. *Amoris Latitiae,* 286.

33. See Anderson, p. 156.

34. TOB 93:2.

35. *Catechism,* 2851.

36. *Families,* 23.

37. Karol Wojtyla, *Sign of Contradiction* (New York: Seabury, 1979), pp. 34–35.

38. See *Families,* 19.

39. Here are two excellent resources for your children: Ruah Woods has produced a K-12 curriculum designed to immerse your children in an authentic vision of their humanity based on St. John Paul II's Theology of the Body (search Ruah Woods curriculum); Ascension Press has an excellent resource called *You* (search Ascension Press You).

40. *Novo Millennio Inuente,* 29.

41. *Novo Millennio Inuente,* 29.

Chapter 10: Saying "I Do" to God Alone

1. Revelation 21:1–3.

2. See TOB 68:2–3.

3. TOB 80:6.

4. TOB 77:6.

5. See TOB 80:7.

6. St. John Paul II, *Letter to Women,* 3. I highly recommend this brief letter, as well as John Paul's more thorough treatment of the dignity and vocation of women in his apostolic letter *Mulieris Dignitatem* (hereafter referred to as *Mulieris*).

7. Stanislaw Grygiel as quoted in "The Church Must Guide the Sexual Revolution" (Zenit International News Agency, August 31, 1999), retrieved from www.ewtn.com/library/Theology/ZSEXREV. HTM.

8. *Mulieris,* 26.

9. *Mulieris,* 26.

10. Thanks to Mary Rousseau for this example. See her excellent article "Eucharist and Gender," *Catholic Dossier,* September/October 1996, 19–23, for a wonderful treatment of the issue of reserving priestly ordination to men.

11. *Catechism,* 500.

12. "Sexuality as Transcendence: An Interview with Fabrice Hadjadj"; https://ethikapolitika.org/2015/04/14/sexuality-as-transcendence-an-interview-with-fabrice-hadjadj/.

13. Address of September 21, 1996.

14. *Catechism,* 2347.

15. John Paul II, "A Meditation on Givenness," published in *Communio* 41, Winter 2014 (originally signed by John Paul II on February 8, 1994), pp. 881–882.

16. See John Paul II, Redemptor Hominis, 1.

INDEX

abduction, 39

abortion, 118, 165, 170

   contraception and, 113, 116–117

   as selective reduction, 127

abstinence

   contraception and, 100, 102, 105, 119–120, 122

   as harmful to marriage, 120

   with NFP, 119, 120, 121

   for unmarried people, 78–79

Adam and Eve

   in Book of Genesis, 6–7, 8–9, 12, 86, 195, 200–201

   New, 11–12, 75, 200n19

   original sin and, 23–25, 26

   See also Eve

adolescence, 69

adoption, 39, 113, 132, 135, 140

   as impediment to marriage, 39

adultery, 10, 46, 48, 62, 81, 101, 112, 113

   Christ on, 49, 60–61

   divorce and, 46, 48, 49, 62, 112–113

affection, guidelines for expressing, 64–68, 82, 83, 122

affinity, as impediment to marriage, 39

age, as impediment to marriage, 38

AIDS, 5, 29

anal sex, 83–84

Anderson, Ryan T., 179, 180

androgyny, 180

Anglican Church, 111, 112

annulments, 37, 45, 46–47, 48–49

   and illegitimacy, 45–46

artificial insemination, 128–129, 136

   of cattle, 132

baptism, 11–12, 28, 29, 44, 143, 192

   as nuptial bath, 12

marriage and, 4, 33–35, 79

Benedict XVI. *See* Pope Benedict XVI

Beyond Gay (Morrison), 140

Bible. *See also* Genesis, Book of

   on contraception, 107

   on flesh vs. spirit, 36

   on God's love for humanity, 2–3

   on Joseph and Mary, 193

   on sex and marriage, 2, 95, 181, 183

   on wives, 49–51

Biddle, Kim, 57

BIID (body integrity identity disorder), 169

birth control, 102–103, 104–105. *See also* contraception; NFP

   the Church on, 110–114, 126–129

   natural vs. artificial, 104–105

   pills, 110, 117–118, 123, 209n25, 26

birth defects, 173–174

Blackwell, Dr. Elizabeth, 114–115

blood and water, symbolism of, 5, 11–12, 35

body and soul, unity of, 36–37, 43–44, 57, 60, 71, 84–85, 145, 163–164, 168, 175

brand identity, 146

Brave New World (Huxley), 125

breastfeeding, 119

canon law, 32, 33

Catechism of the Catholic Church, 20, 35, 52, 90, 129, 164

   on baptism, 12

   on chastity, 67

   on confession, 156, 158

   on creation, 171, 173

   on the devil, 181

   on family planning, 109

   on infallibility of the Church, 21

   on science, 171

Catholic Answers organization, 202n14